CANADA IN FLANDERS
(VOLUME II)

CANADA IN FLANDERS
(VOLUME II)

MAX AITKEN BEAVERBROOK

ISBN: 978-93-5614-608-2

Published: 1917

LECTOR HOUSE

LECTOR HOUSE LLP
E-MAIL: info@lectorhouse.com

CANADA IN FLANDERS (VOLUME II)

THE OFFICIAL STORY OF THE CANADIAN EXPEDITIONARY FORCE

BY

LORD BEAVERBROOK
(SIR MAX AITKEN)

WITH MAPS AND APPENDICES

IN THREE VOLUMES,
VOL. II.

MCMXVII

PREFACE

The narrative of the Second Battle of Ypres was written on the spot and immediately after the action. It was not until long afterwards that it was possible to collect and collate the whole of the battalion diaries. The story, therefore, could only be compiled from the personal reports of the officers commanding units, and in some cases these were not available, and certain regiments did not therefore receive the prominence which was their due. These regiments will, I am sure, readily understand that the omission was not intentional, but due to the impossibility of making sure of all the details of a great and confused action until months after the event. Although the material has become available, I have decided not to attempt to rewrite the story. It is, in its main features, absolutely accurate, and has the advantage which must belong to any narrative written within sound of the guns, and while the impressions of the battlefield are still vivid to the mind. I am, in fact, afraid that any attempt on my part to reconstruct the narrative would spoil whatever merit it may possess.

In the first place, it is necessary, however, to make good some mistakes in the first volume which have been pointed out by persons who were engaged in various actions.

The majority of errors occur in the matter of names, which, in about a dozen cases, have been given inexactly. In some cases it has been possible to make the requisite corrections of initials, rank, or spelling in succeeding editions. I particularly regret the confusion between the two brothers, Sergt. L. G. Newell and Sergt. F. C. C. Newell, both of whom took part in the charge at Langemarke. The first-named, the older brother, died of his wounds after that attack, while the second and younger recovered, returned to the trenches, and won the D.C.M. at Givenchy. With reference to the names of regiments concerned in the Second Battle of Ypres, the King's Own Royal Leinsters have been named by a misprint instead of the King's Own Royal Lancashires, as part of Colonel Geddes' command, on page 35. King Edward's Horse should have the prefix 2nd throughout. I offer my very sincere apologies to both regiments.

As to the position of various units, it is stated on page 45 of Vol. I. that Lieut.-Col. Watson, of the 2nd, was employed with his regiment on a dangerous digging operation to connect a weak point in the line on the night of April 28th, 1915. It should have been added that the entire 1st Brigade took part in this, the 2nd Battalion being on the left, the 3rd in the centre, and the 1st on the right, the 4th Battalion digging in the meanwhile a support trench close in rear. The omission of the description of the part played by the 5th Battalion (Colonel Tuxford) in the

Second Battle of Ypres was a serious one, but this is dealt with in the course of the next few pages.

The only serious accusation of inaccuracy in the tactical survey of any situation is preferred by those who maintain that the sketch of the action at Festubert is wrong or misleading. I have communicated with Colonel J. E. Leckie, of the 16th Battalion, who, as a major, took a prominent part in the assault and succeeded to the command of the regiment, when his brother, Brigadier-General R. G. E. Leckie, was promoted to a brigade. He assures me that the sketch of the two positions occupied by the Canadians in their successive attacks is quite accurate, and, in fact, it is so. None the less, it is easy to see how the idea that there was an error originated. In an attempt to secure largeness of scale in the map, the area is unduly limited in its scope. The position from which the Canadians attacked is not given, and the extent to which the Germans were forced back is only just indicated. In consequence, the words "First Canadian Position" might be held to imply that this was the line from which they sallied forth instead of the first position they occupied before they advanced to the final attack on the orchard. It is a misfortune if the plan underestimates the ground won by the 14th and 15th. No further serious errors have been suggested so far as Vol. I. is concerned.

Mistakes will no doubt be discovered in the second volume. They will be found, however, to apply to the misspelling of the names of individuals and to an occasional mistake or doubt as to the precise position of a particular unit on a certain date, and not, I hope, to any main question of the tactics or strategy of battle.

The contemporary historian cannot hope to avoid these errors. He has at his disposal neither the leisure nor the information of the writer of after years. He must take his information as it comes to him and trust that rough justice is done, believing that his honest misjudgments will be cleared up when the full history comes to be written. In the meantime, he may hope to supply material of value for subsequent examination and use. But for this final judgment we may have to wait some years. In the confusion and isolation of a modern battle men are acutely aware of their own experiences, and can have little knowledge of what is passing to the right or left, while the staff behind have the same difficulty in discovering what is happening on their front. In these circumstances, the eye-witnesses themselves often disagree. Even the historians of the past have not infrequently made mistakes and waged with the pen as fierce battles over stricken fields as were ever fought by the opposing hosts with the sword.

There is, of course, one easy way out of these troubles; it is to have no immediate record, but to await the official publications of after time. The Dominion Government has, and I think rightly, declared against this policy. It has been from the start in favour of publicity so long as there was no danger to national interests. It has not concurred in the suppression of the deeds of regiments or individuals, believing that in a democratic country the greatest stimulus to exertion is the knowledge that one is known and approved by one's fellow-citizens. Its eye-witness accounts, therefore, set in many respects the tone for similar publications, and it has adopted the same liberal view in authorising a contemporary story. In another respect, the Dominion Government has been wise. Enormous sums were spent after the American Civil War in collecting the official records. The units had been disbanded and the witnesses scattered to civilian pursuits all over the country, and the inquiry was in consequence laborious and expensive.

The Dominion Government, warned by this example, have taken prompt measures to secure from day to day and week to week full reports of the movements and actions of all units, at a cost which is trifling compared with what it would cost in after years; in this way the framework has been erected for an official narrative. This is a prudent measure which will be endorsed by Canadian students of history, since there is a growing tendency to demand a full and intelligent documentary record of our progress. All the officers of the Canadian Corps have in one respect or another contributed to the collection of these facts, and have done so often in the face of grave danger and complete exhaustion, when they might well have been excused from troubling about such trivialities as to what posterity would think about them. The members of the Record Officer's Staff have been unwearied in collecting all the available material, and this common sense of duty has laid the foundation of our records on a substantial basis of fact.

For all mistakes which occur, and more particularly for the omissions, I, as Record Officer, take full responsibility, for the Record Officer is no more exempt than others from the fog of battle. But I would point out that my task would be rendered less difficult, and the chances of error or injustice diminished, if the commanders of units would supply exhaustive diaries and reports on all occasions of importance. I have particularly in my mind's eye the case of Brigadier-General (then Lieut.-Col.) Tuxford, of the 5th Battalion, who with his regiment conducted a most heroic defence of the extreme right of the position during the Second Battle of Ypres. His regiment was, in fact, the pivot of the retirement, and, had it given way, very few of the 1st Division would have come back to tell the tale. The General is well known as a man of action and a brilliant soldier, and is perhaps, therefore, though well qualified to write, little disposed to do so, and so it was long after the stress and confusion of the great conflict that I became fully aware of the part that he and his regiment had taken. Yet his defence of the Gravenstafel Ridge was a great feat of arms, well worthy of the 7th Division, the Household Cavalry, and the Guards Brigade, who had fought up and down that bloodstained soil against overwhelming odds in the autumn of 1914.

I hope to make all mistakes good in some final edition of "Canada in Flanders"; if not, posterity will vindicate any who have been wronged by accident. But in return for such confessions as I have made, I would give one word of warning to the critics. The original twelve battalions have become an army corps, and if one division or another happens to find itself involved in a great battle, it is not unnatural that the attention of the public should be concentrated on its achievements, failures, or losses, even though the others are doing their work equally well. Fortunately, or unfortunately, the turn of each division comes, and the 1st is known by Ypres, the 2nd by St. Eloi, and the 3rd by Sanctuary Wood. There is enough glory and enough suffering to go round.

My thanks are due to those who have helped in the production of this volume.

To Chapters II. and III., which deal with the period from the embarkation of the 2nd Division at Folkestone in September to the beginning of March, 1916, Capt. Theodore Roberts has contributed much valuable information and material. So excellent was it, that I have availed myself of his permission to insert many passages in the very words that he employed, and the Canadian public will be a gainer thereby. His services were very valuable in the post he occupied at the Front. The April and June operations involved the reading and careful consideration of a great mass of documents. To reduce them to a satisfactory form entailed an extraordinary effort of intense concentration; for this work I am indebted to Capt. Maurice Woods and to Capt. Talbot Papineau. Capt. Woods in particular has largely contributed to the fabric of the chapters which deal with this part of the story. In placing these services on record, I must make mention of Lieut.-Col. Sims, who performed at the Front the difficult and onerous task of preparing the weekly *communiqué* to the Canadian Press and of organising the collection of the various diaries and other data with great success, and of Lieut. Bradley, who was indefatigable in collecting material.

The kindness of the public in England, Canada, and the United States called for fourteen editions of the first volume of this work within a very few months.

I am encouraged to hope that the attempts to continue the narrative which I began nearly two years ago may not be unwelcome.

The present volume contains no central drama quite comparable to that presented by the Second Battle of Ypres, but I believe it will be found to present an accurate account of much suffering and much glory.

BEAVERBROOK.

CHERKLEY, LEATHERHEAD,
Jan. 27th, 1917.

CONTENTS

CHAPTER III

TRENCH RAIDS

CHAPTER IV

FORMATION OF THE THIRD DIVISION

CHAPTER V

ST. ELOI

CHAPTER VI

ST. ELOI (CONTINUED)

CHAPTER VII

ST. ELOI (CONCLUSION)

CHAPTER VIII

THE BATTLE OF SANCTUARY WOOD

CHAPTER IX

THE COUNTER-ATTACK

CHAPTER X

A LULL IN THE STORM. THE FIGHT FOR HOOGE

CHAPTER XI

THE FINAL VICTORY

CHAPTER I

THE SECOND DIVISION

Canadians in the clash of World Powers—Effect of losses on Canadian people—Tribute of the British—The Service in St. Paul's—"Pure gold"—Eighteen hundred fresh troops cross the Channel—Prompt action of the Minister of Militia—Call for men from the third contingent to refill the ranks—Outstanding feature of the Second Battle of Ypres—Colonel Henderson on volunteer armies—Adaptability of the Canadians—Gallantry and intelligence *v.* lengthy training—The real strength underlying great national movements—The superiority of volunteer armies—The conduct of Canadian and Australian troops—The landings at Gallipoli—Lone Pine Hill—Recruiting for the Second Division—Unbounded patriotism of the Provinces—The Commanding Officers—Mid-winter training—Sailing of the Second Contingent—Major-General Steele—Training in England—Ready for any emergency—Divisional Artillery—A satisfactory inspection—Visit of the Prime Minister, the Colonial Secretary, and the Minister of Militia—The great achievement of Sir Sam Hughes—Words of praise from the Colonial Secretary—The New World ready to redeem the balance of the Old—Our King, Our Country, Our Empire—Special message from the King—Towards the firing line—A startling incident in the Channel—The historic landing-place—The French Canadians in France—A dramatic moment.

The repercussion of the battle of Ypres was immediately felt in Canada. It was an event unique in the history of the Dominion. The numbers engaged, the high proportion of casualties, the character of the enemy, and the desperate nature of the fighting made the engagement the most serious military action in which Canadians had ever borne a part, and the effect upon home opinion was proportionate. The American attack of 1812, the Red River Expedition, the abortive Fenian raid, and even the South African Campaign, were by comparison affairs of minor importance. The Canadian regiment had indeed made a name for itself at Paardeberg, and the 7,000 Canadians who volunteered for service in Africa had set a high standard of soldierly virtue in more than one engagement; but as the European conflict dwarfed the struggle of 1899-1902 for the Empire as a whole, so the share taken by the Dominion in the war against the Central Powers entirely overshadowed the effort she had made against the Transvaal and Free State. Here at last in the clash of World Powers a new nation had come into its own. Twenty thousand Canadian troops, many with less than one year's service, had, almost unsupported and wholly outflanked, held their own for days against the vastly superior numbers of the most highly trained troops in Europe, who, in addition to their usual weapons of warfare, had suddenly and unexpectedly made use of a vile and inhuman method of attack. Of these 20,000 nearly one-third were casualties, and the list of six thousand killed, wounded, and missing came as a shock to a public which had not been hardened as Great Britain had been by the battles of Mons, the Marne, and the Aisne to the colossal sacrifices involved in war. So our land grieved her losses, and set herself to make them good.

From each one of our provinces came the same voice of mingled sorrow, pride and invincible determination. The feeling found expression in the memorial services for the dead held on April 31st in Montreal, in five churches representing all religious denominations. The flags were flown at half-mast and the troops turned out to attend the services. "The achievements of our men," said the Bishop of Montreal, "have brought Canada into a new and more honourable place in the Empire. They endured privation, they suffered greatly, and now they have paid life's greatest tribute with their lives."

May 2nd, 1915.

Nor was Great Britain without her tribute. A memorial service was held in St. Paul's on May 2nd, 1915, for the Canadians who fell at Ypres. The officiating clergy were the Archbishop of Canterbury, the Bishop of London, the Chaplain-General to the Forces, and the Dean of St. Paul's. The ceremony took place not without propriety in the City Cathedral of St. Paul's; for though Westminster Abbey is consecrated by long tradition and the immortal tombs of great monarchs and statesmen of times almost out of remembrance, yet the shrines of Saxon, Norman, Angevin, and Tudor kings are a little remote from the dead of a far-off country with which these recumbent figures were never concerned. But St. Paul's possesses not only the monuments of the great soldiers and sailors who laid the foundations of the Empire of to-day, but enshrines that spirit of patriotic and constrained freedom which has made the citizens of London both "the regular army of Liberty" and the firm supporters of all those statesmen, from Chatham to Disraeli, who have combined freedom with Empire. Here the volunteer army of Canada committed to the Imperial cause would find that its dead might speak without constraint to those of an older time. In this temple of a magnificent sobriety was held the funeral service of the heroes of Ypres. In the stiff and formal tombs of their age lay the mortal remains of Wellington and Nelson, who, if there be remembrance among the shades, might well have been present to pay tribute to men whom even they would have been proud to command. But round the walls hung a more significant witness to the fallen in the countless tablets which still hold the memories of the soldiers and sailors, now long forgotten by history, who in many a desperate battle by sea and land laid the enduring foundations of a Canada which has proved itself not unworthy of its origins. Among these records are those of the City merchants whose purses and patriotism supplied the sinews of war to remind us that the great material resources of the Dominion are not inferior to the patriotism of its sons, and are no less a vital factor of national victory. Here, then, were gathered the representatives of an Empire united both by pride and sorrow. Over the vast assembly which thronged the building on that dim summer evening the half-lights scarcely illuminated the interior of the spacious dome. As those lights grew and shot up into the gloom the massed bands opened with the "Dead March," and a thrill ran through the multitude—one of those waves of emotion which only great occasions can evoke. The Bishop of London was the preacher, nor was his eloquence wanting to the occasion. "It was on that tremendous day when French and British had been overpowered by poisonous gas that the manhood of Canada shone out like pure gold. The example of these men will never die, but will remain as a perpetual inspiration to their successors." Those successors were already on their way.

Within three days of the Ypres fight 1,800 reinforcements from the Canadian Training Division crossed the Channel to bring new blood to the decimated battalions in Flanders. The Commander-in-Chief in France at once dispatched Lieut.-Col. Carrick, M.P., to ask for a further supply of new Canadian formations. The Minister of Militia and Defence, General Sir Sam Hughes, did not wait for any request to deal with the instant need. He called for a draft of men from the 3rd Contingent, still training in Canada, to go abroad and help refill the ranks. The losses of the 1st Division were thus partially made good, and it was able now to inscribe on its banners the proud name of the Second Battle of Ypres.

To the military writer of the future the amazing feature of the Second Battle of Ypres will always be the courage and discipline shown by the Canadians, equal to the best to be found in the armies with which they were associated. The greater proportion of the Anglo-French Armies were composed of Regular soldiers in the broadest sense of the term, and it has been held by most military historians as an axiom that no amount of gallantry and intelligence can make up for a lack of prolonged training and discipline.

Ordinary military writers put the case even more strongly. They maintain in effect that the value of troops depends on the length of service and on the character of their training, and on these things alone. This point of view ignores the other factors which go to the making of a soldier or a regiment—physique, natural boldness and resource, intelligence, and high patriotic motives; and would claim that a body composed of naturally inferior but technically better trained troops could defeat an equal number of men possessing the qualities I have mentioned, but deficient in discipline and experience. I would submit that the Second Battle of Ypres does not accord with the expert theory, but rather teaches the reverse.

The late Colonel Henderson, perhaps the best known of modern historians of war, goes so far as to countenance the suggestion that had either the North or the South in the American Civil War possessed at the start a single army corps of Regulars, the struggle would have been decided instantly in favour of its possessors instead of lasting over four years and necessitating the calling to arms of the great majority of the citizens of the United States! Colonel Henderson states the matter more moderately in a passage I cannot forbear to quote at some length, because it embodies the best which can be said for the professional military point of view. Speaking of American Volunteer troops, Colonel Henderson says:

"The Volunteers had proved themselves exceedingly liable to panic. Their superior intelligence had not enabled them to master the instincts of human nature; and although they had behaved well in camp and on the march, in battle their discipline had fallen to pieces. *It could hardly be otherwise.* Men without ingrained habits of obedience, who have not been trained to subordinate their will to another's, cannot be expected to render implicit obedience in moments of danger and excitement; nor can they be expected, under such circumstances, to follow officers in whom they can have but little confidence. The ideal of battle is a combined effort, directed by a trained leader. Unless troops are thoroughly well disciplined, such effort is impossible; the leaders are ignored, and the spasmodic action of the individual is substituted for the concentrated pressure of the mass.... The Volunteers, although on many occasions they behaved with admirable courage, continually broke loose from control under the fire of the enemy. As individuals they fought well; as organised bodies, capable of manoeuvring under fire and of combined effort, they proved to be comparatively worthless." ("Stonewall Jackson," Vol. I., p. 49; Longmans, 1913.)

Colonel Henderson quoted in support of his view the undisciplined advance and disorganised retreat of the Federal levies at the battle of Bull Run, and the utter failure of the brave French Territorials of the Army of the Loire in 1870-71 to relieve Paris or to make any headway against the Germans when once the French Regular armies had been destroyed at Gravelotte, Metz, and Sedan.

Such views, by ignoring the real strength which underlies great national movements and supports national armies, however ill-trained, lead to that kind of miscalculation which lured Napoleon to his destruction in Spain. They spring chiefly from a study of those periods in history when small mercenary or highly-trained bodies of troops existed side by side with a population whose civic organisation and patriotic ardour were at a low ebb. Such conditions occurred at certain periods of mediæval history, in the Italy of the Renaissance, and during the end of the seventeenth and throughout the eighteenth centuries. But even in those epochs we can notice the victories of the ill-organised levies inspired by Joan of Arc over the highly-trained British men-at-arms and archers, the successful resistance of Volunteer troops in Holland to the veterans of Alva, and the contest waged by the House of Orange with the levies of the United Provinces against the flower of the French Army led by Condé and Turenne. And the system of small, trained armies, and most of the lessons derived from it, were utterly shattered by the armed development of the French Revolution. The Prussian and Austrian Armies which crossed the French frontiers in 1793 were the last word in disciplined perfection. The Prussian Army in particular was the exact model of the instrument which, fighting against similar organisations, had made Frederick the Great. The French Regular Army had vanished with the old régime. In its place was nothing but a mass of ill-trained, ill-armed, ill-supplied National Volunteers, whose only strength lay in a passionate determination to drive the Invader from the soil which they had consecrated to Liberty. The field of Valmy decided the issue in favour of the Volunteers, or, more strictly, of the *levée en masse*, and it was not till the humiliation of Jena and the slackening of French enthusiasm for the Napoleonic cause had given Germany the National Movement which was ebbing from France, that the military *rôles* of the two countries became reversed. The armies which finally drove Napoleon back across Europe to abdication and Elba would have compared unfavourably in technique with the old Prussian Regulars, but they were armed with an enthusiasm for their cause which their predecessors had utterly lacked.

The lessons of history receive a startling reinforcement from the conduct of the Australian and Canadian troops. Both were volunteer and semi-trained troops in the strictest sense of the term—and what was true of the rank and file was, with a few distinguished exceptions, true of its officers and of its higher command. Both forces were confronted, the one in Gallipoli and the other at Ypres, with circumstances of unprecedented difficulty and danger. The landings in the Peninsula and the fierce fighting at Lone Pine Hill were certainly operations of an unusual character in war, and just of a kind, if Colonel Henderson's view is correct, to bring out the unsteadiness and unreliability of Volunteer troops, however brave. The same is true of Ypres. Here we find an attack by a new, horrible, and terrifying instrument of war, accompanied by a massed assault of the flower of the Prussian Army; the left of the position becomes a huge gap with the Canadian trenches in the air. Communication between units becomes more and more difficult in the swaying *mêlée* of the battle, and the senior officers are falling fast; supports for many hours there are none. If our semi-trained troops had broken under these combined stresses, who could have blamed them?

But in the face of these almost unparalleled difficulties, the Canadians showed the world an example of courage, steadiness, and co-ordinated discipline which could not have been surpassed by that Guards Brigade which stemmed the German tide in the first great onslaught at Ypres. The truth would appear to be that although, when other factors are equal between opposing forces, training and discipline will win, yet there resides in intense patriotism, high physical courage and endurance bred of pastimes which are akin to war, and superior personality, a force which can only be equalled by the last word in highly-trained infantry. Sudden and unexpected emergencies, so far from breaking the nerves of great Volunteer armies, as they do those of inferior trained troops, who are confused if the drill book fails them, bring out the resources of an individuality not yet crushed by tradition. The Volunteer adapts himself more quickly than a machine-made soldier.

April, 1915.

But it is time to turn to the fortune of the 2nd Division, part of which was already crossing the Atlantic at the time of the Second Battle of Ypres. The original offer of the Dominion Government had been a full division of all arms numbering 20,000. But the patriotism of the country outran the offer of the Government, and the actual number of the first contingent was 33,000 men. Of these, five battalions, the 6th, 9th, 11th, 12th, and 17th, had been left in England when the 1st Division sailed for France to act as the nucleus of a Drafting and Training Division. But even before the 1st Division had left for England the Dominion Government was feeling its way towards a further offer. The day after the great review of September 7th, 1914, at Valcartier, the Rt. Hon. Sir Robert Borden had cabled Sir George Perley that there were 43,000 men under arms in Canada, and had requested him to sound the Colonial Office as to the dispatch of a second contingent. In the first week of October, 1914, the offer of the 2nd Division of 20,000 men was made by the Dominion and accepted by the Imperial Government, and recruiting for it was started at once.

The 2nd Division consisted of the usual three brigades of infantry, but at the start each battalion was raised as a separate unit, for the purposes of enlistment and training. In fact, in some cases, companies of the same battalion were raised and partly trained in separate localities.

Oct., 1914.

The 4th Brigade was for a time under the command of Col. Denison. Illness intervened, and the high hopes of an officer with a splendid record were completely destroyed. The brigade then passed to the command of Brigadier-General Lord Brooke. The battalions were recruited from such well-known regiments as the Queen's Own (of Toronto), Royal Grenadiers, 21st Essex Fusiliers, 24th Kent Regiment, 28th Perth Regiment, 29th Highland Light Infantry, 7th London Fusiliers, 14th Prince of Wales' Own Rifles, 45th Victoria Regiment, the Brockville Rifles and the Governor-General's Foot Guards. Mobilisation commenced in October, 1914, and the 18th (Western Ontario Battalion) was commanded by Lieut.-Col. Wigle, the 19th (Ontario Battalion) by Lieut.-Col. MacLaren, the 20th (Northern and Central Ontario Battalion) by Lieut.-Col. Allan, and the 21st (Eastern Ontario Battalion) by Lieut.-Col. St. Pierre Hughes.

The 5th Brigade consisted of the 22nd (French Canadians), the 24th (Victoria Rifles), the 25th (Nova Scotia), and 26th (New Brunswick) Battalions. All these regiments began their mobilisation in the latter part of October and the first week in November, 1914, but they completed it for various reasons at very different dates. The brigade was taken over by Brigadier-General Watson, formerly commanding the 2nd Battalion of the 1st Division.

The 22nd Battalion, under Col. Gaudet, was recruited entirely from the French Canadians, and nearly all its officers and men hailed from Montreal or Quebec. Its point of concentration was St. John's. Some two thousand recruits offered themselves, and of these 1,100 were finally accepted or retained, the process of enlistment being completed by November 27th.

The next battalion of the brigade, the 24th (Victoria Rifles), Lieut.-Col. Gunn, was mobilised in Montreal on October 22nd, 1914, but did not complete its mobilisation until May 8th, 1915. There appears to have been a great rush of recruits, no fewer than four thousand offering themselves. The method here was to accept 1,800 men and continue to weed them out by a process of selection for several months until the full complement of the regiment was obtained. A great proportion of this battalion came from Montreal, and, like the 22nd, had carried out most of its preliminary training in the middle of the winter snows.

The 25th Battalion was recruited in Nova Scotia, including a contingent from Cape Breton. Lieut.-Col. Le Cain was in command, and Halifax was its main centre of mobilisation.

The 26th Battalion, commanded by Lieut.-Col. McAvity, was recruited in New Brunswick and mobilised in the first three weeks of November at St. John's.

The 6th Brigade, which when constituted was taken over by Brigadier-General Ketchen, was mainly raised in the West.

The 27th Battalion (City of Winnipeg) was mobilised in Winnipeg and the surrounding districts, and was almost entirely composed of local recruits. Lieut.-Col. Snider was in command. The next battalion, 28th (North-west), under Col. Embury, was more composite in its origin. From Regina came 12 officers and 246 men; from Moose Jaw, 6 officers and 246 men; from Saskatoon, 6 officers and 228 men; whilst smaller detachments were raised at Fort William, Port Arthur, and Prince Albert. It reached Winnipeg on November 1st, 1,025 strong; and it was there able to take part in combined training with the 27th.

The 29th (Vancouver) Battalion was raised entirely in British Columbia and was mobilised very rapidly in the last week of October, 1914. Lieut.-Col. Tobin was in command.

The 31st (Alberta) Battalion, Lieut.-Col. Bell, was mobilised at Calgary in November, and was recruited from that town and from Edmonton, Medicine Hat, Lethbridge, and Red Deer.

The two regiments, which had joined the brigade in Winnipeg on March 1st, were somewhat handicapped in battalion training owing to the bad weather. However, all ranks were kept hard at work at platoon and company training, and route marching was freely indulged in. The 29th and 31st, on the other hand, found the climates of Calgary and Vancouver more fortunate, and were able to carry out battalion training to a fairly large extent.[1]

The sailing of the second Canadian contingent was less spectacular than that of the first.

The 1st Division had started from the mouth of the St. Lawrence as a single whole under the escort of warships—the most formidable Armada which had ever

[1] The Divisional Artillery consisted of the 4th, 5th, 6th, and 7th Brigades of the Canadian Field Artillery, and the 97th, 98th, and 107th Siege Batteries. The 4th Brigade was recruited in Toronto, and commanded by Lieut.-Col. W. J. Brown, the 5th (Lieut.-Col. Dodds) came from Winnipeg, the 6th (Lieut.-Col. King) was raised from various quarters, and the 7th (Lieut.-Col. Stewart) from Montreal, Toronto, and New Brunswick. The Divisional Ammunition Column was under the command of Lieut.-Col. Harrison. The entire artillery of the 2nd Division was commanded by Lieut.-Col. Thacker, until June 25th, 1915, when that officer took command of the 1st Divisional Artillery and was succeeded by Brig.-General E. W. B. Morrison. Mention must also be made of the other units of the Division. The Divisional Engineers were under Lieut.-Col. J. Houleston until September, 1915, when Lieut.-Col. H. T. Hughes took over command; the Divisional train was under Lieut.-Col. A. E. Massey, the Cyclist Company under Lieut.-Col. Denison, and Nos. 4, 5, and 6 Field Ambulances under Lieut.-Cols. Webster, Farmer, and Campbell respectively, with Col. J. T. Fotheringham, C.M.G., as A.D.M.S.

crossed the Atlantic. The 2nd Division left in single ships and without the picturesque accompaniments of the first embarkation.

May to Aug., 1915.

The units had been raised separately and were transhipped separately to their point of union and divisional concentration in England. The voyage was accomplished in safety, and nothing except speculations on possible submarine attacks relieved the ordinary routine of the voyage. A recapitulation of the dates of arrival of the various units and of the vessels which carried them would be tedious. It is enough to say that the transhipment was begun in April, 1915, was in the main completed by May, and that the last body arrived in August. Although some of the units did not join up till August, the division was actually constituted on May 24th, 1915, the first divisional standing orders being issued on that day by Colonel Dennison. On the 25th Major-General Steele assumed command.

The 2nd Division was fortunate in the man who was appointed to command it. Major-General Steele, C.B., M.V.O., had taken part in practically every event in the military history of the Dominion since he joined the 35th Regiment of Militia as an ensign at the age of sixteen during the Fenian raid of 1866.[2]

In December, 1914, he became Inspector-General for Western Canada, and organised the 6th Infantry Brigade. In all these activities he was ably assisted by Lieut.-Col. Ketchen, whose efforts were largely responsible for the success of the recruiting in the West, and who finally took over the command of the 6th Brigade. He, too, like the Divisional Commander, had served in the North-West and in

[2] Major-General Steele's career in the army reads more like a romance than reality. Having distinguished himself as a mere boy in all his examinations while attached to the British Regulars then stationed in Canada, he left the Service, only to rejoin as a ranker in the Red River Expedition of 1870. Here he spent a year in Fort Garry, which was then "the farthest West." After a short time in the Royal Canadian Artillery he went West again, became a Major in the Alberta Field Force during the rebellion of 1885, having raised his own corps of "Steele's Scouts." He was through all the fighting of that summer, and finally broke up Big Bear's band at Loon Lake, a place in the Great Northern Forest where no white man had ever before set foot. In 1898, as soon as the Klondyke gold rush began, he was dispatched at once to secure the frontier, erect customs posts, and prevent American miners establishing claims on the wrong side of a vast and ill-defined frontier. In 1899 he was promoted Lieut.-Colonel, and became the military representative of the Government in the Yukon. The South African War brought him immediately into the field. Within the space of five days he recruited "Strathcona's Horse" from the Western provinces; within a month he had them ready to move from Ottawa—truly a miraculous performance. In South Africa he saw a good deal of fighting in Natal and the Lydenberg district east of Pretoria, notably at Belfast. On August 26th, 1900, he was mentioned in despatches, obtained the Queen's medal with four clasps, and finally took command of a division of the new South African Constabulary. At this stage he was for six months under the direct orders of Lord Kitchener, with whom he became intimately acquainted. In 1906, after a period of mixed civil and military administration in South Africa, he returned to the Dominion to take over the command of the Western Canada military district, a post he occupied until December, 1914. Seven thousand six hundred men went from his command in the West to the First Canadian Contingent, and before he left to take command of the 2nd Division no fewer than 24,000 men in his district had joined the Colours.

South Africa, where he obtained a commission from the ranks.

April to Sept., 1915.

The further training of the units began as soon as each was landed. Up till May 25th those which had arrived took part in the work of the Training Division at Shorncliffe. After that date the 2nd Division was constituted as a separate formation, and as each battalion, battery or squadron was landed it was gradually brought up to full strength. The 2nd Division was, in many respects, more fortunate than its predecessor. It had the best of an English summer, since its time at Shorncliffe ran, roughly, from April to September of 1915; the high green downs above that well-known seaside resort abut on a charming country, and the pleasure of being able to go into a town was added. The men thus avoided the hardships, mud, and isolation of a winter on Salisbury Plain which had fallen to the lot of the 1st Division, and they carried away to France, no doubt, a more pleasant impression of English weather and scenery. All these months they were to be seen tramping the Kentish lanes, the very picture of health and vigour. Their work, of course, was heavy, special care being given to musketry. From the first it was impressed upon every man that he must learn to shoot, and to shoot straight. The musketry courses began in the middle of May, and so great was the number of men to be trained, so limited the time and range accommodation available, that rifle practice went on continuously at Hythe from 5 a.m. until 7 p.m. The 29th and the 31st Battalions carried out their musketry training at Lyd, marching eighteen miles to the ranges and camping on the flats for three weeks. The men, needless to say, were as keen as mustard, and their Regular instructors found them apt pupils. A machine-gun school was set up. Practice in bayonet fighting and the ordinary processes of infantry training went on simultaneously with musketry. The method of preparing new units to take their place in the field is, however, much the same all the world over, and by now only too familiar to millions of the citizens of the British Empire. It is the old story of learning to do things under favourable conditions so thoroughly and completely that in moments of stress they are done almost sub-consciously, leaving the mind free to grapple with anything novel there may be in the situation or in the actions of the enemy. It was in this quality of rapid decision in the face of unexpected emergencies that the Canadian Contingent proved itself pre-eminent.

The Divisional Artillery was far behind the rest of the formation as regards training. Drafts of artillery reached England as late as the middle of August. For some time practice was retarded by lack of equipment, and even so late as October 10th, when the infantry were becoming used to life in the trenches, progress made by the artillery in England was poor. It stands to reason that far more time and trouble are required to make an efficient gunner than an efficient infantryman. The *personnel* of the Artillery brigades was, however, such as to inspire high hopes, and these were fully justified by the 2nd Divisional Artillery when it finally reached the Front.

Ten weeks later the Inspector of Royal Horse and Field Artillery inspected the training, and congratulated Brigadier-General Morrison, D.S.O. (who had returned after serving with great distinction with the 1st Division in France), and Major Constantine on the work accomplished. "All ranks," he reported, "know their work, the drill at the guns is good and quiet, and good effects were obtained. I consider them the best Divisional Artillery I have seen on Salisbury Plain this year."

A break was made in the daily task of training the Division by two weeks' field manoeuvres in August in the valley. Here the Division operated as a whole and existed entirely under Service conditions.

The 2nd Division had now gone through its preliminary training both in Canada and Europe and was ready for the ordeal of battle. It has, however, always been the habit of statesmen, leaders, and commanders to address their troops in the field before the hour of action comes. The Great Causes which inspire volunteer armies to supreme exertion gain added strength from the presence of the leaders themselves.

Aug. 4th, 1915.

The Prime Minister of the Dominion had visited the troops at Shorncliffe in July, 1915 (Vol. I., page 94). He was followed on August 4th by the Rt. Hon. A. Bonar Law, M.P., Secretary for the Colonies, who was accompanied by General Sir Sam Hughes, K.C.B.

The presence of General Hughes was significant, for he above anyone else was the embodiment of Canada in arms. He had performed the amazing feat of raising a huge army in a country remote from Europe to do battle for the Imperial cause. When one remembers that the presence of 7,000 men in South Africa at the beginning of a century only fifteen years old was regarded at the time as a crowning achievement on the part of the Dominion; that the enrolment of 40,000 men for the camp at Valcartier and the dispatch of the First Contingent had been considered only twelve months before this review as a triumph of patriotism and organisation, who would have ventured to predict that in September, 1915, another contingent of equal strength would be about to set sail for Flanders; that by the dawn of 1916 a 3rd Division would be in the trenches and engaged in the death grapple of June; and that far beyond this huge reserves would lie waiting in Canada to create yet other divisions or replace the fallen in the field? Great Armadas had crossed the Atlantic carrying armies beside which those dispatched by the might of Great Britain against Washington and his levies in a day when Chatham still lived, dwindle into insignificance. And the tireless energy of Sir Sam Hughes directed the system which procured the men to meet the demand. Like all strong men he has, and has had, not only friends, but opponents; but if these will set aside the controversies of the present and look down the vista of the future to an impartial and final judgment, both alike will perceive the singleness and simplicity of purpose which constitute greatness of character, and, joined to strength of will, lead to greatness of achievement. As the General looked on the march past of the 2nd Division he might well have been thinking of the pride of work well done; but in reality his heart was with the men, who were going out to fight, suffer, and perhaps to die for their common cause; and in such thoughts there is no room for any pride except that of the aim and the race.

The Colonial Secretary has a natural claim to address a force of Imperial troops, but in this case there are special reasons why Mr. Bonar Law should have been given a cordial welcome. He is Canadian born and British trained, and therefore represents a natural link of union between the Dominion and the Mother Country. Direct and business-like, at once enthusiastic and unimpassioned, he is the natural interpreter between the newer nations and the old.

The conditions of the review were not happy. A heavy thunderstorm had broken the summer weather, and the troops were wet through long before the inspection began. The men, of course, were not worried, and it struck more than one observer that the driving rain and heavy cloud-wrack behind it gave a solemnity to the occasion which might have been lost in the mere picture of green glades, tall immemorial trees, and brightly-dressed spectators. Rain, after all, has about it a certain air of reality for anyone who is going to Flanders. As the artillery removed itself on its own devices, the long columns of infantry, platoon by platoon, began to swing past the saluting base, where stood the Colonial Secretary and the Canadian Minister. The dull afternoon light shone on the rippling bayonets, beneath which thousands of men, superbly fit, marched by to prove to Canada and the Empire that the New World was still ready to redress the balance of the Old. Something of this seems to have stirred in the Colonial Secretary's mind as he addressed the officers. In simple language he told his hearers that when he watched them marching past he thought how strong had been the call of duty which had brought them there. The world knew what they had sacrificed, and that every one of them was prepared to face danger and death and to give a good account of himself when the opportunity came. He realised their courage and their devotion, and he thought also, when he saw so many young faces, that, after all, their sacrifice was not perhaps so great as that of those whom they had left behind in anxiety as to the fate of their dearest. He himself was born in Canada—he was proud of what Canadian troops had done and of the future which lay in front of them. "After the war things would never be quite the same again." Already by an arrangement with the Mother Country and the self-governing Dominions it was understood that when the time came for peace, the Dominion Governments were to have a say in the negotiations. That marked a great step onwards, but it was only a step. It had long been his hope and was now his belief that as a result of the war the time would come when the whole of the self-governing Dominions, in proportion to their population and resources, would share with the Mother Country in the duty and honour of governing the British Empire.

Sept. 2nd, 1915.

The 2nd Division had at least the sense that they were contributing to the making of history. Nor were they without the further assurance that their efforts were appreciated. On September 2nd, 1915, his Majesty the King, accompanied by Lord Kitchener, inspected the Division before it left for the Front. Once more, under a grey and gloomy sky, it marched out—this time to parade before its Sovereign. The 2nd Division was only following in the steps of the 1st, which had already received that supreme honour. But the 1st Division had already earned the King's accolade in the field, and there was a rigid determination on the part of the 2nd to do the same. So, as line after line of infantry went by the saluting point, the unspoken homage was in the heart of every man: "One King, One Country, One Empire."[3]

Sept. 14th, 1915.

Major-General Turner (Vol. I., p. 107) had taken over the Division from General Steele, who had been appointed to command the troops in the Shorncliffe area. Preparations were now begun for departure. The Divisional Supply Column had already started on September 5th. The real crossing, however, began on September 13th, 1915, when the transport, with the 4th Canadian Infantry Brigade, the Borden Machine-Gun Battery, the Divisional Signallers, the 4th Canadian Field Ambulance, and all the motor ambulance wagons of the Division, left Southampton for Havre. On the night of September 14th the Headquarters Staff and the bulk of the Division embarked, including the 4th Brigade, Canadian Field Artillery. The rest of the Divisional Artillery, the 5th, 6th[4] and 7th Brigades, were left behind for a time to complete their training, proceeding later to France on January 18th, 1916.

Eight battalions were left in reserve and absorbed in the Training Division at Shorncliffe—the 23rd, 30th, 32nd, 36th, 39th, and 43rd, to supply drafts for the Infantry, the 48th for the Pioneers, and the Royal Canadian Regiment afterwards incorporated in the 3rd Division. The 2nd Canadian Division Headquarters in Shorncliffe were then closed.

The voyage of the 2nd Division was not to be a long one like that of the 1st, from Bristol in the West of England to St. Nazaire on the coast of Brittany. The high, white cliffs of Folkestone by day and the light of its lamps by night are clearly visible from the high downs above Boulogne in fair weather; while the light of Gris Nez flashing like a wheeling spearshaft has long been familiar to the Canadian troops. It was for Boulogne that the 2nd Division set out—to the harbours below the heights from which the statue of Napoleon on its great bronze column

---

[3] The Special Message from the King to the 2nd Canadian Division was published after the inspection:—

"Officers, Non-commissioned Officers and Men of the 2nd Canadian Division,—Six months ago I inspected the 1st Canadian Division before their departure for the Front. The heroism they have since shown on the field of battle has won for them undying tame. You are now leaving to join them, and I am glad to have the opportunity of seeing you to-day, for it has convinced me that the same spirit which animated them inspires you also. The past weeks at Shorncliffe have been for you a period of severe and rigorous training; and your appearance at this inspection testifies to the thoroughness and devotion to duty with which your work has been performed. You are going to meet hardships and dangers, but the steadiness and discipline which have marked your bearing on parade to-day will carry you through all difficulties. History will never forget your loyalty and the readiness with which you rallied to the aid of your Mother Country in the hour of danger. My thoughts will always be with you. May God bless you and bring you victory!"

[4] The 6th Brigade was formed by reorganising the 8th Howitzer Brigade from the Reserve Brigade at Shorncliffe.

still looks out, as he did all the summer of 1805, at the white cliffs on which he was never to set foot, to the coast, too, whence Cæsar first saw the almost fabulous land of Britain. Those conquerors of the modern and ancient worlds would have marvelled had they beheld the sailing of 20,000 men of French and British birth from the other side of the Atlantic across the narrow salt-water trench, once the confluent of the Thames and Rhine, to defend the land of Gaul against that Teuton menace which both of these had overthrown.

Who of the millions that have undergone the experience will ever forget their first crossing of the Channel in a troopship? The absence of any lights and the swift drive of the engines give the sense of a stealthy escape from the unseen perils of the deep. Dimly visible for a moment is a dark shape of another transport or some destroyer of the escort. The men who can crowd below are perhaps asleep, but to the remainder, shivering a little on deck in the sea breeze, the whole air and the chopping seas seem to breathe something of danger, of the mystery of the dark, and the romance of the High Adventure yet ahead. It was in this atmosphere that a serious collision occurred. The Staff of the 4th Brigade under Brigadier-General Lord Brooke and the 10th Battalion were aboard a paddle-wheeled steamer when a dark mass suddenly shot out of the night and rammed her amidships. The shock threw everybody off their feet; no one could tell at first whether it was a German cruiser or a friend; and had panic broken out among the massed humanity of over a thousand souls on board it would not have been surprising. But the Volunteer troops showed themselves in calmness and discipline the equal of any Regulars. The instant the collision occurred the troops were paraded on deck with the life-belts which had been provided for them. For a time it was thought that the ship was going down. But the men ranged on deck remained steady in the ranks, and the parties told off to loose the rafts carried out their duties swiftly and surely. The incident adjusted itself. The stranger, which turned out to be one of our own destroyers, had by a fortunate chance struck the great wooden paddle-box of the steamer, and though the latter was for a time out of control, no irretrievable damage had been done. The transport carrying the Divisional Staff stood by and endeavoured to tow her in, but the hawsers and steel cables parted under the strain of the rough weather. It was necessary to send for tugs from Boulogne, and, finally, at five in the morning, that port was made. All through the night an escort of destroyers which had raced up at the first news of the accident circled round flashing their searchlights over the seas to guard against a possible submarine attack, but no enemy appeared to disturb the work of rescue. The remaining ships of the Division, despite the heavy weather, made the passage in security, and the whole body began to pass up country to effect its junction with its comrades of the 1st Division.

The landing in France possessed one feature both of racial and historic importance. The 1st Division had included one company of the 14th Battalion, which was entirely composed of French Canadians, and many others of the same race were scattered among the various units. The 22nd Battalion of the 2nd Division was entirely recruited, as has been recorded, from the French of the old province, and its appearance on the sacred soil of France serves to awaken a host of memories.

There is no parallel in history that matches the picture of the descendants of the men who founded Port Royal and Quebec under Champlain in the first decade of the seventeenth century returning, after three hundred years of absence and a hundred and fifty years under a different flag, to fight once more for the soil whence their ancestors sprang. The German menace has welded the two great nations of the West on the two sea-boards of the Atlantic and linked the centuries together beyond imagination and almost beyond belief. In the firing line at Ypres were found side by side not only the successors of the British who had stayed in their island home and of the French who had remained in France and dealt with the British since on many a hard-fought field in Europe, but the sons of those who had struggled together before the entrenchments of Ticonderoga or on the fateful Plains of Abraham. When after the Seven Years' War in 1763 the Empire of the West passed finally to Great Britain under the pressure of British sea-power and the military inspiration of Chatham, France must have mourned what seemed the irrevocable loss of her sons. Yet in France and Flanders to-day they are risen again for her service, returned across the Atlantic by that same sea-power that once claimed them, and are now warring on the very fields their fathers held, with the same courage and fortitude their race displayed in the eighteenth century against Great Britain.

The French are of all people the most susceptible to an appeal to the imagination. One can imagine their feelings when they learnt that a whole regiment of French Canadians had landed with the 2nd Division. Very strange must have been the meeting between these two branches of a race separated so long by the Seas of Time!

Gradually it dawned on these people that among the strange soldiers from across the ocean were men speaking their mother tongue—not the French, perhaps, of modern Brittany and Normandy, but French none the less. One must picture the joyous effort to find the common idiom and accent, the older country casting back in memory across the years to the point where the two streams of speech had divided, the younger nation of the older speech casting forward to catch the new French which had sprung up since the division. The scene is one for the painter or the novelist, and this wonderful journey's end in lovers meeting must leave an ineffaceable imprint on the memories of both England and France. Dramatic moments are few in modern war, but this was one of them—a fitting pendant to that other scene when the joint memorial to Wolfe and Montcalm was unveiled on the heights of Quebec.

CHAPTER II

PATROLS

An interval of calm—Process of forming the Second and Third Divisions—St. Eloi—The sector of Bailleul—Work of the Army Corps Staff—Changes in the Higher Command—The first experience of the Second Division—A demonstration opposite La Douve Farm—Dummy trenches—Smoke sacks—Veterans of the Third Brigade act as instructors—Bombardment of the Fifth Brigade—The gallant deed of Major Roy—Steadiness of the French Canadians—New Brunswickers on their mettle—Heroism of Sergeant Ryer—Canadians at home in patrol work—Stolidity of the Germans—Inventiveness of Canadians—Plucky rescue of Corporal May—Deadly land mines—Lucky escape of the Winnipeg boys—A thrilling adventure in the air—Capture of a German 'plane—Singular recovery of a Colt gun—The value of model trenches—The formation of a Brigade—Difficult night work—Havoc wrought by storms—Useful work of Labour Battalion—Holy ground.

Sept., 1915.

With the junction between the two divisions the work of the Canadian troops in Flanders enters on a new and broader phase. The meeting took place in time midway between the tempest which raged on the plains of Ypres in May of 1915 and that scarcely less violent iron-storm which, in the same month of 1916, burst in the fields of St. Eloi. An interval of calm, or such calm as modern war knows, was permitted for that reunion. It is well for the soldier that there should be such intervals, for the strain of modern action, were it never relaxed, would destroy the mind and nerve of man as surely as the continuance of its shell fire must destroy the body. But though modern armies cannot always be locked in desperate conflict, the reader may not find the ensuing chapters altogether dull. He will be able to trace the steps by which the original 1st Division added unto itself first a second and then a third, and developed into an army corps. He can watch the multiplication of the Staffs, the promotion of Brigadiers to command divisions, of Colonels to brigades, and of Majors and Captains to regiments; the process of the division of labour as the specialists develop in bombing, mining, or machine-gunning; the foundations of schools of instruction behind the line; the methodical study of the arts of patrolling and raiding. He can survey, in fact, the full range of those methods by which large bodies of men carrying rifles gradually develop into a self-sufficient army far greater in numbers than the British troops that the Duke of Wellington commanded, not so far away, on the field of Waterloo. As a stream draws into it confluent after confluent until it attains the dignity of a river, so the original Canadian Expeditionary Force, by the flow of men across the Atlantic, is becoming an army; and it is the history of this process that the next few chapters must relate. In artillery alone is the development a slow one, and here the 2nd and 3rd Divisions were for long dependent on the assistance of the British gunners.

The scene is laid in a sector to the south of Ypres and to the north of Armentières. Its more southerly position in the line is marked by the greater number of spinneys, small eminences, and commanding heights, such as that of Kemmel, from which the enemy's lines can be overlooked. But portions of it are a dead level, and it is very far from the well-covered hills of the real southern line. The main features are still those of Flanders—the slightly rolling flat where the transparent richness of the crops which spring from the sand and the clay seems no deeper than the paint of a fresco on the wall, and the scraggy trees and ragged woods mock one with a delusive memory of forest cool and shade. As the army grows the winter draws on, and the fine, hot autumn days and brilliant nights with the moon high in the heavens behind the trenches turn to the rains of November and the mists and frosts of Christmas. The ground grows wet underfoot and the air is clammy and cold. Such is the winter season of Northern Europe, when most of the campaigners of history allowed their troops to hibernate in warm and comfortable billets.

The 1st Division had spent the later summer on a sector the right of which rests on the northern edge of Ploegsteert. As the 2nd Division came by degrees into the fighting line the Canadian sector was extended northwards until the left of the Corps finally rested on a spot a little to the south of St. Eloi. The moves which resulted in the final disposition were not all made in a day, but it would be tedious to do more than note in passing the various shifts the new corps made with the II British Corps to the south of them and the V British Corps to the north. Roughly speaking, the northern line ending by St. Eloi was taken over by the 2nd Division while the 1st Division remained in the Ploegsteert area to the south. The dividing point was a little to the north of Wulverghem, facing the German trenches halfway between Messines and Wytschaete. For the sake of clearness one might call it the sector of Bailleul.

The distinguishing feature of the line is length rather than depth—the precise converse of the subsequent St. Eloi position. The line from that place to Ploegsteert is not excessive for a corps of three divisions, but it is distinctly so for one with only two. In fact, on March 1st, when the whole three divisions were assembled, the frontage was occupied by six out of the nine brigades, and this six brigade frontage was throughout the normal one. But the 3rd Division was not in full existence till the middle of January, 1916, and in the meantime the reliefs could only be effected by such elements of corps troops as happened from time to time to be in readiness. Thus on October 3rd, when an additional two thousand yards were taken over, and the 2nd Division occupied our final position to the north, the only corps troops available for reliefs were Brigadier-General Seely's force, consisting of three regiments of the Cavalry Brigade and the 1st Canadian Mounted Rifle Brigade. The 42nd Battalion (Royal Highlanders of Canada) and the 49th Battalion (Edmonton Regiment) did not arrive till the middle of that month, the 2nd Canadian Mounted Rifle Brigade till towards the end of it, the Princess Patricia's Canadian Light Infantry and the Royal Canadian Regiment till November, and the various units which finally formed the 3rd Division were not completed till January. This necessarily entailed a somewhat extended sojourn in the front line area by the various brigades of the first two divisions.

The task, therefore, of interchanging the different units was one that required careful working out on the part of the Corps Staff. The ordinary divisional front is held by two brigades, with a third at rest well in the rear. The business of interchanging them becomes as mechanical as that of a bridge-player opening a long and strong suit; every unit knows to within two or three days its time in the front line, support line, reserve line, or rest billets. As the units of the 3rd Division began to arrive, matters, of course, became simpler, but in the last months of the year the Corps found itself compelled to make heavy calls on the endurance of the various battalions.

Sept. 14th, 1915.

To return to the narrative. The 2nd Division arrived at Caestre on September 14th. On the previous day the Canadian Corps had been formed. Upon his appointment as Corps Commander, General Alderson relinquished the command of the 1st Division to Major-General Currie, who was in turn succeeded in the 2nd Brigade by Brigadier-General Lipsett. Major-General Turner was already in command of the 2nd Division, and he was succeeded in the command of the 3rd Brigade by Brigadier-General Leckie. The 16th Battalion was taken over from Brigadier-General Leckie by his brother, Major Leckie. The changes in the Higher Command were now for the moment complete. The duty of the 2nd Division was to relieve the 28th British Division in what may be called for convenience the Kemmel section of the line, which stretched north from the ground of the 1st Canadian Division. As in the case of all inexperienced troops, they were given a "trial trip," and their officers went in with the 84th and 85th British Brigades for a few days to learn the tricks of the trade and the lie of the land.

Sept. 23rd, 1915.

The relief was finally accomplished by September 23rd, 1915. The 4th Brigade, 2nd Division, took the north of the line; the 5th Brigade the south; while the centre was stiffened by the hardened veterans of the 3rd Brigade, 1st Division. The 6th Brigade remained in reserve at Kemmel.

Sept. 25th, 1915.

The first experience of the 2nd Division and of the new Canadian Corps was a curious one, as a glance at the dates will suggest. The last week of September was the time of the great Anglo-French offensive, which to us spells Loos and to our

Allies Champagne. The advantage of the initiative is the uncertainty for the enemy as to where the real blow will fall. Until he knows, he dare not shift his reserves. The ingenuity of the Canadian Force was, therefore, exercised to produce without loss of life the appearance of an attack which would pin the Germans opposite to their ground and prevent them from going to the assistance of their sorely-pressed colleagues to the south. The new corps rose gallantly to the demand for theatrical effect, and a demonstration was arranged along the whole line, but particularly in front of the 1st Division, opposite La Douve farm. It must have been exciting for everyone to think out methods of simulating a bogus assault to keep the Germans on tenterhooks. On the night of the 24th the guns opened on the enemy wire and cut great gaps thirty yards wide in it as though to open the way for the assaulting columns. Dummy trenches were dug close behind the firing line to hold the supports of the supposed assailants. In the early dawn of the 25th the Germans could see great and dangerous activity in the Canadian trenches, which hummed like a hive of bees about to swarm. At 5.45 a.m. sacks full of wet straw were fired and thrown on the parapets whenever the wind blew towards the enemy. That same morning real gas was covering in grim earnest the rush of the British over the stricken field of Lens and to the Hohenzollern Redoubt. To intensify the effect, the platoon commanders shouted orders and blew their whistles, while scaling ladders and the shimmer of bayonets were shown above the edge of the parapet. Our troops then opened fire, both with rifles and machine-guns. The Germans, in the face of this provocation and menace, became convinced that an attack was imminent, though reflection might have convinced them that serious assaults are seldom so well advertised. They put down a heavy barrage behind our firing line to prevent the arrival of supports, and thronged their own second-line trenches. This was precisely the intention of the Canadian Command, whose gunners shelled the communication and support trenches severely. About six o'clock in the morning, when it was too late to move troops to Loos, the false smoke thinned, and the enemy could see clearly that no attack was in progress. The fire died away; but the German bulletin announced the successful repulse of a determined advance. It is not surprising that the Canadians have achieved a certain unpopularity among their *vis-à-vis* in the trenches owing to their predilection for "slickness." Such incidents, as the men know well, relieve the monotony of trench warfare.

Sept. 26th to 30th, 1915.

From September 26th to 30th, following this episode, certain changes were made in the British line on the right of the Canadian Corps. The 12th Division was pulled out, to be sent further south, and a new division, the 25th, was brought up to take its place. During the change the 3rd Brigade took over a part of the British line and acted as instructors to the inexperienced troops of the 75th British Infantry Brigade for the space of a week, when the scholars took over from the tutors. Their place in the 2nd Division was occupied by the 6th Canadian Brigade, commanded by Brigadier-General Ketchen, and until then in reserve at Kemmel.

All three brigades of the 2nd Division were now in the front line, and, as has been mentioned, they were extended two thousand yards to the north to complete the final frontage of the corps. They possessed in Divisional Reserve Brigadier-General Seely's force, which had been replaced in the firing line by the 2nd Infantry Brigade. The line of the 1st Division was held by this brigade and by the 1st Brigade, while the 3rd enjoyed a well-earned rest as corps reserve. These two brigades were, however, holding the frontage of three, and it must be observed once more that the forces behind the entire British line were at this period hardly sufficient to supply adequate reliefs, much less to resist a strong attack. This state of affairs was merely the result of the general lack of preparation of the British Empire for the duration and scale of the land war. In the first week of October five brigades were in the front line of a six-brigade frontage, and their total reserve was four battalions of infantry and six regiments of cavalry. During the month, however, the situation was improved, since the 42nd (Royal Highlanders of Canada), under Lieut.-Col. Cantlie, and the 49th (Edmonton Regiment), under Lieut.-Col. Griesbach, arrived on October 10th, and the 2nd Canadian Mounted Rifle Brigade, under the command of Colonel Sissons, on the 26th.

Oct. 5th, 1915.

The beginning of October was not, however, by any means without its incidents, both tragic and glorious. On the evening of October 5th, while the great struggle round Loos was still raging, the 5th Brigade was subjected to its first severe bombardment. The perpetual pillars of yellow and green smoke, slashed with black *débris* spouting to heaven, and the earth-shaking roar of heavy shells, are enough to try the nerve of the most trench-hardened warriors, and this brigade was but a week in the trenches and entirely new to the experience. In these cases all depends on the example and leading of the officers. It may be recorded here how that example was set. Brigadier-General Watson had been moving continually up and down in the front of his brigade, and was passing through the line of the 22nd (French Canadians). He passed Major Roy of that regiment in the muddy trench and spoke a word to him. Hardly had he turned the traverse when out of the sky fell one of those huge abominations fired from a trench mortar. There it lay in a trench full of men, ready to explode any second. Like a flash Major Roy took his risk and dashed to save the lives of the rest. As he stooped to pick up the great greasy cone of steel and hurl it over the parapet he slipped in the mud, and the shell exploded in his arms. There died a very gallant gentleman, and with him all doubts as to the steadiness of the French Canadian regiment under shell fire.

Throughout the early part of October the enemy exhibited great activity in mining on the front of the Corps. It was the turn of the New Brunswickers to show their mettle in a first raid into "No Man's Land." The fibre of the race that province breeds has become indurated by generations of contest with the elements, and has taken on something of the unbending hardness of the North. They were now to test these ingrained qualities against a new antagonist, for immediately on their front the enemy one day blew up a great mine.

Oct. 13th, 1915.

The 26th (New Brunswick), under Lieut.-Col. McAvity, was ordered to make a reconnaissance on October 13th, and the company commanded by Major Brown held the post of honour. If the mine crater could be occupied with advantage, then it was to be held by the attacking party; if, on the other hand, it was useless to hang on there, the crater was to be abandoned. Imagine the infantry, bombers and bayonet men in four successive lines, straining on the leash till the artillery had finished pounding and the smoke-bombs which had been prepared to cover the advance from the sight of the German trenches had been let loose. Thrilling is the moment when warriors climb their trenches to the assault. The New Brunswickers were untried. But before dawn, at four o'clock, out they came from a saphead dug in advance of their trench, and raced for the crater over forty yards of open ground. The weight of a threefold decision lay upon them. Major Brown and Lieutenant Fairweather, of the 26th, and Lieutenant McPhee, of the Engineers, had to survey the ground, determine whether to hold on or retire, and guard against counter and flank attacks. One party at their order rushed to within throwing distance of the German side of the crater, where the enemy occupied a saphead from which noises of tapping had been heard, and held off assault with bomb and rifle. Shielded by their efforts our officers examined the ground, while Major Brown extended the supports right and left of our saphead to ward off a flank attack. Both advanced support parties were met by high-explosive bombs and a heavy crossfire from enemy machine-guns. In the words of Captain McMillan, of the 26th:—"In the face of a shower of bombs from the front, and enfiladed from both sides by machine-gun fire, the first and second lines went forward and gained the crater. After a careful reconnaissance made by the officers in charge it was found inadvisable to remain in the crater, and the order to retire was given. Nor did that order come a moment too soon. Just as the officers and party cleared the crater, a mine trap, whose existence had been suspected, was fired by the Germans and the whole force barely escaped destruction. At this moment the ground between the crater and our trench was covered with a hail of bullets from the machine-guns of the enemy, and by flying shells and bursting bombs." The explosion stunned everyone within reach. Sergeant Ryer, a well-known scout and trapper in civil life, remained unshaken. "Instead of retiring at once, he kept in the open, using his rifle as opportunity offered with good success, accounting—it is believed—for eleven of the enemy." After he had helped to cover his comrades, with an indifference to orders not unlike Nelson at Copenhagen, Ryer turned to the wounded. The losses of the 26th had been severe. Imagine a ground swept by machine-gun fire "with a noise like a giant tearing calico," the shattering crash of bombs, and the perpetual spit-fire rattle from the enemy. To live in it seemed impossible. But Sergeant Ryer, his fancy shooting done, tried to give assistance to Sergeant Cotter, who had led the first line to the German sap. Finding him beyond all aid, he turned to Pte. D. Winchester, who was badly wounded, unwound one of the wounded man's puttees, passed it under Winchester's armpits and around his own shoulders, and crawled back to the trench, struggling under the weight of his comrade. Pte. Daly came to his help, and between them they dragged Winchester into safety.

For all kinds of patrol work between the lines the Canadians showed an inherent aptitude from the start. The art of woodcraft, the inherited instinct of men whose fathers and grandfathers had been mighty hunters before the Lord, gave the corps supremacy almost at once over their adversaries in these contests of small groups in the dark.

Except for one brief period, when a particularly adventurous Saxon corps developed a tendency to dispute the mastery of "No Man's Land," the Canadians throughout the winter of 1915 ranged almost at will over that doubtful territory. They won the right by their conspicuous victories over larger bodies of the enemy in struggles where good shooting, steady nerves, and individual initiative were more vital to success than drill or routine. They excelled in the most fascinating of pursuits which modern war has left to its votaries. The sharp night air, the rustle in the grass or the trees which may mean an enemy, the stealthy crawl with the fingers on the trigger, the fitful flare of the star-shells, the rasp of barbed wire, the knowledge that life depends on one's own personal swiftness of action, wake again in civilised man the old instincts of the hunter and the hunted. Life runs keen in the veins because Death lurks under every shadow. In spite of their personal courage, the disciplined stolidity of the Germans is hardly adapted to this peculiar kind of sport. They lacked the range of inventiveness of their opponents, and by posing opportunities of quick action they lost the initiative of attack. Instances without number could be given of these small engagements on the front at night in which every regiment has borne its share. One could almost select one's instances at random and do no injustice to the general picture.

Oct. 20th, 1915.

On the night of October 20th, 1915, a patrol from the 4th (Central Ontario) Battalion, in charge of Sergt.-Major Matheson, became enveloped in a heavy fog in "No Man's Land" and lost its way. While trying to regain direction, Pte. Inwood was wounded. Corporal May went to Inwood's assistance, and found him lying in the German entanglements. In attempting to remove Inwood from the wire, the corporal's foot struck a tin can, and the sound drew an instant volley of fire from the enemy's parapet. Inwood received another wound in his body and May was hit in the thigh and shoulder. The corporal remained with Inwood in the German wire until the latter's death, and then crawled into the cover of a clump of bushes close at hand. In the meantime, the other members of the patrol had been forced back to our trenches by a converging fire from the enemy. Sergt.-Major Matheson, accompanied by Sergt. Norwood, went out and searched unsuccessfully for the wounded men. At dawn the Sergeant-major went out again, this time with Pte. Donoghue. These two separated soon after leaving our trench, the better to cover the ground in their merciful quest. Donoghue found Corporal May in the little clump of bushes near the German wire, dressed his wounds, and slowly, tenderly, and under the constant menace of death, removed him to the head of one of our saps.

On the same evening Lieutenant Cosgrave, of the Engineers, supported by a small party of the 15th (48th Highlanders), under Lieutenant McLaurin, of the 16th (Canadian Scottish), who had reconnoitred the ground beforehand, went out two hundred yards from our trenches and blew up a heavily-wired and fortified house.

The weather during the latter part of October was inclined to be misty, and this led to a considerable activity on the part of the patrols in front of the line by night, and of the digging parties behind it by day.

Oct. 23rd, 1915.

But a new horror was added to life—the discovery of land-mines laid down by the Germans between the lines, some fired by trip-wires after the fashion of the spring gun in forbidden woods, others electrically connected by wires with the hostile trenches. On the 23rd, a whole party of the 8th (Winnipeg Rifles) nearly fell victims to one of the former kind, and Pte. Green, who actually touched off the wire, was blown to atoms.

The end of the month was marked by one or two very daring reconnaissances by Lieutenant Owen, of the 7th (British Columbia) Battalion, up the bed of the Douve River, and by a great aeroplane battle.

The aeroplane battle occurred upon a morning warm and bright with sunshine. The conditions were admirable for flying and observing, and, as usual, a German Albatross took advantage of them. Soaring high against the warm blue of the sky, over Bailleul, over the headquarters of a division, over our brigades and trenches and back again, it glinted like silver in the morning sun. The snow-white blobs of bursting shrapnel from our anti-aircraft guns followed its graceful sweeps and curves—followed and followed, but never caught it up; and thousands of our men stared after it. But a more dramatic spectacle was in store for the watchers on the brown roads and in the brown trenches.

A British machine appeared suddenly low against the blue, mounting and flying out of the west. The men in the Albatross were evidently so intent on their task of observing the landscape beneath them and keeping well ahead of our blossoming shrapnel that they failed to observe the approach of the British 'plane as soon as they should have for their own good. They were heading west when they saw their danger, and instantly the Albatross swerved round and sped towards home. But the British flier had the heels of the German and the advantage of the position. It circled and dipped, and down through the clear air aloft came the rippling "tap-tap-tap" of the aerial machine-guns. Again and again the enemy's frantic efforts to escape were frustrated by the skill and daring of the British pilot and the hedging fire of the British guns. Suddenly the gun of the German 'plane jammed and ceased; the pilot was hit and wounded; the Albatross commenced a rapid descent, in which it was followed by the British 'plane to within a thousand feet of the ground. Then, under heavy shell-fire from German batteries, the victorious machine rose and flew away undamaged, and the unfortunate Albatross struck the earth between the front and support trenches of the 14th (Montreal) Battalion and turned turtle. The German pilot was dead; the observer, slightly wounded, crawled to our support trenches and surrendered. The German batteries kept up a hot fire of high explosives and shrapnel on the machine with the object of smashing it beyond hope of repair before the Canadians could salvage it. They made several direct hits, but our men sapped out to the wreck and managed to bring most of it in, piece by piece. Among the articles brought in was the machine-gun that had jammed in the heat of the fight. This was found to be a Colt gun. Closer examination proved it to be one of the original guns of our 14th Battalion—to whose lines it had just made such a dramatic return! The gun had been abandoned during one of the desperate and confused fights of the Second Battle of Ypres half a year before.

Sept. and Oct., 1915.

In these months of September and October great efforts were expended on improving the line. Work in the front positions was done by the occupying battalions, and the troops in reserve came up night after night to assist their labours and to create new secondary positions and drive through fresh communication trenches. Even the training of new units was occasionally and rightly sacrificed to the performance of this essential task. The weather was, on the whole, favourable for these operations, with the exception of three days of rain early in September and a wet week late in October. The 1st Division, long on the ground and fortified by the experience of what good trenches mean for comfort and safety, was pre-eminent in these exertions, as would be proved by the trench-map with its continuous increase, month after month, in the black and zigzag lines of new work. Each tiny scrawl on the surface of such a map represents the labours of hundreds of men, extended over many nights. Second and third lines grew apace, so that a sudden attack of the enemy would still leave trenches to be held and would reduce the German bite to mere nibbles at the forward trench. The communication trenches are driven true and straight from well in the rear, and up these the ration parties toil in safety night after night under their burdens of food, water, ammunition, and R.E. material to feed the front line. These parties know well enough the difference between well-made lines and bad ones. Stooping under the heavy weights as they struggle on through the dark, they will bless in army fashion a smooth and dry surface underfoot and a sound high parapet which protects them from the casual German shells which are searching for them, or the intermittent whistle of the long-range bullet humming on its errand in the dusk. Messengers or stretcher-bearers with their burdens can move backwards or forwards even by day along the well-built hollow, and all those who pass are protected both from the arrow that flieth by night and the terror which walketh in the noonday. Very different is the story of a badly-kept line. It finds carrying parties struggling in, hours late, exhausted by wading through mud and water, and delayed by continually climbing out and walking outside the trench to avoid impassable sections. Here an unlucky shell or a casual bullet may take its toll. The men struggle back with difficulty, arriving hardly before the dawn, and with their period of supposed rest and recuperation turned into the most arduous of labours. It is not too much to say that the efficiency of a regiment or division can be tested by a comparison between the state in which it takes over and that in which it leaves its trenches.

The creation of secondary positions is as important as that of communication trenches, and on this task the Canadian Corps worked unsparingly throughout the autumn.

The disposition of a brigade is two, or on occasion three, battalions in the front line and one or two in support or reserve trenches. But in most cases even the leading regiments will not have their whole strength in the firing trench. One or two companies lie close up in support or reserve to reinforce any threatened point. The nearness of these supports is a very present help in time of trouble, and gives confidence to officers and men, who would be nervous if they knew that no assistance was nearer than a mile away in distance and an hour in time. But these lines must be dug under cover of dark, so the men toiled with the spade through the nights of autumn and blessed the dawn which put a term to their labours. Their record is written on the scarred earth from St. Eloi down to Ploegsteert. Let us hope that the corps which took their place in March was duly grateful for the blessing of a well-constructed line.

Nov., 1915.

With the end of October and the beginning November, however, trouble began. The mists of early autumn had enabled some of the back-line digging to be done by day, without undue attention from the German gunners, but with the rain of the end of the first-named months the efforts of weeks began to dissolve in hours. As a sudden thunderstorm fills all the ditches to the brink, so two days' rain in the horrible clay of Flanders turns every trench into a miniature mill-race. Traverses, parapets, and parados, which in the summer sun had assumed the solidity of Egyptian monuments, collapsed like melting jelly as the torrents tore under the foundations. Men struggled waist-high in water to repair the damage, only to hear the heavy splash of falling earth and sandbags as the rain broke away the trenches as a cheese-scoop cuts out cheese. Many of the communications became impassable, and parties had to walk outside them even in broad daylight and in plain view of the enemy's observers. The situation of the Germans, at any rate, was no better, and our gunners had their revenge on them when they also were compelled to walk in the open. The last fortnight of November was, however, fortunately drier, and the Canadian Corps were able by increased exertions to make their trenches safe and habitable for the winter. The weak places in the trenches were revetted with chicken-wire, and strutted wooden paths two or three feet high, like the crossings of a swollen stream, were placed in the worst parts of the communication trenches, so that even if men's feet were in water, they had a firm foothold beneath them instead of a deadly morass. In this work they were assisted by the 11th (British) Labour Battalion, which was attached on November 1st to the Canadian Corps. A scientific system of drainage was devised and carried out.[5]

One can cast one's eye southwards from Voormezeele and St. Eloi through Vierstraat to Kemmel, and from Kemmel and Petit Bois to Wulverghem, Neuve Eglise to Hutte and Ploegsteert, and everywhere line upon line of Canadian trenches score the ground like a succession of gigantic furrows. Far beyond the line extends till it strikes the grey seas of the Channel on the north and the snow-clad Alps on the south. The labour of these vast field-works would have built the Canadian Pacific, and one may wonder how long these gashes in the earth will survive the passions and ideals of the men who created them. For some years after the

[5] On November 27th, 1915, the Princess Patricia's Canadian Light Infantry, led by Lieut.-Col. Buller, rejoined the Canadian Corps after a long separation.

war soldiers will be able to move freely over the ground where once the bravest man dared scarcely show his head, and say, "Here we charged and here we stood our ground"; or, "It was there the captain fell." Then the kindly work of Nature will crumble the well-built trenches and cover them with grass, and the industry of man will drive the plough once more over the stricken fields of history, and Ypres and St. Eloi will become as Valmy or Gravelotte. None the less, certain great earthworks or craters will remain, and, like the hoof-prints "stamped deep into the flint," will serve to remind the Canada of the future that a line on the soil of Flanders is for the nation holy ground. These upheavals of the raw earth, covered in time by the grass and turf of centuries, may survive almost as long as the great emplacements of the Bronze Age which, after four thousand years, still guard the loop of the Thames by Dorchester, command the valley under White Horse Hill, and ring with a double forty-foot ditch the immemorial Temple of Avebury.

CHAPTER III

TRENCH RAIDS

The manner of raiding in "No Man's Land"—Winter in grim earnest—The use of the grenade—Changes in methods of warfare—The musket and the field gun—Adaptability of Canadians—Rehearsal of each assault—Good work of the Headquarters Staff—General Lipsett—A bold decision—A gap in the wire entanglements—A desperate venture—A welcome storm—Canadians in the German trenches—The exploit of Captain Costigan—A hot twenty minutes—German prisoners—Bridges placed across the Douve—Lively times in Ploegsteert—Good work of the Seventh Battalion—A series of failures and a stirring success—A "crack shot"—"Missing"—Its significance—-The German line pierced—Careful work of the General Officer Commanding—At work in the enemy's wire—Into the jaws of death—Canadians disguised—The Huns caught napping—Captain McIntyre's report—A timely shot.

Nov., 1915.

The winter had now set in in grim earnest, as the rains and mists of November bore witness. The nights were longer, and with them stretched out hour after hour the possibility of activity denied to the infantry of either side in the long summer days. For great actions or extended movements the sodden soil afforded no scope. The sharp edges of conflict are stationary—sunk in the muddy trenches and nailed down to machine-gun emplacements. But while the fronts of the great war machine are thus held, they are never still. The wear and tear of conflict go on day and night, week after week, month after month. Behind the infantry in their earthy strongholds the great guns of the artillery hide, long-sighted and tireless. Some 30,000 shells a month pour out from their unseen lips—nearly double the number given in exchange by the Germans. But, after all, gunnery is, in the main, an affair of daylight; the dark has given birth to the adventure of the midnight escalade. "One form of midnight activity," says Sir Douglas Haig, in his report of events from December 19th to May 19th, 1916, "deserves special mention, namely, the raids or cutting-out parties which are made at least twice or three times a week against the enemy's line. They consist of a brief attack with some special object on a section of the opposing trenches, usually carried out at night by a small body of men. The character of these operations—the preparation of a road through our own and the enemy's wire, the crossing of the open ground unseen, the penetration of the enemy's trenches, the hand-to-hand fighting in the darkness and the uncertainty as to the strength of the opposing force—give peculiar scope to the gallantry, dash, and quickness of decision of the troops engaged, and much skill and daring are frequently displayed." The Commander-in-Chief adds that the initiative has, on the whole, been with the British, and that statement would certainly be true of the Canadian section of the line. The objects of such expeditions might roughly be described as threefold:—To gain prisoners and information; to lower your opponents' moral—a form of terrorism; and to kill as many Germans as possible before beating a retreat. Two features of the attempts of this character undertaken by the Canadian Corps will at once arrest attention; the immense pains taken to rehearse the actual performance beforehand and the lavish and successful use of bombs as a weapon of offence.

The grenade, indeed, seemed to have passed into history with the fortress warfare of which it was the product. It has always required for its effective use an enemy tethered to his ground and impervious from his cover to rifle fire. In open fighting the rifle must always have the mastery of any hand-thrown weapon because of its superior range. Now the importance of fortifications or fixed defences has always depended on the nature of the weapons employed by man. The original dyke, moat, or vallum, from the Stone Age to the Fall of Rome and the rise of the Middle Ages, gave the defender the advantage both of cover against arrow or javelin, and of the psychological moment for the counter-attack, sword or spear in hand, as the advancing force floundered in confusion against a sudden obstacle. It was used as the Duke of Wellington used the ridge of Busaco and many other crests of the Peninsula to inflict the maximum loss on the assailant, and to keep reserves well in hand for a counter-stroke, the power and place of which could not be foreseen by the enemy. It possessed, of course, the disadvantage of all field works of a non-continuous nature: it might be outflanked and surrounded. It was to guard against this danger that Imperial Rome in the second century constructed a permanent line of works, wherever Nature failed in her protection, from the mouths of the Rhine to the mouths of the Danube, and from Carlisle to Newcastle, and thus produced the only parallel to the gigantic trenches which bestride Europe to-day. The defence of such a system implied, of course, a great Central Power; and as that Power sank into impotence, the fortress keep of stone, impervious to anything but treachery or starvation, arose in its place to protect the local potentate against his neighbour. But these great structures again vanished into smoke before the blasting force of gunpowder. Earthworks were the next answer of the defence to the new attack, but these in their turn failed because no country had the population, the wealth, or the will to keep an adequate garrison on the whole of a threatened frontier, while an army superior in the field could outflank the defender or compel him to give battle in the open. The musket and the field gun became, therefore, the supreme arbiters of war, and sieges a mere incident in their struggles. Napoleon simply carried the process to its logical conclusion. But the advance of science brought new developments in its train. First, it gave weapons so terrible that men could hardly live against them in the open field, and the advantage was to the prepared defence. This in itself would have mattered little, for

Metz would have fallen in 1870 by starvation though it had been as strong in guns as the Russian fortress of Port Arthur. But science also gave populations great enough to hold with a continuous garrison, as did the Roman Empire, the whole line of national frontiers. With this the inherent weakness of the field work, its liability to outflanking, vanishes; and we come back once more to fortress warfare, and with it to the grenade. In all sieges the grenade is there, from the seventeenth century to Badajos, Sevastopol, and Port Arthur. The opposing trenches are impervious to rifle fire, but not to the lobbing of high explosives thrown in a curve from anything up to forty yards. Neither side was quite prepared for this development, and the original jam-tin bomb with a protruding fuse lit by a match was indeed a sorry device begot of native ingenuity and urgent need, and was soon improved upon. The 1st Canadian Division showed their adaptability by taking very readily to the new weapon. The Guards acted as their instructors, and the Canadian Corps set the pace at once by being the only troops that attached to each brigade a bombing-school of its own.

The result of this earnest preparation was seen in the success of the bombing assaults in the encounters of the winter of 1915-16. Perhaps more admirable, because more rare, was the careful rehearsal of each assault given to the units behind the lines. The photographs taken by the aeroplanes and the results of dangerous personal reconnaissances were used in this service, until an accurate model of the enemy's trenches could be dug and each man could go through the precise task he would have to perform at the actual moment of crisis. Rarely were these ground plans found to be wrong. But the Staff which could conceive and carry out such a laborious undertaking deserves to be given the kind of praise which history has bestowed on the Headquarters Staff of the great Von Moltke. They had grasped the true principle underlying all success in war. You must practise and practise the expected together and disseminate all available knowledge through all ranks, so that when the unexpected comes, as it must in battle, every man knows the situation and the probable conduct of his neighbours, and can act on his own initiative without throwing the whole plan into irremediable confusion.

The doctrine, at any rate, was justified by its results. Early in November the Officer Commanding the 2nd Infantry Brigade (Brigadier-General Lipsett) decided that conditions on his front were ripe for the proving of his belief that strong parties of determined troops, properly equipped and led and operating on carefully-planned lines, could enter the German trenches and inflict casualties out of all proportion to their own losses, make prisoners, and get away. These objects were fully realised. At this time "No Man's Land" on the whole Canadian front was well in our control, and so completely so in the area through which the River Douve meanders from the German position before Douve Farm to a point at which it cuts our trenches just north of Red Lodge, that German patrols seldom ventured beyond their wire entanglements. The Scouts from the 5th Battalion, commanded by Lieut.-Col. G. S. Tuxford, reported a gap in the wire before the point of their intended attack twenty yards in width and leading to the hostile parapet. The scouts of the 7th, however, found that a screen of trees protected the defences before the point selected by their battalion for entry into the German trench. The Commanding Officer of the 7th (Lieut.-Col. V. W. Odlum) then decided that such wire-cutting as was required for his share in the raid should be done by hand.

The night closed in chilly with a promise of rain. The moon was frequently obscured by clouds. Lieut. W. D. Holmes, Sergeants Merston and Ashby (7th Battalion), and Corporals Odlum and Babcock crept out and were busy with the enemy's wire by nine o'clock. They worked on this job until midnight, lying flat when the moon was clear, and cutting fast when it was clouded. As the task was one which caused both muscular and nervous fatigue, hot cocoa was carried out to the wire-cutters at intervals during those three hours. During that time two lanes were cut completely through the German entanglements. They ran diagonally so as not to be observed from the German parapet, and converged on the point of attack. Satisfied with his work in the wire, Lieut. Holmes then took up his bridging party and spanned the River Douve in three places. One bridge was laid at a point within sixteen yards of the German parapet. Sergeant Ashby and Lance-Corporal Weir were conspicuous in this enterprise.

The raiders from both battalions were to enter the German trench at 2.30 a.m., but the attacks were entirely separate as to their striking points and their control.

The 5th Battalion party, under Lieuts. J. E. Purslow and K. L. T. Campbell, was checked directly beneath the German parapet by an obstacle which had been overlooked by their reconnoitring party. That obstacle was a trench or ditch about 12 feet wide and 6 feet deep, full of water from the overflow of the Douve. In the water, rising from the bottom of the ditch to within a couple of feet of the muddy surface, were coils and tangles and strands of barbed wire. Five men of the party fell into this ditch and were with difficulty rescued. The officers made several attempts to negotiate it, only to learn that it could not be crossed either by swimming or wading. As further investigations failed to disclose a passage across the wired and flooded ditch, the party bombed across it into the heavily-manned trench. This grenade fire, delivered at a considerable distance from the 7th Battalion's point of attack, doubtless served well in misleading the enemy as to the extent and exact location of the threat against his front. Also, it must have caused him numerous casualties.

Their supply of grenades exhausted, the 5th Battalion party returned to their own line.

In the meantime, the British Columbians (7th Battalion) had left our front-line trench by way of a gap in our parapet in front of Irish Farm. Led by scouts along the Douve, they crossed the bridges, passed the lanes through the enemy wire, and scaled the hostile parapet, and commenced operations.

Capt. C. T. Costigan, grenade instructor for the brigade, led one party of thirteen men, and Lieut. McIllree led another. These parties were composed of bayonet-men, grenadiers, grenade-carriers, wire-men, and shovel-men. Every man wore a black mask, and none carried any badge or mark of identification. Each bayonet-man had a small electric lamp fastened to his bayonet in such a way that he could flash it without shifting his grip on the rifle.

Lieut. A. H. Wrightson followed with the rifle party and telephone. His command consisted of five riflemen, a telephonist, a linesman, and two stretcher-bearers.

Before the raiders reached the German wire a sudden heavy downpour of rain commenced. Under the black screen and splashing patter of the storm our men went over the enemy parapet. Capt. Costigan and Lieut. McIllree dropped into the trench together—on top of a German sentry crouched beneath a sheet of corrugated iron, seeking shelter from the rain. McIllree shot the sentry, seized another German, disarmed him and threw him down, then clubbed yet another of the enemy with the German rifle. He was then overtaken by his men, and they all moved down the trench to the right, bombing, bayoneting, and shooting as they went. In the meantime, Capt. Costigan—a medium-sized officer of the most charming manners—had dispatched three of the enemy with his revolver and bombed his way along the trench to the left for a distance of three bays before being joined by his party.

The trench was heavily garrisoned, and (as we afterwards learned from the prisoners) the men had been warned by their officers to expect an attack, but all the forewarning had not forearmed them sufficiently for their salvation.

For twenty minutes the Canadians toiled terribly in the outraged stronghold of the enemy, by the light of star-shells from the German support trenches, under a tumult of fire from artillery and machine-guns in both lines and the crashing of their own bombs. The dug-outs were full. While our raiders made prisoners of the occupants of some dug-outs by dragging them bodily forth, and dead men of others by simply throwing grenades in at the narrow doorways, our artillery made a barrage in the rear of the invaded trench and our machine-guns searched with their fire all the roads by which German reinforcements would be likely to move. Lieut. Wrightson, with his rifle party, remained at the point of entry into the German trench during the bombing. He communicated the progress of the affair by telephone to the Commanding Officer of the 7th Battalion, and the officer in charge of operations (Capt. L. J. Thomas) guarded against a German counter-attack from the rear and passed prisoners over the parapet to our scouts. The scouts took the prisoners as they came over the parapet to our bridge-covering parties; these in turn passed them back to a strong party which supported one of our listening posts, and from the listening post they were handed back to and through the gap in our front line.

When the allotted time of twenty minutes was up, Lieut. Wrightson gave the signal for the bombing parties to get out and come back.

As soon as our men were clear of the enemy's parapet our artillery dropped its fire from the German communicating roads and rear positions to the bombed trench, in the hope of catching the reinforcements which the enemy was sure to have got up by this time at all costs to repulse the invasion. It is probable that our gunners' hope was realised.

The return of the raiders across "No Man's Land" was safely accomplished. Captors and captives retired immediately from our front-line trench by the rising and waning illumination of star-shells shooting up hysterically from the enemy's bewildered positions. They moved back to safety under a brisk fire of a variety of weapons.

But this condition of being "under fire" is nothing to write about so long as one happens to be far enough under it.

Lieuts. Holmes and Wrightson, with their scouts and riflemen, did not come in until they had withdrawn all our bridges from the Douve.

The artillery and machine-guns put the finishing touches on the offensive operation. At about four in the morning every British and Canadian gun cut loose again and drubbed the German positions for twenty minutes. Machine-guns spat from every grey bush behind Irish Farm. The woods about Red Lodge and all the hedges on the Ploegsteert Road were red and alive with flashes of field-guns and howitzers. From Romarin way several big naval guns joined in the game.

Thus the enterprise at La Petite Douve was accomplished without a hitch. A handful of men of the 7th Canadian Battalion had gone into the German trench, killed at least fifty of the enemy, and brought away twelve prisoners. They had knocked parapets, dug-outs, and machine-gun emplacements about. The artillery had knocked things about, too, in their part of the enterprise, and who knows the extent of the casualties caused by our high explosives, our shrapnel, and the fire of our machine-guns?

The moral of the enemy had been shaken and his nerves unstrung. Fame and decorations had been won, and fresh glory for Canadian arms; a new branch of the science of trench warfare had been demonstrated and proved; and against all this one Canadian soldier had given his life and another a little of his blood.

The next episode begins with a series of failures and ends with a striking success. A large tree felled across the Messines-Armentières road by artillery fire, at a point within one hundred and twenty yards of our front line, had been gradually built into a formidable barricade by the enemy. Several attempts by our artillery to demolish this strong point failed, owing to an obstructive screen of large trees along the roadside. This barricade grew in strength daily. Strong wire entanglements were put across its face and across the ditches on its flanks, which ran parallel to the road from our position to the front line of the enemy. The garrison moved in and out by way of the roadside ditches.

Several gallant attacks were made on this position before it was finally taken and demolished. In an unsuccessful attack led by Lieuts. N. W. F. Rant and A. V. Evans, of the 2nd Canadian Mounted Rifles, Lieut. Rant was wounded by the explosion of a German grenade.

Dec. 8th, 1915.

A week later, on the night of December 8th, after a careful reconnaissance by daylight, Lieut. John Galt, Jr., of Lord Strathcona's Horse, and fourteen grenadiers and riflemen of his regiment, assaulted the barricade. The enemy held the position in force, and his fire was too heavy for the Strathconas. Our party was driven in, and Lieut. Galt and two of his men were left wounded on the ground. Of the twelve who got back to our lines, eight were wounded.

Dec. 14th, 1915.

On the night of December 14th-15th, the 5th Battalion and the 3rd Battery Canadian Field Artillery took the barricade in hand. Preliminary work was done by our artillery on the 12th, 13th, and 14th. During the bombardment of the position on the 13th, twenty Germans broke from the cover of the barricade and made a dash across the open for their own lines. Sergeant McGlashan, of the 5th Battalion, a crack shot and an opportunist, dropped five of the enemy before they could reach their parapet.

The 5th Battalion had constructed an emplacement for a field gun in our front line where our trench cuts the Messines-Armentières road. From a flank of the emplacement they sapped out towards the barricade.

Dec. 15th, 1915.

Early on the morning of the 15th an 18-pounder from the 3rd Battery Canadian Field Artillery was brought down the road by an armoured car to within a couple of hundred yards of the prepared emplacement. From that point it was man-handled into position in our trench by Capt. G. V. Taylor and his gun crew. Attacking parties from the 5th, commanded by Lieuts. K. T. Campbell and K. A. Mahaffy, and supports under Lieut. E. H. Latter, took up position to right and left of the gun and just outside the parapet.

It was now four o'clock in the morning. On the minute our artillery opened against the German trenches with shrapnel and high explosive, and Capt. Taylor's gun cut loose at the barricade, point blank at 120 yards, firing five rounds a minute for five minutes. Then our guns in the rear lifted their fire from the enemy's front line to his reserve trenches, and the attacking parties of grenadiers and riflemen advanced to the site of the barricade. Four dead and two living Germans were found in the ruins of wire and sandbags. The living were captured and sent back to our trench. Live wires were discovered in the bottom of a ditch on a flank and immediately in rear of the position. These were cut in a hurry, in the belief that one or more of them connected mine locations near at hand with the hostile trench. Our men then mined the ruined barrier and retired to one of our saps. The German artillery and machine-guns now became active, and retaliated heavily against the wrecked barricade and our front line and winter trenches.

During the examination of the prisoners it was learned that three wounded Canadians—one of them an officer—had been passed back through Messines a few days before. It was suggested more in a reliance upon hope than upon fact that those men may have been Lieut. Galt and the survivors from the attack of December 18th, when Lieut. Galt and two men were left behind. All we know is that his name appeared in the list of "Missing"—a word which means a greater tragedy than any other in the casualty list. The dead have died in their glory, and of them we know the best and the worst; the wounded we expect and hope to see again; but the missing remain for months nothing but a supreme and torturing anxiety.[6]

[6] Lieut. John Galt was taken prisoner, but died of his wounds very soon afterwards.

Jan. 30th, 1916.

On the night of January 30th-31st, 1916, two battalions of the 6th Canadian Infantry Brigade (Brigadier-General Ketchen), supported by artillery, machine-guns, and trench mortars, succeeded in an important attack against the unsuspecting enemy on their brigade front. The objects of this operation were the same as those of the 7th Battalion's offensive in November, to obtain prisoners and information, to cause casualties, apprehension, and material damage. This enterprise exceeded that of our 2nd Brigade in that it pierced the German line at two widely separated points.

In their conception and plans of attack the General Officer Commanding the 6th Brigade and his Staff gave the same careful attention to details as had their comrades of the 2nd Brigade two months before.

The 28th (North-West) Battalion's objective was a point on the northern side, and that of the 29th (Vancouver) Battalion a point on the southern face of the Spanbroekmolen salient. Here, a little to the south-east of Kemmel and about the centre of the Canadian line, the German line runs sharply in to a western thrust over some 1,900 yards, and the attacks were like the jaws of pincers gripping the base of the protuberance at that distance from each other. The two objectives were about eleven hundred yards apart. The wire in front of these selected points was cut solely by hand, as one of the chief features of this attack was to dispense with the customary artillery preparation and so take the enemy by complete surprise.

The operation, as has been stated, consisted of two widely separated and individual attacks, delivered simultaneously, both maintained in the hostile trenches for the same number of minutes and simultaneously withdrawn. Scout-Sergeant Turner and Corporal Conlin, of the 28th Battalion, worked in the enemy's wire from 10 p.m. to 1.45 in the morning, and stayed there until joined by the attacking party, with whom they entered the German trench at about twenty minutes to three. The enemy's entanglements had been strongly reinforced during the previous day, under cover of a heavy fog; but Turner and Conlin stuck to their difficult and dangerous task and completed it without an error.

The raiders of both battalions advanced from their positions of readiness in "No Man's Land" at half-past two sharp. The 28th Battalion party, thirty strong, commanded by Capts. D. E. MacIntyre and K. C. Taylor, lost a few minutes in negotiating the trunk of a fallen tree, and were still strung out in the German wire when sounds of exploding grenades and an increased flaring of star-shells told them that their comrades of the 29th were already in violent touch with the enemy. There was no time to lose. Lives hang on fractions of seconds in such work as this. The two captains and the two tireless wire-cutters were still in the lead. Together they crawled up the sloping face of the big German parapet, and each threw a grenade into the crowded trench. Four explosions followed. Sentries shouted and fired their rifles. Capt. MacIntyre accounted for one of the sentries with the second shot of his automatic. Then the four leaders jumped down into the 10-foot-deep trench, into the midst of confusion and rage and fear. The other raiders followed

He was buried by the enemy, and the words "Here lies a British Officer" inscribed on his tomb.

them with a rush.

Here were thirty Canadians with blackened faces[7] and armed with sudden death in a trench full of Germans. Many of the Germans were "standing to," many had but then scrambled from their dug-outs, their blankets still about them, and their feet still unbooted. Make the picture for yourself, with the help of these extracts from Capt. Macintyre's report:—

"The trench seemed full of men running both ways.... Almost at once Corporal Conlin fell at my feet shot through the head. Behind Conlin was a Hun. I shot him through the stomach. The noise was frightful, and I could not tell where it was coming from. The flares made it nearly as light as day. I was knocked down by something once, but don't know what it was.

"After six minutes I blew the horn, and all the men heard it and the squads retired to the point of entry. Capt. Taylor held the right and Sergeant Cameron the left. I asked them if all their squads were out, and they said 'Yes.' Then I told them to 'beat it,' and we all jumped."

The casualties suffered by this party were two men killed and two officers and eight men wounded. Capt. Taylor, though wounded in the leg while in the very act of invading the trench, did terrible execution. It is claimed for him that he killed fourteen of the enemy, shooting some and bayoneting others. He was wounded in eight places, but returned to our lines unaided when the affair was over.

The majority of our casualties were caused by a machine-gun which enfiladed the invaded trench. This gun was fortunately put out of action by a bomb from our trench-mortars just before the retirement commenced. The 28th Battalion party brought out no prisoners, but inflicted thirty-nine casualties by actual count.

While the North-Westerners were thus engaged at Peckham, the raiders of the 29th Battalion were as busily employed in their chosen place of trench at Spanbroekmolen. The officers in charge of the Vancouver Battalion's assault were Lieuts. G. I. Gwynn, N. E. O'Brien, and L. A. Wilmot. Lieut. Wilmot and his men cut the wire, then acted as guides to the others, and accompanied them into the trench. The leading men of the right and left parties went over the parapet together, using the loophole of a machine-gun emplacement as a step. Sergeant Dungan bayoneted the first two sentries encountered by the left party. Lieut. O'Brien entered a dug-out and captured one of its inmates. A machine-gun opened fire on the raiders, but the gunner was promptly shot by Lieuts. Wilmot and O'Brien and the gun and the dug-out of the crew were bombed. Other dug-outs were also bombed. The right party, on the other flank of the central machine-gun emplacement, did equally fine execution. The work of Lieut. Gwynn was conspicuous.

Things had gone very well with the raiders thus far, when Lieut. Wilmot was wounded by a grenade. In spite of his injury he kept his head clear and a grip on the situation. Seeing that a number of prisoners had been taken and that the alarm of the enemy had become general, he ordered a retirement, and then signalled to

[7] The one thing most likely to be seen by the flare-lights sent up by the enemy is the face of an opponent. Those advancing in "No Man's Land," therefore, blacken their faces to avoid being seen.

our artillery to open fire. The return to our lines was accomplished without accident.

The 29th Battalion killed at least twenty of the enemy, did considerable damage to dug-outs and machine-guns, and brought back three prisoners. Lieut. Wilmot, Sergeant Kirkland, and two men were wounded.

These two successful raids illustrate not inaptly the various phases through which advance patrol work has gone. The first stage, as soon as trench warfare set in, was the casual encounters of hostile parties in the dark. The second was the organised trench raid by night, in which the Canadians led the way. The last stage was reached in midsummer, before the Canadians fought on the Somme, when the 19th Ontario Battalion made a most successful daylight rush into the enemy trenches, led by Lieuts. B. O. Hooper and S. S. Burnham. They disposed of forty or fifty of the enemy, and after remaining in the enemy's lines for five minutes returned with very valuable information as to the enemy's dispositions. And these, as I have said, are instances, chosen almost at a venture, to show in what manner and under what conditions we go raiding in "No Man's Land."

CHAPTER IV

FORMATION OF THE THIRD DIVISION

Coming events cast no shadows before—General Seely's command redistributed—The Seventh Brigade in the trenches—Heavy bombardment at Messines—Fortified positions of the Huns battered—Good work of the Artillery—Three privates distinguish themselves—Death of a daring explorer in "No Man's Land"—Visit of H.R.H. the Prince of Wales and the Colonial Secretary—Canadians co-operate with British—A terrific bombardment—The Huns establish themselves in British trenches—Canadian guns aid the British—"Tobin's Tigers"—The Tenth Battalion in a serious encounter—A fierce medley in the dark—An unfortunate day—Two Generals wounded—A survey of the strategic position—-The force of massed artillery—A new era—Mr. Lloyd George's work—Iron lips produce conclusive arguments—A successful ruse—Ingenious device of Captain Costigan—A swollen river aids the Canadians—A hero indeed—An exchange of front—The value of salients questioned—The problem of transferring a sector—The Battle of St. Eloi a joint affair—Description of the ground—The process of exchange described—Adequate reasons for changes—A critical moment—Second Canadian Division supports the British—Six huge craters created by exploding mines—Activity of Northumberlands and Royal Fusiliers—Timely assistance of Canadians acknowledged—The "Canadians' Trench"—The enemy cleared out of debatable land—Good fighting of the enemy at St. Eloi—Trenches filled with the dead of both combatants—The Sixth Canadian Brigade to the relief.

Dec., 1915.

The main event of the New Year was the formation of the 3rd Division. Authority to create this force had been received in the last week of December, and at the same time the 7th and 8th Brigades had come into being. The 7th Brigade, which was commanded by Brigadier-General MacDonell (who handed over the command of Lord Strathcona's Horse, R.C., to Lieut.-Col. C. M. Nelles, C.M.G.) consisted of the Princess Patricia's Light Infantry (Lieut.-Col. C. H. Buller), the Royal Canadian Regiment (Lieut.-Col. C. H. Hill, D.S.O.), the 42nd Royal Highlanders of Canada (Lieut.-Col. G. S. Cantlie), and the 49th (Edmonton) Canadian

Battalion (Lieut.-Col. W. A. Griesbach), all of which had been acting for some time as corps troops. The 8th Brigade was made up of the six Canadian Mounted Rifle regiments, which had up till now been part of Seely's force. They were made into four battalions of infantry, known as the 1st (Lieut.-Col. A. E. Shaw), 2nd (Lieut.-Col. C. L. Bott), 4th (Lieut.-Col. S. F. Smith), and 5th (Lieut.-Col. G. H. Baker) Canadian Mounted Rifles, and placed under the command of Brigadier-General Williams. Early in January the 3rd Division was constituted out of these two brigades, and Major-General Mercer was appointed to the command. Coming events cast no shadows before, and there was no fore-knowledge of the ill-luck which was to attend one of the distinguished officers, and the death in action which awaited the other. All seemed fair for the prospects of the 3rd Division, which was within a few months to pass through the most terrible ordeal that the Canadians had yet sustained. The creation of this new force scattered Brigadier-General Seely's command.[8] The Canadian Mounted Rifles, as we have seen, were incorporated in the 3rd Division, while the Cavalry Brigade was removed altogether from the Corps Command. The 2nd King Edward's Horse was dispatched on January 14th to General Headquarters, and the remaining units, the Royal Canadian Dragoons, Strathcona's Horse, and the Royal Canadian Horse Artillery, were attached on January 26th to the 1st Indian Cavalry Division at Friville.[9]

General Seely commanded a Brigade holding the front trench line since May of 1915, and it was unfortunate that the fact of his commanding a Cavalry Brigade compelled him to abandon the advanced command on the redistribution of the cavalry units. In the opinion of the Higher Command and of all Canadian officers who came in contact with him, he exhibited conspicuous intelligence, coolness, and courage in a degree which qualified him for high command and a distinguished military career.

Jan 7th, 1916.

By the end of the first week in January the 7th Brigade was able to begin its share of trench duties, and took over from the 1st Brigade of the 1st Division. Their first turn of duty as a Brigade was a long one, lasting for full three weeks. The month was, on the whole, a quiet one until the trench raid of January 30th/31st, described in the previous chapter. The weather turned from wet to fine and cold, and the most persistent reminders of winter were the occasional fogs, which set-

[8] This had consisted of the Royal Canadian Horse Artillery, Lord Strathcona's Horse, 2nd King Edward's Horse, Royal Canadian Dragoons, and 1st, 2nd, 3rd, 4th, 5th, and 6th Canadian Mounted Rifles. The Fort Garry Horse did not come out until February 24th, 1916. Brig.-General Seely had commanded his Brigade with marked ability, and its dispersal was much regretted by the troops.

[9] The 3rd Divisional Train, under Lieut.-Colonel C. H. Lougheed, and the Machine-Gun Companies accompanied the Division to France in January, 1916. The Divisional Signal Company was formed from units in the field in December, 1915, and placed under the command of Major T. E. Powers. The Supply Column was also formed in the field. The 9th and 10th Field Ambulances, under Lieut.-Colonels C. A. Peters and A. W. Tanner respectively, went to France on April 3rd, 1916 and the 8th Field Ambulance, under Lieut.-Colonel S. W. Hewetson, followed a month later. The 3rd Divisional Engineers, with Lieut.-Colonel T. V. Anderson in command, arrived at the Front early in April.

tled down like white blankets on the flats and enabled parties to move about with impunity in the day-time.

The artillery bombardment on both sides formed the main feature of the month. Although the corps was not able to keep up the great superiority over the Germans in the number of shells fired in November and December, very heavy bombardment of the trenches in front of Messines took place. The enemy, perhaps in reply, shelled the front trenches somewhat severely. On the whole, however, their bombardments were characterised by the usual features—a wide dispersement of shells over a large area, Dranoutre being heavily bombarded during the early part of the month. This kind of attack is annoying rather than serious. The policy of the Canadian gunners was very different. It was to concentrate on objects of real importance. Organised bombardments of sections of the enemy's front were carried out by the artillery, and the combination of the heavy batteries and field guns was most effective. German mounds and fortified positions near the front lines were battered in, and all machine-gun emplacements were carefully registered in case of sudden emergencies. It is the custom of the enemy to occupy farm buildings as redoubts, and two direct hits were obtained by the gunners at La Douve Farm on January 7th. Germans were seen scattering as the result of these shots, and were instantly pursued by shrapnel. It is necessary to lay some stress on the work of the artillery, which is liable to suffer neglect; only the infantry can know the relief of hearing the guns roaring over their heads.

Jan. 16th and 17th, 1916.

Throughout the month of January considerable liveliness in patrol work was kept up, and if encounters between parties were infrequent, this fact was due to Teutonic caution. Some encounters, however, did take place, and there was fighting on the 16th and 17th on the front of the 3rd Infantry Brigade.

Jan. 22nd and 23rd, 1916.

On the night of the 22nd and 23rd the 8th Battalion (Winnipeg Rifles) made a careful reconnaissance of their front—a task in which Privates Bole, Gunn, and Matkin, scouts of the regiment, particularly distinguished themselves in a short, severe encounter with the enemy. Here again the lack of automatic pistols and sufficient ammunition proved a handicap in the struggle.

The incidents in which good work was done are almost too numerous to mention, but a particular interest attaches to the death of Lieut. Owen, of the 7th British Columbia Regiment, well known as a daring explorer in "No Man's Land." Lieut. Owen and three of his men encountered some fifteen Germans in the sudden and nerve-breaking way which characterises a patrol battle. A fierce fight with revolvers and bombs ensued, and four Germans at least were seen to fall; then the bombs ran out, and a retreat became imperative. The officer ordered the men to retire, saying, "I am coming right after you," and remained, covering the retreat by revolver fire. He never returned, and when his party went back to seek him they found him lying in the wet ground with a bullet through his head.

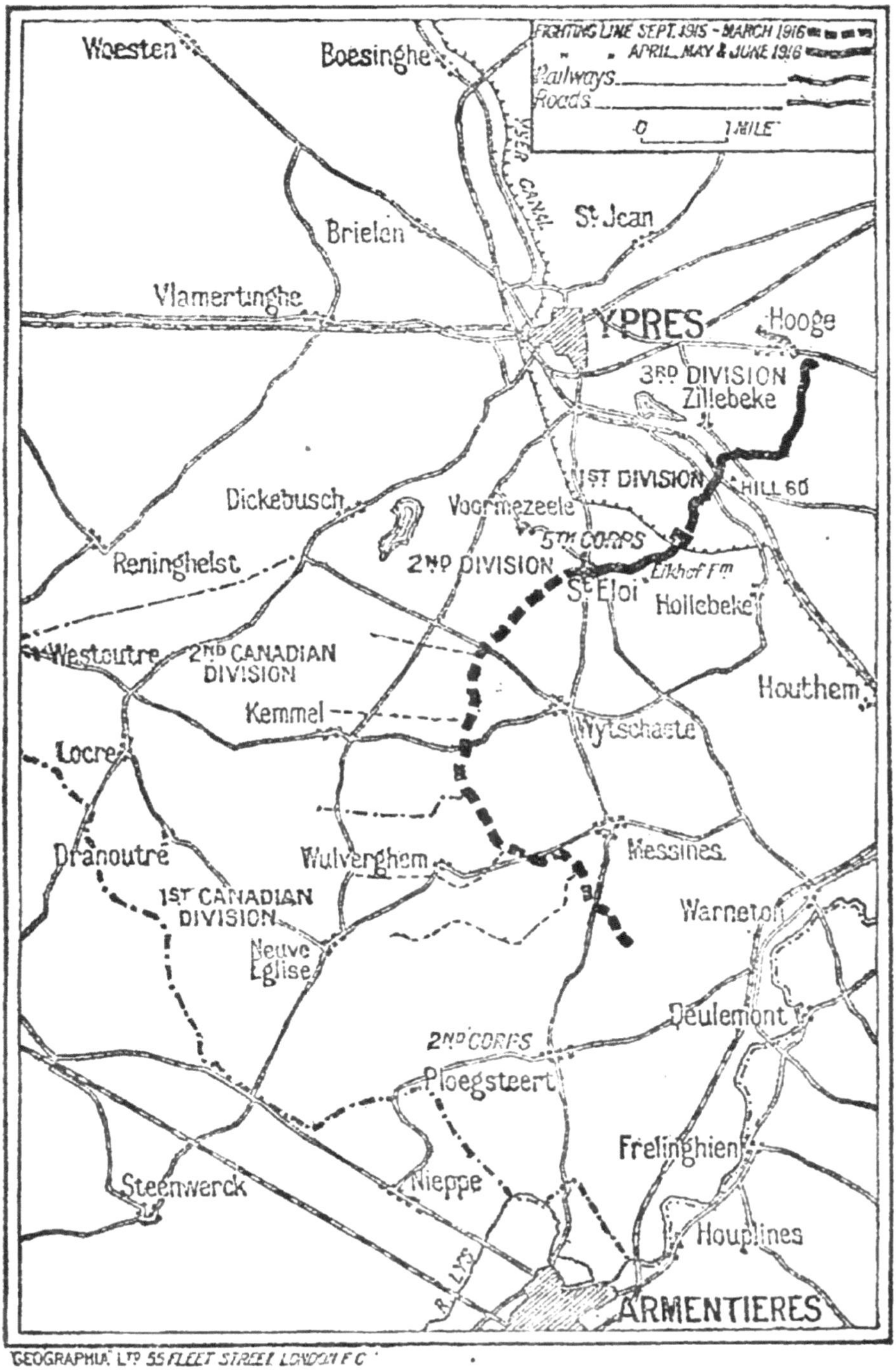

Map—Ypres-Armentières area

The end of the month, which passed in comparative quiet until the assault of the night of the 30th, described in the previous chapter, was chiefly marked by the arrival of two distinguished visitors.

Jan. 28th, 1916.

On January 28th H.R.H. the Prince of Wales spent a day with the Canadian Corps, surveying the whole field from the eminences behind the lines and passing down a portion of the front trenches. He met and conversed with the various Brigadiers and a few of the Regimental Commanders. On the 30th, Mr. Bonar Law, Secretary of State for the Colonies, whose interest in the corps is well known, arrived, and addressed the 31st (Alberta) Battalion.

Feb., 1916.

In February began that period of close co-operation with the V British Corps which was destined to last for nearly seven weeks owing to the persistent fighting at the Bluff and about the Mound of St. Eloi. So long is the range of modern artillery that the guns of neighbouring corps and divisions can be of the greatest assistance to the actual combatants by firing slantwise into the enemy positions around the field of action, while an infantry demonstration may hold up his reserves.

Feb. 13th, 1916.

About three o'clock in the afternoon of February 13th a terrific bombardment was directed against the British trenches north of the Bluff, a high artificial mound covered with trees immediately north of the Ypres-Comines Canal; a series of mines was exploded in the neighbourhood of Hill 60 and in the direction of Hooge and of Sanctuary Wood. As the dusk fell several assaults were delivered along the line defended subsequently by the Canadians on the day of June 2nd. The majority of these assaults were repelled, but the Germans broke through the Bluff north of the canal, and succeeded in establishing themselves in the British front trenches, where they stayed until they were expelled on March 2nd. This action was the beginning of many woes to both combatants. The moment the trouble started the V (British) Corps called up the Canadians and asked for the help of their guns. This was readily accorded, and throughout the evening of the 13th and the day of the 14th a combined Anglo-Canadian shoot was directed with success on the German positions in front of the Bluff.

Feb. 16th, 1916.

Further relief to the British was afforded by an extension of our line on the night of February 16th, 700 yards to the north, as to set free the Northumberland Fusiliers. This task was given to the 6th Brigade, and brought it into the trenches which flanked the line on the right of the St. Eloi position, and from which the final relief of the Northumberlands was made in the battle of the first week of April. The 29th (Vancouver, "Tobin's Tigers"), supported by the 28th (North-West), took over this additional task.

Patrol fighting went on steadily all this time. Early in the month of February a particularly exciting action was fought between a large party of the 10th (Western Canada) Battalion and an equally numerous party of Germans. It had been decided to creep up, cut the German barbed wire, and bomb their front-line trenches. Lieut. Kent and Sergeant Milne, of the 10th, with two privates, succeeded in cutting the wire, and were joined by a column of fifty men. While waiting immediately in front of the German trench for the best opportunity of bombing the enemy positions, a patrol of thirty or forty Germans stumbled across them from the flank. A fierce medley in the dark followed, the Germans attacking with bombs and revolvers, and our men with grenades, bayonets, and knobkerries.[10] The enemy machine-guns took the alarm and fired blindly into the scrimmage. Eventually the German patrol was dispersed with heavy casualties, and the 10th returned with five prisoners.

Feb. 23rd, 1916.

The 17th was an unfortunate day for the Canadian Corps. Brigadier-Generals MacDonell and Leckie were both hit by stray bullets and seriously wounded during their tour of the trenches.[11] On the 23rd, the 9th Brigade of the 3rd Division was formed. It consisted of the 43rd Canadian Battalion, under Lieut.-Col. R. McD. Thomson; 52nd, under Lieut.-Col. A. W. Hay; 58th, under Lieut.-Col. H. A. Genet; and 60th, under Lieut.-Col. F. A. de L. Gascoigne, and was placed under the command of Brigadier-General F. W. Hill, D.S.O. The 3rd Division had now its three brigades; and with a sharp brush between the 42nd (Royal Highlanders of Canada) Battalion and some over-adventurous Germans, the month came to a close.

The Canadian Corps was now approaching the second crisis in the history of its various divisions; this was to lead them through three months of continuous fighting steadily northwards across the blood-stained fields of St. Eloi and Hooge until they almost reached the scene of the Second Battle of Ypres. To grasp the inner meaning of these movements and the consequences to which they led, it is essential to take a wider survey of the strategic position which the Allied Commanders had to face on the Western front. Two great bodies of the German reserves were known to be in existence, the first opposite Verdun, the second in the region of the northern British line. Whether this last concentration was a defensive measure against a possible British advance, or portended a third German assault on the Ypres salient, could not in the month of March be known for certain. One fact at least was clear. The persistent and violent offensive against Verdun which marked that month made it incumbent on the British armies to come to the assistance of the French. This was done in two ways. A fourth army was assembled out of the growing hosts in France, and the Arras sector of the line given into its charge—a step which released a French army for the heroic contest before Verdun—while a series of attacks was delivered from the original British line, any of which might

[10] These were made locally in the trenches, and consisted of about two feet of hedge-stick, covered at the top with nails bound round with wire.

[11] General Leckie was assisted back to safety by Major E. McCuaig, of the 13th Battalion. This officer, while temporarily in command of the Battalion, subsequently repulsed a very severe German attack on the line north of St. Eloi on April 19th, 1915. The 13th were very heavily bombarded, and lost 10 officers and 225 men, but held their ground.

have been the beginning of an assault on a larger scale. The actions of the Bluff, of the Mound of St. Eloi, and of Vimy, were designed to show the enemy that in the northern line we were "ware and waking," and to pin the enemy reserves to the ground. Nor, it may be added, were the Germans slow to take up the challenge.

Mar. 2nd, 1916.

Indeed, the whole series of actions with which the remainder of this volume is concerned began with the German assault on February 12th on the Bluff, when the troops of the V British Corps, who held the line on the left of the Canadians, were driven from the position on the Bluff and the front-line trenches to the north. Preparations had been made for the recapture of the lost positions, and the advance took place on March 2nd. The Divisional Artillery of the 1st and 2nd Canadian Divisions[12] co-operated that day with the gunners of the V British Corps in a terrific bombardment of the ground to be taken. As a result of this fire a large section of the German front-line trenches and communication trenches north of the canal was reduced to ruins, and the successful assault of the British on the morning of March 2nd met with little resistance. The lost ground was regained and consolidated. This action was one of the first to demonstrate the increased blasting force of massed artillery, which became the standard weapon of offence on either side during the battles of the next five months. The continued piling up of munitions and guns during the preceding twelve months had begun to modify profoundly the tactics of the Western front, and it would be alike an error and an injustice to judge the performance of the infantry in the spring of 1916 by the standards of the previous year. The old British idea of a solid and immovable front line held almost entirely by the fire of a rifleman to a yard of trench, was beginning to give way in the stress of circumstances and the example of the French.

A line more lightly held by the aid of machine-guns and wire entanglements, and a greater disposition to yield or gain ground, were the signs of a new era. But chiefly the enemy's guns were our teachers, for their iron lips pronounced very conclusive arguments.

However, if the main work of the Canadians in the attack on the Bluff lay with the Canadian gunners, the infantry were by no means idle. They assisted the V Corps by a demonstration on their front, and by massing three battalions of the 4th Infantry Brigade behind their left flank to come to the aid of the British in the event of a counter-attack. All arms contributed to the frontal demonstration. In the early morning of March 2nd smoke-bombs were loosed from the trenches as though in prelude to an attack, and a great blare of musketry and machine-gun fire roared up and down the line. The Germans sprang to arms and hurried supports up their communication trenches into their lightly-held front line. It was for this that our field guns had been waiting, and with continued bursts of fire they ranged the denser masses opposite as they came crowding into the trenches. The retaliation

[12] The remaining three Brigades of the 2nd Division—the 5th (Lieut.-Colonel G. A. Carruthers), the 6th (Lieut.-Colonel W. B. M. King), and the 7th (Lieut.-Colonel J. S. Stewart) Canadian Field Artillery—had crossed to France in January. The 4th Brigade C.F.A. had been out since September, 1915.

of the German artillery was singularly ineffective, probably because their attention was now wholly occupied with the line further north. This operation produced one striking incident of ingenuity in warfare. At one point in the corps position the stream of the Douve, flowing rapidly with the winter rains, ran through our trenches and disappeared into the German line. This fact suggested to Capt. Costigan, D.S.O., of the 10th Battalion, a new method of alarming the Hun.

This enterprising officer suggested that a raft loaded with high explosive might be floated down the current and exploded in the enemy's lines.

The stream was, however, narrow, and, as anyone who has thrown sticks into a river will remember, the tendency of a floating object is to get stuck on some obstacle or corner on the way down. Capt. Costigan therefore proposed to accompany the raft himself until it was within certain reach of the objective. He and Corporal Witney came out of the trenches and carried the raft to the river. After floating down some distance, he found the stream continually obstructed by low overhanging boughs, and to avoid any chance of failure he continued to pilot his dangerous convoy to within thirty yards of where the German barbed wire, stretched across the channel, barred any further progress. Here he waited in the water until the light of a flare gave the signal for the general demonstration. The fuse was then lit and the load shot fair at the enemy's obstruction from a distance of thirty yards. The explosion was a very fine one, and so perturbed the gentle soul of the enemy that he fired off several concealed machine-guns, the existence of which the 10th Battalion had long suspected but the location of which they had never known. Writing in cold blood, it is easy to represent such a feat of arms as ordinary, but when one considers what the action really entailed, the exploit was heroic even as we count heroism to-day. It was something which an ordinary man could not have done and could not reasonably have been expected to do. The long stumble in the dark with sudden death in one's hands, the plunge into the icy stream, the physical struggle with the sweeping boughs and jutting bends, the swift drift down towards the enemy, and the calm waiting in the cold, dark water for the given signal, serve to show that the most romantic deeds of the hero of fiction can be matched and mastered in the battlefields of to-day.

That the whole demonstration was a success is witnessed by the following telegram from the V Corps:—

> "SINCERE THANKS FOR YOUR MOST VALUABLE CO-OPERATION. SHOULD ENEMY RENEW COUNTER-ATTACK TO-MORROW AT DAWN OR LATER, HOPE YOU WILL AGAIN HELP US."

Mar., 1916.

Early in March orders were issued by the 2nd Army Commander for the exchange of fronts between the V and the Canadian Corps. The sector held by the V Corps runs from the Ypres-Roulers Railway just north of Hooge down south as far as St. Eloi. It constituted the southern half of the Ypres salient, and was by common consent about the worst portion of the whole British line. In the autumn of 1914 during the first battle of Ypres, it had been heroically defended by the Guards Brigade, the Household Cavalry, and the 7th Division, seldom mustering more than 5,000 men at any given time, against the successive attacks of two German Army Corps and of the Prussian Guard lasting for a month.

The V Corps had now held it for little short of a year, and had during that period incurred heavy losses. Nor is this to be wondered at when one considers the number of general and minor actions which had taken place in the area since the great attack on Hill 60 in April, 1915. The trenches round Hooge had continually changed hands. Fierce divisional actions had been fought there on June 16th, July 30th, and August 8th, 1915; while later in the autumn an unsuccessful British assault had been launched against the Bellewarde Lake line. Of minor actions there had been no end, while the great bulge of the salient rendered every trench in it liable to that most deadly of dangers, a direct lateral fire from heavy guns placed to the south or to the north. Salients are valuable as examples of the British soldier's willingness to die rather than to live. They make a great many widows and orphans and splendid material for patriotic speeches. For the rest, their utility may be questioned—and has been.

Mar., 1916.

The transfer of a sector from one Army Corps to another is one of those operations which the layman thinks of as done by a single sweeping stroke of the Commander-in-Chief's pen. In reality, it is a slow and intricate process—nothing less than the gradual interchange of all the population of two countrysides and all the means of feeding and clothing them—a wave of immigration and emigration affecting more than 120,000 people, and this has to be carried out with the minimum of disturbance, since the inhabitants of the two areas must be ready to man the trenches and fight a battle at any stage in the process of change.

The Staffs are in the position of two householders who are exchanging residences and moving their families under the immediate threat of a burglary at either or both houses. If it is done on too large a scale, there will be confusion, but, on the other hand, every day that the move is protracted, there will be mixed Staffs and units in the same battle line and sector—a state of affairs not conducive to the efficient management of a sudden crisis. Far behind the front line trenches the ramifications of the services extend; for though a brigade may be holding a frontage of a couple of thousand yards, its section runs back through miles of land crowded with reserves, with light and heavy artillery, with transport services, hospitals and depots, and all the paraphernalia of modern war. The trench line is like a tooth, the depth of the roots of which is only discovered when one tries to pull it out. To the Staffs, at any rate, the period of movement is one of strain and anxiety, and the total changes were not completed under a period of three weeks, during which time both corps were engaged in heavy and continuous fighting.

The battle of St. Eloi was indeed a joint or rather a successive affair carried on by units of two Corps, the Canadians and the V (British).

Mar. 17th-April 8th, 1916.

The moves began as early as March 17th, when the heavy divisional artillery, supporting the 3rd Canadian Division, were taken north, and were completed by the night of April 8th. The Corps Command of the two sections was not handed over till April 4th. A glance at the map will show the problem which confronted the Corps Commanders. The V Corps held exactly the southern curve of the Ypres salient from almost due east of the town.

The left of its 24th Division rested on Bellewarde Beek, and its line continued along the rise through Sanctuary Wood to a high point south-east of the extremity of Zillebeke Lake, known as Mount Sorrel. We shall have occasion later to study this ground with more particularity, for the force which holds it holds Ypres in the hollow of its hand. Here the salient headed back violently, running almost due east and west, took a southerly turn again, crossed the railway to Comines, passed Hill 60 of glorious and tragic memory, and struck the Ypres-Comines Canal by the Bluff. This was the sector of the 50th British Division—south again was the 3rd British Division holding what was destined to be the field of St. Eloi from the canal to Bois Quarante.

At the village of St. Eloi there was another of these violent turns of the line which leave the opposing forces facing each other due north and south. The total length of this corps sector was about six miles, but the curves of the trenches and the ground would make the actual number of yards to be held considerably greater. It was, roughly, broken up into three sections of two miles each belonging to a single division. With Bois Quarante the salient of Ypres came to an end. The Canadian Corps line to the south reaching to Ploegsteert has already been described. It was devoid in the main of salients and had become increasingly peaceful since the fierce fighting in the streets of Comines and Wytschaete in the autumn of 1914.

It was held, when the 3rd Canadian Division was formed finally in the middle of February, by three divisions on a frontage of six brigades. The 3rd Division had no line of its own, but sent its brigades up indifferently to relieve those of the other two divisions. It was therefore selected as the first of the infantry formations for transference to the new Canadian front.

A moment's consideration will make it clear that to exchange two bodies of men in the front line would mean an open gap in the defence during the period of the full relief. As in the game of "Fox and Geese," though the metaphor is perhaps not very complimentary to the enemy or ourselves, a single hole in the ranks lets the fox through. The change can therefore only be made in two ways. It can be begun by moving the reserve troops of the two corps into each other's positions and pushing them up into the front line in succession until the process is complete, or by a swifter and more direct method of marching the reserve division of one corps to relieve a front line division of the other, this division in turn becoming a temporary reserve for its neighbouring corps. In accordance with the former plan, the 3rd Canadian Division was taken up in the third week of March and took over from the 24th Division in the Hooge-Zillebeke sector, while the 24th Division came back to the rest area of the Canadian Corps, whence they in turn displaced a front line Canadian Division. The process once set on foot by the initial move becomes more or less automatic. But it is necessarily slow. It would be in the last degree inadvisable and dangerous to substitute larger bodies of troops in a single night and place each on ground with which it is thoroughly unfamiliar. Even the ordinary visits of officers to their new trenches a day or so in advance would be no protection against confusion in the dark on ground unknown to a whole brigade or division—and this lesson was written in letters of blood in the first week of April over the stricken field of St. Eloi. The 3rd Division move was therefore made by degrees. It began on March 18th with two battalions of the 8th Brigade to the V Corps camp behind the lines, while two British battalions took their place in Canadian reserve. The next day the exchange of the remainder of the Brigade was effected, while in the course of the night the two original Canadian battalions took over their share of the British trenches. On the day of the 20th the entire 7th Canadian Brigade marched from its own reserve area into that of the V Corps near Poperinghe, and went into the firing line the following night. The 9th Brigade followed them on the 23rd, and became the supporting brigade of the whole division. The relief of the north section of the line was now complete, and the divisions changed on the night of the 21st. In the meantime as each British unit was pulled out it came swiftly and surely into the place of the Canadians. The change can be put most simply in a mathematical form. If *A* represents the British in the trenches, *B* the British in reserve, *C* the Canadians in the trenches, and *D* the Canadians in reserve—*B* and *D* change places. That is the first move. On the following day or night approximately *D* relieves *A*, and *B* relieves *C* in the trenches. That is the second move. There remains only the substitution between the two units *C* and *A* and the full relief has been accomplished, and each party stands complete within its new area. The process in a corps will be slow, since the unit of exchange will be only two battalions out of thirty-six, or at most of a brigade.

Mar. 23rd-25th, 1916.

Thus the 24th British Division as soon as the 3rd Canadians had got into place, began to relieve the 1st Canadian Division. On the night of the 23rd two of their battalions took the lines of the two battalions of the 3rd Canadian Infantry Brigade in the trenches, and the change was finished by the night of the 25th. Next came the turn of the 1st Canadian Brigade, which was out by March 28th-29th.

Mar. 28th-29th, 1916.

On that night the 50th British Division began to move to the rear as the leading columns of the 1st Canadian Division came up to take its place. The process was continued until the 2nd Canadian Division in its turn stood in the trenches of the 3rd British Division. The length of time and the order of the moves are best indicated by the days in which the various high commands took over their new responsibilities. The 3rd Canadian Division took over from the 24th British Division, as has already been mentioned, on March 21st. The 24th British Division from the 1st Canadian Division on March 30th, giving ten days for the double change. The 1st Canadian Divisional Staff assumed responsibility for the area of the 50th Division on the night of April 3rd, four days later. The 50th relieved the 2nd Canadian Division on the same night, while the 2nd Canadian Division did not relieve the 3rd British till the fatal night of April 4th-5th. Reading the map from north to south, we find the 9th and 7th Brigades holding the front of the 3rd Canadian Division; the 3rd and 1st Brigades in the same order as that of the 1st Division, while the 6th Brigade covered the whole frontage of the 2nd Division opposite St. Eloi. The Corps Commanders changed their functions on April 4th, and by the 7th-8th the V Corps were safely ensconced in the Canadian area.

Mar. 27th, 1916.

But in describing this move in its completeness we have run ahead of history. While the columns of weary men were tramping through the dust of the day, the delicious cool of the evening, and the chilliness of the night march, and the great batteries were being slowly removed from position to position, an event had occurred which added greatly to the difficulty. If the transfer of a corps can be done in peace so much the better for all concerned. In this case a fierce conflict was raging on the front of the 3rd British Division before the 2nd Canadian Division had taken over from them. After the fighting at the Bluff in February and March, it had been determined that the V Corps should assault the enemy's position at St. Eloi, and this attack had no doubt originally been intended to be the business of the corps concerned. For other reasons, which it is not necessary to relate here, the Canadians were brought up half-way through the intended action, which began on March 27th. The strategic reasons for a move on the British front in answer to Verdun have been indicated; the tactical reasons for a change in the *personnel* of the line were strong.

None the less, the obvious disadvantage of changing the higher command in the middle of an action would have been overwhelming but for one single reason. The mineshaft and the mines, the explosion of which would hurl the charge, were by the end of March ready for use. Every hour's delay meant a risk of their discovery and a counter-explosion by the enemy, when the labours of weeks would have been lost for ever. In these difficult and conflicting circumstances it was decided by the higher authorities to send the 3rd British Division to the attack opposite St. Eloi, and to bring the Canadian 2nd Division up to their support and relief as soon as the first stage of the fighting was over.

On the night of March 27th the mines were exploded, with cataclysmic effect, and six huge craters full of dead or wounded Germans took the place of the enemy's front trenches. The Northumberlands and the Royal Fusiliers of a British Division were over the parapet in a moment and dashed on the shattered enemy position. A heavy barrage of artillery fire was kept up by the various divisional artillery brigades to prevent the counter-attack; in this the Canadians took their share, as the Commander of the V Corps telegraphed in the following message:—

> "The handling of the trench mortars reflected the greatest credit on the officers and men concerned."

April 2nd, 1916.

In the meantime, the 4th Canadian Brigade had been giving most valuable assistance in linking up the right of the attacking regiments with the old line. They had driven a communication trench during the four days of doubtful fighting through from the trenches on the right of the St. Eloi position to the new line—and it was christened forthwith "The Canadian Trench." Further demonstrations were made by our infantry up and down their front and were duly and generously acknowledged as before by our brothers-in-arms of the V Corps. "Thank you very much for all the most valuable help you are giving. Your assistance has contributed very largely to the success which we have achieved." But the attack of the Northumberlands, though it had attained its immediate objective, had not been uniformly successful. It had begun to encounter all those difficulties which were to confront the 6th Canadian Brigade. The centre attack went right through the crumbled *débris* of the craters, and a position was established some two hundred yards south of them and four hundred yards in advance of the old British line. The 3rd Division fought throughout with the greatest gallantry and resolution. On the right, the efforts of the 4th Canadian Brigade succeeded finally in establishing touch, but the left remained in the air, and Crater 5, the easternmost of the big craters, was still in the enemy's hands. Finally, after four days' fighting, it was necessary to make what was practically a renewed assault on April 2nd and clear the enemy out of the debatable area. This was done with the utmost gallantry by the 3rd British Division and a new line well beyond the craters finally established. But this last effort absolutely exhausted the energy of the troops concerned. They had fought like heroes, but there are limits to human endurance, and it was imperative to bring up the Canadians to their support. A considerable number of German prisoners passed through the lines of the Canadian troops in support, and the reports speak of them as fine upstanding men in the main, but too young from our military point of view. The Divisional Command was able to extract from them much valuable information as to the distribution of the German regiments. There can be no doubt that the enemy infantry fought well at St. Eloi, and with a nerve and initiative that they have seldom displayed. They may have been new troops, but they were not old men driven on by their officers to certain death in massed formation, and they were all the more formidable for that.

It was now necessary to move the 2nd Division into action. The 6th Brigade led, and the 27th and 31st Battalions were its spearhead, with the 28th and 29th in support and reserve. The Northumberlands had been in the new line for about forty-eight hours, but they had been unable to place it in a good condition for defence. Their trenches were the remains of German second or third line defences choked with the dead and wounded of both combatants; their communications were only to left and right; firing trenches or platforms there were practically none; the earth was a sodden pulp and the skies full of falling shells; the schemes for the reconstruction of the lines put forward by their divisional command, wise as they were, had not been carried out owing to extreme weariness and the want of material; the position of the enemy was unknown, and doubt and darkness enveloped the whole situation. It was under this cloud of danger and uncertainty that the 6th Canadian Brigade advanced to the relief.

CHAPTER V

ST. ELOI

Canadians in a serious engagement—The old German line—The new British line—The effect of the eruption—Trenches little better than drains—The Second Division in "No Man's Land"—The situation described by General Turner—A gap in our line—The call for additional guns—Welcome relief—The importance of rear exits—Evacuation of the wounded—Our weak spot discovered—Prompt and intelligent action by General Turner—Steadfast endurance—The bravery of Privates Smith and Bowden—Conspicuous gallantry of Captain Meredith—Miscalculation—The enemy dashes through the zone of our artillery—Desperate situation of the Canadians—Communication by telephone intermittent—Confusion in the trenches—Under bombardment for sixty hours—The enemy's artillery preparation begins—Pandemonium inevitable—Clogged rifles and machine-guns—A brave struggle for existence—A moment of doubt—The enemy gains the craters—An unfortunate mistake—Unorganised retirement—Precipitate action—A case for help—Dilemma of the Higher Command—Trench mortars put out of action—Full story of the retirement cut short by death—A hand-to-hand encounter—Failure less welcome than success—Reasons for retirement only appreciated by those experienced in trench warfare—The Fates unpropitious—The error of the craters—Success denied though well deserved.

April 3rd, 1916.

On the night of April 3rd began the most serious engagement in which Canadian troops had been involved since the Second Battle of Ypres. The 2nd Division was ordered to occupy the ground won by the 3rd British Division in the two successive actions on March 27th and April 2nd. To understand the protracted battle which ensued it is necessary to have a clear grasp of the ground over which it was fought. The opposing lines opposite St. Eloi ran almost due east and west, instead of the north and south frontage which marked the usual direction of Allied and German trenches. The old German line had been a salient north pushed out towards St. Eloi and receding from it right and left. The new line captured by the 3rd British Division was a salient thrust due south into the German position and receding again slightly on its right and abruptly on its left, to meet the old British line. In other words, the old British line had been the arc of a bow turned north and the new line became the arc of a bow pushed south. The distance between these bows never exceeded 500 yards, and both of them were less than 1,000 yards in length from end to end, with a direct frontage of 600 yards. In the middle, running as the string of both concave bows and separated by 200 or 250 yards from either old or new line, was the original German line blown to atoms in most places and represented throughout the centre part of its length by a series of four huge mine-craters. These crowned the mound of St. Eloi, a rise in the ground which dominated the surrounding country.

To hold the craters and the mound was to look down into your enemies' trenches. The explosion of the great mine had leapt to heaven in a colossal shower of yellow smoke and *débris;* it could be seen from miles away and shook the earth like the sudden outburst of a volcano. The effects of the eruption on a narrow space of 600 yards were tremendous. Trenches on both sides collapsed like packs of cards under the shock; old landmarks were blotted out, and right in the centre of the arc of the bow stretched a line of huge tumbled *débris*. In front lay the new trenches captured by the 3rd British Division on April 2nd. Behind lay the remains of the old line, while the crater stood as an almost impassable bar between troops holding the one and troops holding the other. To get to the new front trench, you had to enter it from the left or the right, and a line to which supports cannot be brought up from the rear is always in grave danger. So much for the general position; its particular features have yet to be considered.

We have learned from a study of the French reports at Verdun what can be effected by concentrated artillery fire on a selected area. The frontage at St. Eloi was that of 600 to 1,000 yards, and against it was directed for over three weeks a colossal concentration of German fire, answered shell for shell by our own artillery. Under the combined efforts of the artillery of both sides and the result of the mine explosions, the whole face of the country was altered. The "high hills were laid low and the valleys were exalted" until an officer of the 3rd British Division who had stayed behind to assist the newcomers, twice confessed himself utterly unable to recognise the ground destroyed by man as bearing any resemblance to the ground he had known designed by Nature.

In this change will be found the explanation of much that followed. But there was to be added another cause, the inclemency of the weather. In this battered soil was nothing but mud. Every shellhole was a pond, every step might lead one up to the waist in the sticky element, and earthworks fell in from the flood as much as from the shell-fire of the enemy. It is then under a doubtful star that we must conceive of the whole action being fought. The trenches in the first firing line were little better than scattered drains—behind was the crater barrier—underfoot were the mud and the water, and above the unceasing whine of the shells. The air was heavy with a damp mist, even by day, and by night all objects were magnified and uncertain till a shell-hole appeared a crater, an advance of fifty yards like one of 500 yards, and an hour grew into years! The battle was fought in "No Man's Land"—a *débris* of shattered trees, sudden pool-holes, and upraised earth, "where no man comes, nor hath come since the making of the world."

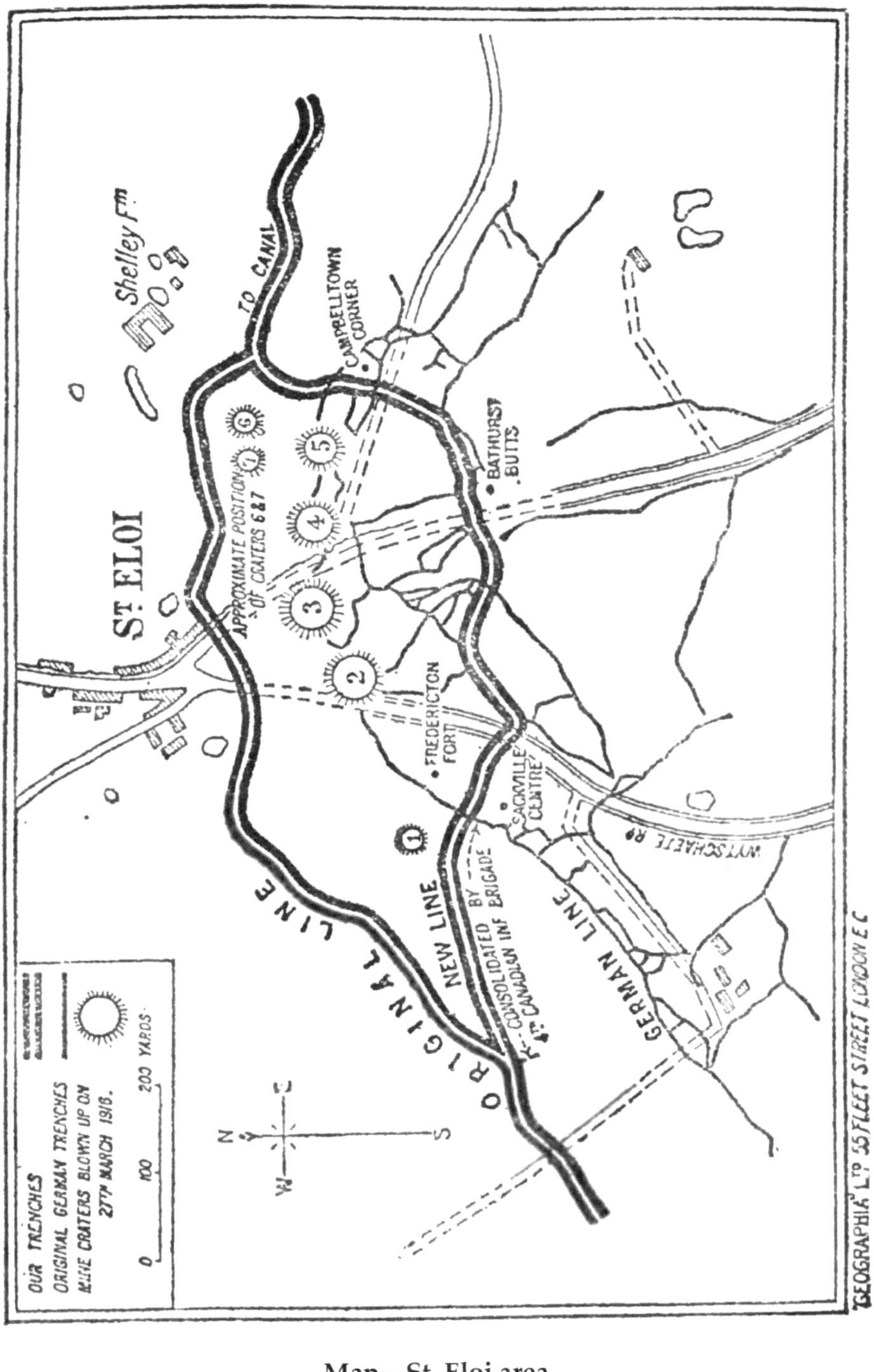

Map—St. Eloi area

Into this area the 2nd Division came on the night of 3rd April. The 6th Brigade, under Brigadier-General Ketchen, took over the immediate front, while the 5th and 4th Brigades were in reserve. The post of honour was given to the 27th (Winnipeg) Battalion, commanded by Lieut.-Col. Snider, on the right of the line and to the 31st. (Alberta) Battalion, under Lieut.-Col. Bell, on the left. The 29th (Vancouver) Battalion, under Lieut.-Col. Tobin, was in support of the 27th, while the 28th (North-West) under Lieut.-Col. Embury, occupied a position behind the craters and in the centre, with its left supporting the 31st. It is on the first two regiments that attention must be concentrated for the moment, for they had to occupy the southern thrust of the line and to file into their new positions from the old line on either flank.

A glance at the map will show the position, while Gen. Turner has given a lucid description of the state of the various defences three hours after the men were in. From the right of the old British line, the Canadian communication trench, built by the 4th Canadian Brigade—as elsewhere mentioned—broke straight out to the left and ran east with a touch of south, until it met the original German firing trench at a point known as Sackville Centre, of which we shall hear more in the future. The General described it as 250 yards in length, "a wet, shallow communication trench." This was held by a company of the 27th, under Lieut. Wilson. Continuing to our left the line crossed the first of the two roads (that to Wytschaete) which run from north to south and meet in St. Eloi; here the front, after going south-east for about fifty yards, swung round due east until it reached Bathurst Butts, near the second road; it then bent sharply north, so as to complete the salient by striking the old German firing trench again at Campbelltown Corner.[13] This bit was about 540 yards in length, and consisted of a deep *untraversed* firing trench, with a few firing platforms *facing north*: that is, the wrong way.[14] Apparently the 3rd British Division had been unable to turn it about after they took it by storm. The last two hundred yards were—adds the General—badly battered. The frontage was fairly evenly divided between two companies of the 27th. The left-hand company thus secured the most shaky point in the frontage—a 200 yards which proved a miniature gap of Alsace to the Germans. From Campbelltown Corner to the original British line the circuit was completed by one company of the 31st. Here the old British line continued due east to the canal and was occupied by two more compa-

[13] The whole of this line from the Canadian communication trench to Campbelltown Corner consisted of German communication, or second and third line, trenches, which had been battered in turn by the guns of both sides.

[14] A traverse is the projection of earth back into the firing trench which divides it into sections or firing bays. Its object is to give cover against flank fire, so that if an enemy enfilades you he cannot sweep right down the length of the trench. A trench without traverses is therefore very dangerous.

The firing platform is a ledge of earth from one to two feet high, on which a man must stand in order to see or fire over a parapet. It follows from this that until he gets up on the platform he can, in a good trench, walk about freely, without exposing his head to the enemy. Here, of course, the trench was a German one, and in consequence the parapet and platform were on the north side of the trench, whereas we wanted them on the south side. The first thing to do in capturing a trench from the enemy is to seize the sandbags of the parapet and to drag them across to the other side and then make a new platform below them.

nies of the 31st, with a third in support.

Machine-guns were also posted at intervals along the line. It was found necessary, owing to the extent to which these were being constantly put out of action, to call for additional guns. These were supplied by the 5th Brigade, the 22nd, 24th, 25th, and 26th each sending up a Lewis gun and team; but they were not available till the night of the 5th just before the German attack, when they were posted by Lieut. McLorg, of the 28th.

The relief, in the language of the official reports, was successfully concluded during the night of the 3rd and 4th. How much doubt, how much discomfort, how much danger a single sentence can cover! As the Canadians slipped and struggled along the wretched drains, or clambered over the places where shell-fire had destroyed them, they found everywhere the men of the 61st British Brigade, 3rd British Division in a state of considerable exhaustion. They had been fighting what was practically a continuous general action for five days under terrific shell-fire. The last push, which had driven the Germans 200 or 250 yards south of the craters, left the British in such casual shelter as they could obtain, encumbered with the dead on both sides and with their own wounded, whom they were unable to evacuate. A firing trench with no direct way in or out from the rear exposes its occupants to every horror and hardship and danger. The supply of food, water, and ammunition, is intermittent and uncertain, while the knowledge that supports may take hours to come up in case of attack is added to the mental torture and physical staleness induced by a persistent bombardment by heavy guns. But the presence of wounded men in a crowded trench passes the limit of horror. The dreadful nature of the injuries inflicted by high explosive, the irrepressible cries and moans of pain; the impossibility of bringing relief to the sufferers form a combination of sight, sound and sensation which if protracted for many hours absolutely unnerves the unwounded survivors and forms the nightmare of their sleep for years.

April 3rd and 4th, 1916.

Even with fair weather and solid defences a night relief has its trials; under the conditions of the night of April 3rd, its success was an achievement. As the 27th (Winnipeg) and the 31st (Alberta) succeeded to this bed of thorns, in the pitch dark of night, they discovered that the officers of the 61st (British) Brigade, through no fault of theirs, but owing to the lie of the ground and the conditions of the assault, could tell them practically nothing of the whereabouts of the enemy. They looked out into a noisy darkness which covered the Unknown. Such a state of affairs is by no means uncommon in trench warfare. Furthermore, while the line throughout could nowhere be held continuously, that portion of it between Bathurst Butts near the second road, and Campbelltown Corner could only be held by small bombing posts linked together by visiting patrols. By daylight it was altogether untenable for any body of men in sufficient number to resist a resolute attack. There was thus a gap sparsely and insecurely occupied by patrols of the 27th between the left of that regiment and the right of the 31st Battalion. This was the joint in the harness, and against it the Germans directed a continuous shower of heavy explosives.

It was obvious to the Higher Command that if the position was to be made secure or even tenable, a drastic scheme of consolidation must be set on foot. General Turner grasped the situation firmly and clearly; and after consulting General Haldane (3rd British Division) put forward the following plan. He proposed to repair the front line, to dig communication trenches through the intervals between the craters, so as to link old and new lines together, to make good the damage done to the old line, and finally to dig another trench about halfway between the firing line and the craters where supports could be kept handy. Dummy trenches were also to be made in the lips of the crater and both lines wired. The work was carried out by small parties, one N.C.O. and a few men of the 28th, centre support battalion, and most of them were overwhelmed by the German onrush on the morning of April 6th.

This plan would have saved the situation had time or opportunity been given to carry it out, but the Fates ruled otherwise.

The first thing to do was to evacuate the British wounded, and this gruesome task was accomplished during the morning to the accompaniment of heavy shelling, which began at ten o'clock and lasted at intervals nearly all day. Lieut. McCaw and his company, holding the bad part of the line, endured, without shifting an inch, a terrible bombardment which destroyed the greater part of their position from under their very feet. Out of the 90 men present (for 40 had been sent back as there was no cover for them), 67 were killed or wounded—a notable example of endurance. The trenches were blown out of existence and men lay down in the open under what cover they could find. As one wounded man was seen to fall, Private Smith dashed out to render first aid under the shower of high explosives; he was himself struck down at once. Private Bowden went in his turn to the two men, dressed their wounds, and remained with them until they both died, with no cover against the rain of shell except a shovel over his head.

Wading in many places waist-deep in the mud, Capt. Meredith, of the 27th, who behaved with conspicuous coolness and gallantry in the action which ensued, found that the day's bombardment had practically wiped out the position he was to occupy. There was a little cover on the right, just east of the second road; but to the left, in the Gap itself, it was impossible to do more than put out isolated groups of sentries and bombers, to crouch in shell holes, or behind improvised shelters, and trust that one would not be observed. A single fact speaks volumes; although Capt. Meredith had only 110 men for his company, it was found impossible to get cover by daylight for more than a few isolated posts, and the remainder of the men had to be sent back in the early morning of April 5th, to come up again on their weary journey as soon as it was dark. There was, in a word, no longer a line for over 250 yards of the front. Some 40 men were trying to hold the position of a strong company of 200.

Night, April 5th and 6th, 1916.

On the following night, that of the 5th and 6th, it was decided to relieve the two sorely-beset companies of the 27th. Capt. Gwynn, of the 29th Battalion, was to take over from Capt. Meredith the left of the line, and Lieut. O'Brien, of the same regiment, was to relieve the company of the 27th on the right. It was during the concluding stages of this relief that the German attack took place. The blasting fire of our artillery had been well maintained on the German second and third line trenches, and it was supposed that this barrage[15] had proved effective in preventing any considerable force of the enemy reaching through to their own front line. This did not prove to be the case. The German 214th Battalion, with some units of the 216th, had—according to the accounts of prisoners—succeeded in passing through the barrage into the front line, from which they launched their assault.

On the night of the 5th, the Germans had dashed through the zone of our artillery fire in a succession of small parties in extended order, and had thus, by choosing their occasions, escaped with comparatively small casualties, and massed in strength within striking distance of our front. It may be said that throughout the action the Germans showed a far greater aptitude for fighting in small parties than is usual with them, and that they nowhere attempted the mass formation attack which has generally been a prelude to their defeat.

But while the Germans are forming up for the assault at dawn, we must return to the fortunes of the Canadians. The working parties are out for the second night in succession, and a strong second line trench with barbed wire entanglements has been constructed in front and south of the craters. Behind and north of the craters a third supporting line is being dug, while the reliefs of the 29th are struggling up through the delays of mud and barrage to reach the battered 27th.

Night, April 5th and 6th, 1916.

Capt. Gwynn, of the 29th, had already been informed that the left of his line would only be occupied by machine-guns, bombing, and sentry posts, and with some 40 men, picked out for these danger posts, he went on ahead of the remainder of his company and found Capt. Meredith near Bathurst Butts at 2 o'clock on the morning of the 6th. The position was rapidly becoming desperate. One of Capt. Meredith's subalterns, Lieut. Dunlop, had been out under a rain of shells to try to find the original line to the left, held by the 31st, and the posts holding it. He returned to say that he could find no vestige of either the trench or the posts. Everything had been wiped out; and two machine-guns and their crews perished with the exception of a single man, who crawled back wounded hours after. A party of the 31st who had made a similar attempt to keep connection from their right, returned with the same news. Under the circumstances, Capt. Meredith could supply no guides into the unoccupied chaos of shell-holes which represented his left, and the two officers having completed their relief in the small fraction of surviving trench, returned to the nearest telephone, at Fredericton Fort, to get orders from the Colonel of the 29th Battalion. It was at this point in the line alone that the telephone was working, and that only intermittently, in spite of the heroic conduct of the signallers in going out into the open again and again to repair the shattered

[15] A barrage is a concentration of shell fire on a particular point or frontage so as to make it impassable to the enemy. It is also called "curtain fire" by the French. It can be used to prevent an attack on one's own front line, or check reinforcements coming to the enemy first line from the second or third lines.

wires. Lieutenant Browne of the 22nd (French Canadians), of the 4th Brigade, with his machine-gun party, remained behind with the 40 men of the 29th on the left of Bathurst Butts. The two officers and the men who had been relieved reached Fredericton Fort successfully at about 2.45 a.m., and found there several officers of the 27th, and also Lieut. O'Brien of the 29th, who was trying to relieve Lieut. Wilson's company of the 27th. Less fortunate than Capt. Gwynn, he had not succeeded in finding the officer he was to replace, but none the less he appears to have got his men somewhere near the trench he was to occupy. This place he found full of stray units, ration-carrying parties of the 27th, many of whom had lost their way, and having placed his men in position, he also returned to the telephone at Fredericton Fort in the hope of finding someone in authority.

The Canadian communication trench was by this time practically abandoned under heavy shell-fire. For the rest, then, one must conceive the remains of the front line as held, where there was any cover, by isolated groups of the 29th, intermingled here and there with men of the 27th who had not been relieved or who had missed their way, and with a gaping space on the left. Beyond this, the line on the left still held firm for the moment.

The 27th Battalion, the relief of which was by now more or less complete, had suffered a terrible experience. It had been almost continuously under heavy shell fire in hopeless trenches for about sixty hours, during which sleep, rest, or refreshment had been practically out of the question. Major Kitson had conducted the defence of the first line with skill and judgment, and the Company Commanders, Capt. Meredith, Lieut. McCaw, Lieut. Wilson, and their subalterns had shown great courage and coolness in the face of adverse circumstances. Lieut. R. E. N. Jones, of the same battalion, met a gallant death in the early morning of the attack in an attempt to keep touch with and collect the left of the regiment during the retirement. He went out into the open under a terrific fire and was killed almost instantly.

April 6th, 3 A.M.

It was by now three o'clock of a misty morning; and as the officers around the telephone dug-out discovered that the line was cut, and were taking counsel together, the German artillery preparation began.

The shelling—heavy but intermittent—rose to a roar and the night overhead became pandemonium, while the ground underneath shook with the concussion or dissolved under the explosions. Officers endeavoured to rejoin their units, but it most cases found it impossible, and every group turned to their official or natural leader for orders. It is easy for those whose experience of the movements of bodies of men is confined to reviews in peace time, or to the organisation of a big political demonstration, to consider that this state of affairs is not to be expected of an army. Such a view simply springs from ignorance of conditions. Not here was a broad plain, smiling in the sun, on which battalions could be moved with uniformity; or the familiar pavements, where every street turning is known to the marshals of the delegations; not here the frictionless chess-board of the war game, with its moves pondered silently long in advance. The ground on which to move is certain death;

the shattered and almost impassable trenches; the vast distance away in time of any supports; the blindness in the sense of direction which affects nearly every man on unknown country in the dark; the line of craters behind and the noise of the shells overhead: these are the elements making up the picture of the situation which, on that April morning, the 6th Canadian Brigade had to face. The rifles and machine-guns on which armed men are accustomed to depend for their lives, were half-clogged and useless. The very position of the enemy was unknown. But the native hardihood of the race asserted itself; groups made up of every unit formed themselves for the struggle for existence, fought where they could and retreated or died when the choice became retirement or passive annihilation.

April 6th, 3.30 A.M.

On this scene of incertitude and disturbance the day began to break. It was the hour when men rub their eyes and shiver in the cool air and stand to arms to meet that period which is most likely to bring the attack. The light of dawn, stealthy and suspicious, was showing in the east over a scene of ruin and desolation, and in this valley of dry bones something began to move. To the group of watchers in the trenches dark forms advancing could be seen through the mist. They came straight on without hesitating up the St. Eloi-Wytschaete road, towards Sackville Centre. It was known to our men that some Pioneers were out in that direction wiring the front. A whisper of doubt ran along the line. Were they the enemy or one of our working parties gone astray? One group evidently had made up its mind, and a sputter of fire broke out—how different in volume and intensity, alas! from the full-throated crash of musketry from a strongly-held, well-filled trench! It was enough, at any rate, for the Germans. They had thought to find nothing alive in the area on which their guns had wrought such havoc. The dark line turned half-right and swung round like a wave, seeking an inlet through some rocky barrier. Instantly every gun and rifle which would work was brought to bear. But the result was one to break the hearts of men trained to regard their weapons as their unfailing friends in the hour of need and danger. The foul mud splashed over them in torrents by the bombardment had worked into breech and magazine, and men threw down their choked rifles with curses, and snatched for one left behind by some dead or wounded man. But these, too, after a shot or two, refused to do their work! All along the line the remaining Lewis guns jammed, groups were too isolated to make a concerted counter-attack with the bayonet; and the Germans passed along our front until they found the fatal gap in the line. As they came opposite the last post on our left, Lieut. Browne, a machine-gunner of the 22nd French Canadians, turned his Lewis gun and what rifles the party had full on to them at short range. Some fifteen or twenty Germans were seen to fall, and the remainder threw themselves flat on their faces. Then the inevitable happened, and the gun went out of action. As the fire dribbled away to the crack of a single rifle, the enemy jumped up, swung to the left of the outpost, and headed straight through the undefended breach for the craters 150 yards behind.

The light had now grown brighter, and the officers at Sackville Centre could see the Germans breaking through to Craters 2 and 3. They turned their remaining men half-left rear, and fired with every rifle which would work. But the damage was done. The working parties on the second line, which was being built in front of the craters, had been withdrawn before light, and the small groups of the 28th Battalion in the craters themselves must have been overpowered by the 200 or 300 Germans who broke in on them. Once over the rim, the enemy were for the moment safe, and they promptly set about digging themselves in, and getting the machine-guns they had brought with them into position.

In all, then, some 200 or 300 Germans succeeded in occupying the two craters on the right of our position. From this point they began to work towards our left, and in the course of the day or the following night became possessed of Craters 4 and 5. This movement would have placed them in the rear of the men of the 31st Battalion at Campbelltown Corner had that still been occupied. As a matter of fact, however, the extreme right and south position of the 31st had been abandoned and destroyed in the course of the preliminary bombardment. At dawn a tremendous fire had been directed on the top line towards Shelley Farm,[16] and the trench between Campbelltown Corner and the old British line became untenable. To stay in it was certain and useless death. Part of its garrison got back into the original line. Other parties occupied the two small and ancient Craters 6 and 7, immediately in advance of it, under the impression, arrived at without due thought, that these were Craters 4 and 5; while one platoon cut off by the barrage moved to their left into an old advanced trench which afforded them some cover.

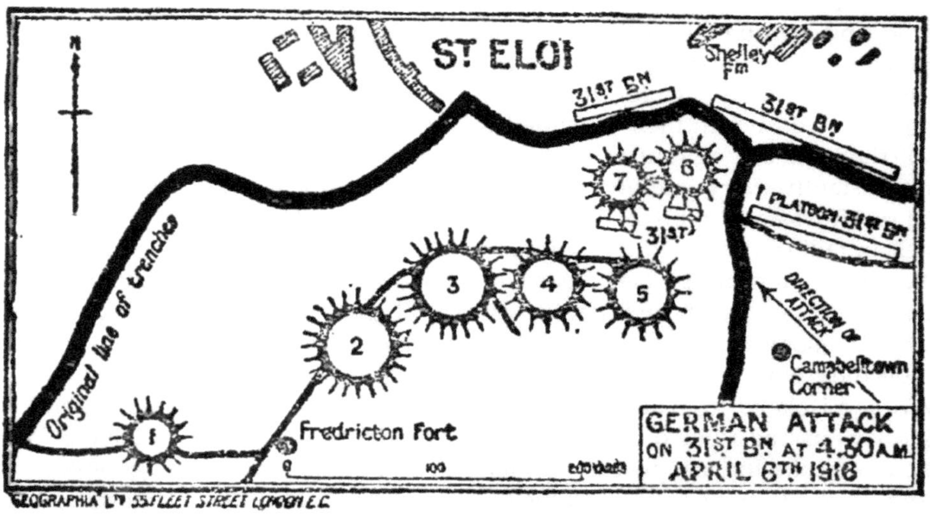

Map—St. Eloi

April 6th, 4:30 A.M.

At 4.30 in the morning, or an hour after the attack on the 27th, about 200 of the enemy made a second attack and attempted to overwhelm the party holding

[16] The Farm was not named after the poet, but because of the number of shells it received.

Craters 7 and 6; Major Doughty, of the 31st, organised the defence with skill and resolution. He allowed the Germans to advance within effective range, and then brought a concentric fire to bear on them. The isolated platoon enfiladed them on the left, the men in the craters enfiladed them on the right, while the original occupants of the old front line just behind and to the left of the craters mowed them down from the front. The attack recoiled in confusion.

Some fled, others threw themselves down into shell-holes and lay there unobserved as long as the daylight lasted. Our line was suffering now the fate of a taut rope cut in the centre. Each end recoiled instinctively to its point of connection with the old British trenches. It cannot be maintained that the retirement on the right, albeit it was from an untenable position, was carried out in a very skilled or organised fashion. This fact was due partly to the general nature of the ground and the situation, which has been sufficiently dwelt on, and partly to the number of different units on the same front. The time of relief—and the relief of the 27th was not yet fully accomplished though nearly so—with two sets of officers and men on the same front moving contrary ways, is always a period of some little confusion, and for that reason reliefs are not carried out at dawn, because it is the likely time for an attack. In this case the circumstances made it impossible to get the reliefs up earlier. But, apart from this, there were small parties of Pioneers scattered about in or in front of the line. It was not, of course, the business of these latter to await the Germans, but to get back into their own line, but the precipitancy and thoroughness with which they executed this movement added to the prevailing disturbance. At any rate, on the right every party from Bathurst Butts and the extreme right of their original line was between two fires and in imminent danger of being surrounded. So the scattered groups began to retire towards Sackville Centre and Fredericton Fort, where Capts. Gwynn and Meredith were organising the defence. Their party consisted of some subalterns of both their regiments, sixteen men of the 27th, and five Pioneers. These officers determined to hold on in spite of the heavy machine-gun fire from the craters in the rear, and to give time for the more easterly parties to rally on them. They got the telephone to work and asked for reinforcements; they tried to establish a continuous line down the Canadian communication trench, which had been deserted at its easterly end, and they asked for fire to be directed on the captured craters from the guns and trench mortars. Col. Snider, of the 27th, was the nearest Commanding Officer to them, and he did his utmost to come to their assistance. Their last request verged on the heroic, for their own trenches were only a hundred yards beyond those of the enemy, and their precise position could not be known to our gunners far to the rear. All this time men were falling fast. The cover was poor, and to show one's head was to invite an almost inevitable bullet. None the less, Lieut. Jackson, of the 29th, volunteered to go out with four men of the 27th and try to locate more precisely the positions the enemy had taken up. So murderous was the fire that within a few minutes he and one private returned alone. The other three had been killed almost instantly.

The requests for assistance from guns and men from the Brigade could not be very adequately met. The Higher Command were under a double difficulty. In the first place, so heavy was the German fire on the communication trenches that it was impossible to move supports up to them in the daylight hours of that morning. In the second place, the continual breakdown in the telephone service made all information as to the precise state of affairs in the front line impossible to obtain from minute to minute. In so far, however, as messages came through they continued to confirm the original evidence which had given the Brigade a radically false view of the whole situation. The view of the Brigade was that the Germans were simply a small raiding party who had broken through a weakly-held part of the line and seized on Crater 2, and possibly Crater 3. There they were, surrounded on every side except that by which they had come in, by parties of our troops in the closest proximity to them. Capts. Gwynn and Meredith were close behind their line on the right; and it was quite wrongly believed that Major Daly and the 31st were cheek by jowl with them in Craters 4 and 5 on the left; in the centre, of course, was our main force. To start a heavy bombardment was therefore impossible, for it would have killed more Canadians than Germans; it would have been using a steam-hammer to crack a nut and cracking one's own finger instead. A bombing and rifle attack was the only way to deal with such intruders. That was the obvious argument, and it would have been correct had the premises on which it was based borne any relation to the facts. The difficulties with which General Ketchen was confronted can best be appreciated in the light of the fact that he was not definitely informed till 5 o'clock on the morning of the 6th that the two Craters—2 and 3—were lost, and that all communication with the front then ceased for two and a half hours! As it was, under the urgent pressure of Col. Snider, of the 27th, and Capt. Gwynn, artillery fire was finally opened on Crater 2.

The trench mortars in our original right-hand trenches, whose gunners were near enough to see what they were doing, were out of action. Eventually, however, some 18-pounders were turned on the enemy. Capt. Gwynn, who observed the bombardment by Fredericton Fort, was doubtful of its efficacy, but the testimony of prisoners taken during the ensuing night proves that the garrison of Crater 2 lost heavily, though not heavily enough to induce them to retire. But the main reliance was placed on a bombing and infantry attack from the north and north-east, and the 28th Battalion, which had not yet been in action, was ordered to come up from its trenches behind the centre of the position and assist in the assault.

In the meantime, the isolated parties of the 27th and the 29th were making their way back as best they could from the east to the rallying point in front of Crater 1. The stories of these successive retirements will, in the main, never be told—for too often they were cut short by death. The machine-gun teams of the 5th Brigade were also involved in the retreat. Lieut. Browne commanded the 22nd, Sergt. Naylor the 24th, Lieut. White the 25th, Lieut. Lockhart the 26th. Of all these, only one gun was brought out of action—that of Sergt. Naylor, of the 24th Battalion, who showed great presence of mind in mitigating the confusion of the mixed units in the retreat, and saved the majority of his team. The character of the force is well illustrated by the private occupations of his team. The sergeant was a storekeeper, Lance-Cpl. Rose a patternmaker, Lance-Cpl. Duley a bank teller, Private Arundel a ledger-keeper, Private Clarke a salesman, Private Burchell a private secretary.

April 6th, 7 A.M.

The parties of the 25th and 26th were never seen again. They must presumably have perished, and their stories with them. One tale, however, survives—and that is the march of Lieut. Browne of the 22nd (French Canadians) and his detachment across the front and through the lines of the enemy. As has been already related, Lieut. Browne found himself on our extreme left with a Lewis gun when Capt. Gwynn went back for instructions. He fired on the Germans and saw them pass behind him to the crater. "The enemy," he says, "marched in absolute silence until I opened fire, and they extended and began to shout as they ran forward. In my opinion the enemy did not think that the front line was occupied, which would account for their advancing in close order until struck by our fire." As the enemy swung round his left, there was no outbreak of fire from the Lewis gun of the 25th Battalion—it had been buried and its crew presumably killed. Every gun and rifle save one having jammed, and the enemy being well behind the line, Lieut. Browne took his decision. "Not being able to do any effective work and believing the other crews to be out of action; also seeing the enemy closing on the left towards the craters, I decided to retire to the second line, there to unite with the garrison to make a stand." The party, which consisted of five men of the 22nd and a few others, accordingly started back north, following in the wake of the advancing Germans. There was, however, no garrison in our newly-dug second line south of the craters, for the working party had gone. Instead they encountered the barbed wire the working parties had put in front of the trench. The Germans, by now on the edge of the craters, fired on them as they were struggling through. Lance-Cpl. Lambert, Private Rattè, Private Brisebois, and a man of the 25th fell, but as they gained the other side they came across a digging party which had lost its way, and had not gone back with the others. Hastily gathering these men, Lieut. Browne charged for the spot where they had been fired on. Not a man had a rifle which would work, but they rushed in like the paladins of romance on the armed Germans who were in the trench. These they killed in hand-to-hand conflict with the butts of their rifles. Alter this notable feat of arms the party got into the new second line trench and proceeded along it towards Fredericton Fort. As they came running down the trench, the Germans came out of the crater against them, but Lieut. Browne's detachment managed to elude the enemy. Picking up some of the 29th, and the gun crew of the 24th on the way, Lieut. Browne succeeded in reaching Fredericton Fort, where he found Capts. Gwynn and Meredith. Of his original section only two remained alive. None the less, each new group had rallied round this officer, and were "ready for a fight at any time." Such a story of valour and discretion exceeds all that fiction has ever imagined. At 7 a.m. on the morning of the 6th, all telephone communication with the officers at Fredericton Fort ceased. The last message which came through to Capt. Gwynn (as appeared subsequently) from the Canadian communication trench was a simple and tragic one: "*We are retiring.*" Isolated by now on both right and left, and with the enemy in front and rear, Capt. Gwynn still held firm until he was reasonably certain that the last party from the abandoned line had come in. Finally, some two hours afterwards, no orders having been received, as indeed they could not be, he decided to retire. His men were falling fast in an impossible position and no alternative was open to him.

Fortunately, a message asking for the support of the machine-guns in our original trenches on the right had got through, and under cover of their fire and the shelling of the Crater 2 by our 18-pounders, Capt. Gwynn conducted a successful retirement to the old lines. In this emergency the 27th and the 29th were ably led, and seconded their officers' efforts to the last. The news of this final movement on the right did not reach the Brigade until some time later in the day.

With this retirement the first phase of the battle comes to an end. The new line has been indubitably lost with the exception of a few outpost positions like the minor craters, and the remainder of the prolonged struggle is devoted to the attempt to reoccupy by a series of counter-attacks ground which has been abandoned, and to oust the enemy from the craters. It will be well to defer to a later stage a full consideration of all the circumstances which prevented a successful issue, but something may be said with advantage on the fighting from the night of April 3rd, when the Canadian 2nd Division took over, to the morning of the 6th, when the German advance succeeded. It is inevitable that the mere event should leave behind it a certain trace of bitterness. To lose trenches, however indefensible, can never be pleasant. Failure must differ from success whatever the real merits of the case may be. And it is part of the tragedy of modern warfare that the real conditions which make such a retirement unavoidable can never be understood to the full by those who have not gone through the experience of a general action in trench warfare. No word painting, however vivid, can make the picture actual to minds which have mercifully been preserved from the experience and to eyes which have never seen a modern battlefield. The shock of squadrons, the bayonet charge, or the exchange of point-blank volleys between opposing battalions has become familiar to us in history-books, and the artist can draw them to the life. It is easy to grasp the recoil of a column down the hill-side under the furious impetus of an overwhelming assault. But to be killed in sections by high explosives and machine-guns in a trench which is rapidly ceasing to exist, so that the agony is prolonged for hours, is an ordeal more difficult to grasp. The mere reiteration of its horrors dulls the sense of the reader as the actuality strains the nerves of the soldier. Every sentence would have to end with the word "shell." The knowledge that to stay is useless because no attack will be made while anyone remains alive; that to bring up supports is impossible under the barrage, and that anyone who came would merely share your fate; the impossibility of keeping pace with the destruction of your only cover; the biting fire from rear, front and flank; the impotence of gripping a useless rifle—these things are indeed worse than the bitterness of death! The men of the 6th Brigade were right in retiring as soon as the line was broken and had become indefensible, and when no supports could be brought up to their assistance. But, apart from the unavoidable necessities of the case, the 2nd Division suffered from ill-luck. In all military operations luck is of primary importance, because even the best planned and most carefully executed schemes are met by such unexpected changes and conditions that they go to ruin through the Unforeseen. Every commander must expect a reasonable share of the favours of fortune. That share was in this action conspicuously lacking. The mistake about the identity of the Craters 4 and 5 was the beginning of all the trouble. Had the 31st Battalion occupied these instead of Craters 6 and 7, when they were blown out of Campbelltown Corner, they might have checked the whole enemy advance and made the Germans in Craters 2 and 3 what they were for long believed to be by the Higher Command, an isolated group partly surrounded by the Canadians. The initial mistake was the precipitate action and belief of the 31st Battalion, due to the fact that no one knew the ground as it had been transformed by mine and shell fire. But the results of the blunder were cumulative.

The counter-attack on the night of the 6th-7th—dealt with in the next chapter—by the 27th and 31st Battalions confirmed and exaggerated the error by failing to get to the real craters, although the men of these battalions were firmly convinced that they *had* done so. They found men holding what they thought to be Crater 5, and naturally believed them. The result was to immobilise our artillery during the crucial phase of the action and for days afterwards. Had we known that the whole crater line in the centre was held by the Germans, we could almost certainly have blown them out of it. As it was our gunners were crippled by the fear of destroying the positions of their own infantry. Such a mistake is no doubt "the luck of war," and in the ordinary course of events it would soon have been rectified by the photographic pictures taken by our aeroplanes. But here came the crowning blow of a malignant fortune. All through the first fortnight of the action a great gale blew. It not only hindered our actions on the surface of the earth, but it absolutely stopped them in the air. No aeroplane could go up in it, and the vital facts of the position were hidden from the commanders until the morning of April 16th.

Confronted by all these adverse circumstances, the companies of the 27th, 29th and the 31st did all that mortal men could do. In the face of heavy casualties, and holding positions under intolerable artillery fire, they stood their ground firmly so long as defence was possible, and retired, in rallying groups when to hold on was merely suicide they did not command success; they deserved it.

CHAPTER VI

ST. ELOI (CONTINUED)

Counter-attacks—Obstacles to victory—The ground described—The enemy deceived—Ravage wrought by heavy guns—Impassable ground—Schemes based upon unreliable information—Forward movement ordered—The 28th severely shelled at Voormezeele—Confusion regarding the occupation of the craters—Raid on Craters 2 and 3 fails—Wrong craters attacked—The Canadian infantry in Craters 6 and 7—Enemy patrols walk straight into Canadian trenches and are taken prisoners—The actual situation revealed by aerial photographs—Unit follows unit to certain death—The brave 28th—Heavy casualties—Determination of the Higher Command—Sniper Zacharias—A gallant deserter—Imperative order to take the German positions—Crater No. 1 captured—Unfortunate lack of reliable information—Four Privates hold an exposed position for 70 hours—Individual acts of bravery common—Good work of the Lewis gun team—"Get on at any cost"—Brave though fruitless attempts—A glorious failure—Repeated counter-attacks unsuccessful—The third phase of the Battle of St. Eloi—A parallel of Verdun—The enemy seizes a dominant position—A deadlock—General Turner's suggestions—Reconstruction of the old British line under General Watson—The inglorious drudgery of digging—Perilous position of Canadians in advanced positions—Carrier pigeons used as messengers for the first time—Value of position problematical—Superior trenches of the enemy—Useful work of aircraft—Historic ground—First and second great actions of Dominion Army contrasted—Failure and success enter into the education of a nation.

April 6th, 1916.

With the morning of April 6th began that series of counter-attacks against the Germans which continued at intervals during the remainder of the action.

Here, in estimating the causes of success or failure, three factors are of primary importance: the general lie of the land and the consequent disposition of our troops on it; the concentrated fire of the enemy's heavy artillery; and the state of the weather and the subsoil. None of these factors was in our favour, and though taken singly their hostility need not have proved fatal, taken in conjunction they formed as grave an obstacle to victory as any general has encountered.

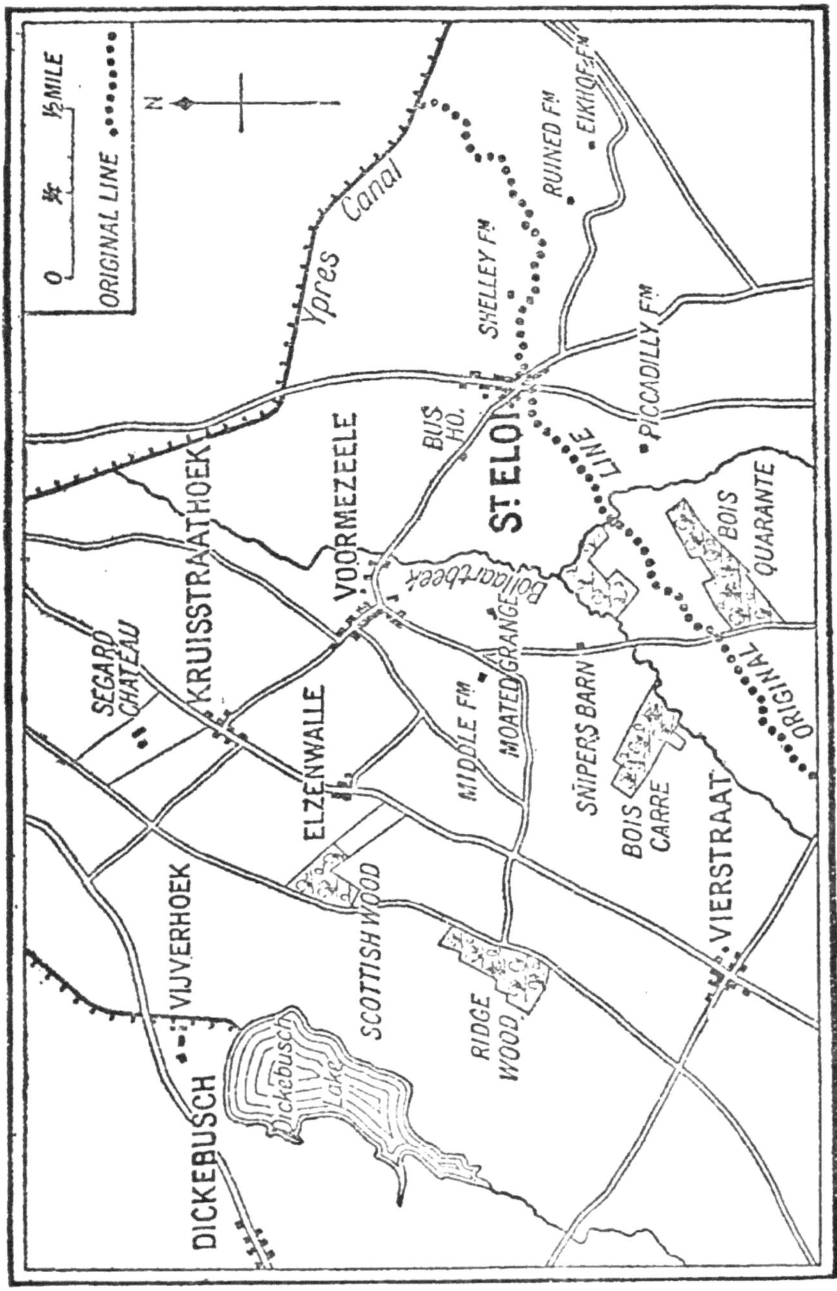

Map—St. Eloi area

The knoll of St. Elbi is in itself of no great magnitude. From the plateau which it crowns the ground drops suddenly to the south and the German second line trenches. But though it possesses this local advantage it is in its turn dominated both by the rise at Eikhof Farm some 1,000 yards to the east and by gun positions well back in the German line. This drawback was aggravated by the fact that, like most positions, such as Hooge or Hill 60, in the Ypres salient, it could be subjected to a converging fire from the front and either flank. The German observers could thus look north past the knoll, and watching any signs of the movements of our troops far behind the line, turn on them a rain of shells from at least three points of the compass. The Canadian Higher Command was compelled in consequence to order the dispositions of the troops accordingly. The divisional frontage was taken by only one brigade with two battalions in the advance positions. The centre and support battalion had to find cover farther back, while the reserve battalion was right back near Dickebusch nearly three miles away. Such a dispersion cannot but be disadvantageous. But the configuration of the ground would have been of less importance had there been no great concentration of German guns to face. Such a collection of heavy pieces takes days to assemble or disperse, and is not therefore to be looked for on the side of the defence. The enemy, *ex hypothesi*, should have been taken by surprise when the craters were blown up and the 3rd British Division attacked, and plenty of time given to the assailants to consolidate the new position before a great concentration of guns could be brought to bear on them. But this did not happen, by a simple piece of bad luck, as has been related in Chapter IV. In February the British Division holding the Bluff to the north of St. Eloi, just east of the Canal, and included in the subsequent Canadian position, had some trenches there snatched from them. They took the matter calmly; got up the heavy batteries, including even the monstrous 15-inch guns, blew the Bluff practically to pieces, and took back the lost ground on March 2nd. This performance caused keen irritation to the Germans, who looked round for the best spot on which to retaliate, and selected St. Eloi. The troops then who carried the new line, and the Canadians, who had to hold it, found a ready-prepared artillery concentration against them from the moment they started. The whole area was laid waste, and the old British line in the centre, and many of the support and communication trenches behind it, were rendered untenable.

Depth then, not length, is the distinguishing feature of the section occupied by the 2nd Canadian Division. And here the third factor comes into play, the state of the soil. In war, distance, time, and energy are interchangeable terms. The interval between a line and its supports is not to be measured by the number of yards between them, but by the time it will take to traverse and by the amount of fatigue involved in the process. Undisturbed earth under rain forms mud, but in a country which is not marshy it can be crossed somehow. But earth disintegrated by high explosive and drowned in water becomes pulp. One can wade through water, or struggle over mud, but this stuff was neither. As men splashed from shell-hole to shell-hole—and the surface of the earth consisted of nothing else—they sank up to the armpits and could find no grip for their feet. One of the strongest men in the 2nd Division has declared that after sixty yards of this work he was incapable of going further.

To make new—or, worse still, to repair old—trenches out of this material was impossible. Add darkness for a night attack, and the picture is complete. Even by daylight, parties reported in the utmost good faith that they had reached such and such a point on the map, when, as a matter of fact, they had done nothing of the kind, for all the old landmarks had vanished. Yet it was on this information that schemes of attack had to be based.

Morning, April 6th, 1916.

On the morning of the 6th, as soon as the enemy attack was known of at Headquarters, a forward movement of the supports and reserves of the 6th Brigade began. Two companies of the 29th were already up with the 27th in the original British trenches and the new Canadian line beyond, and a bombing party followed them into the former position. The 28th occupied Voormezeele in the support centre line, where they were subjected to as severe a shelling as any experienced in the forward trenches. Two battalions, 18th (Western Ontario), commanded by Lieut.-Col. Wigle, and 21st (Eastern Ontario), under Lieut.-Col. Hughes, of the 4th Brigade, took their places at Dickebusch in reserve. Two counter-attacks were then organised. The attacks were to be simultaneous and converging. From the right of the line the bombers of the 27th and the 29th were to head an assault against Craters 2 and 3, which lay to the south-east of the original line. From the left-centre of the line, the bombers of the 28th and 31st Battalions were to re-occupy Craters 4 and 5, should these have been abandoned, moving in a south-westerly direction. The men of these two regiments had to come up from well behind St. Eloi on to ground with which they were utterly unfamiliar, and from which all landmarks had been blotted out. As they advanced through the half-ruined communications in the full light of day, the German observers caught a glimpse of them and a tremendous barrage of fire was turned on them. Dashing through this, they saw in front of them the outlines of two craters and immediately assumed that their objective was before them. No one knew at the time which craters on our left were in German hands, and as has been noted before, the 31st under Major Doughty, when they evacuated their forward position at the time of attack, were firmly convinced that they had seized Craters 4 and 5, whereas they had actually occupied Craters 6 and 7, and from these repulsed the assault.

It was into these two craters that the bombers of the two battalions broke, and found one still occupied by a party of the 31st, and the other abandoned under a rain of shells. They reported accordingly, and the original error was again confirmed in the minds of the Brigade. In the meantime, the raid on Craters 2 and 3 had come to grief. It was delivered across the open, where the only cover was shell-holes, in face of a sweeping machine-gun fire from the German redoubts in the craters, backed by their gunners behind their lines. To advance in the face of this hail of death was impossible, and finally the attempt was abandoned.

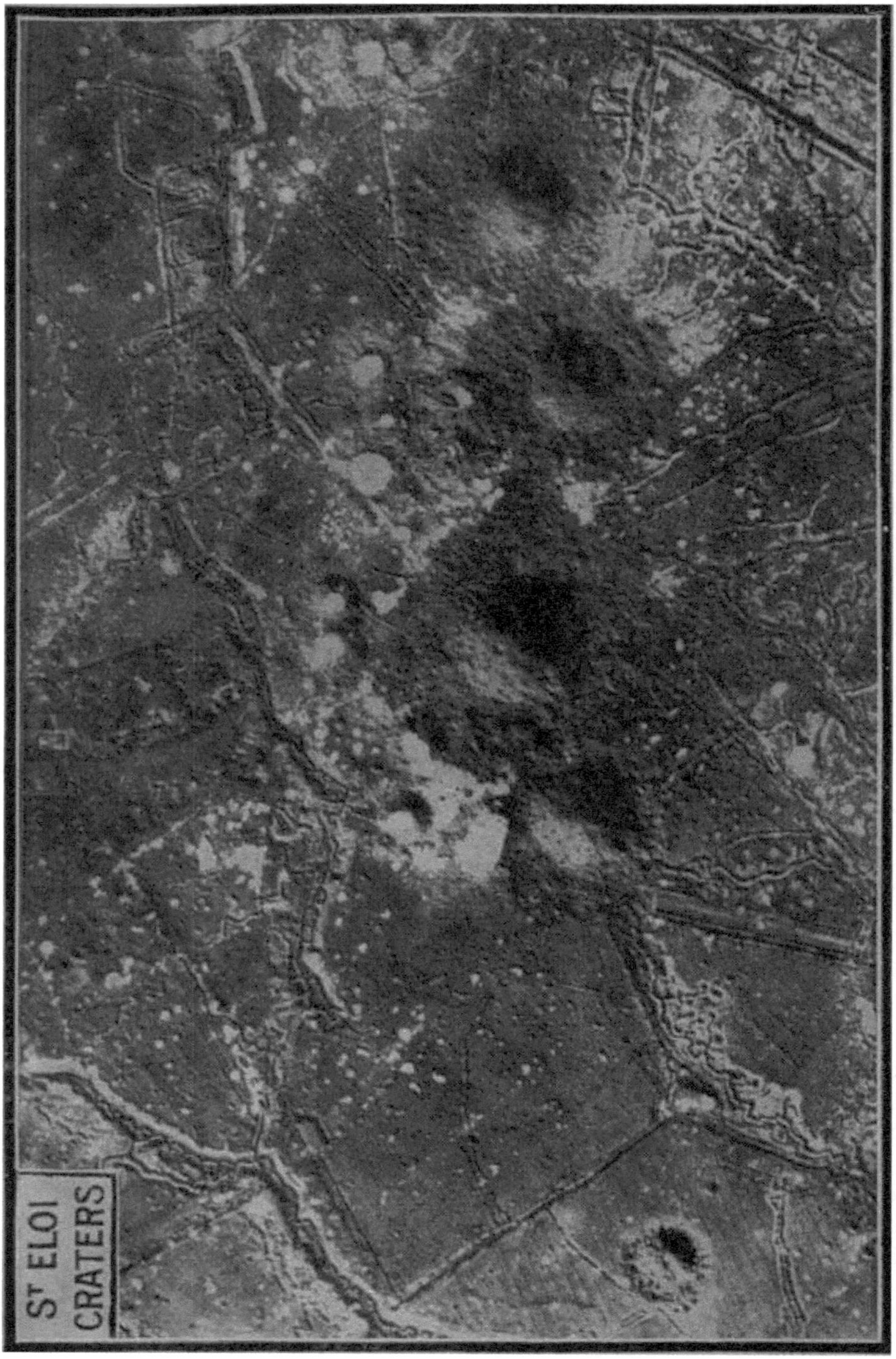

St. Eloi Craters

6 P.M., April 6th, 1916.

An attack organised for 1.30 a.m. on April 6th was postponed while our artillery bombarded the craters. All through the day the German barrage hardly lifted, but it was decided to make a new push against Craters 4 and 5, then supposed to be Craters 2 and 3, as soon as the dark descended. But at dusk the Germans themselves took the initiative for a moment. When the 31st had repulsed the attack at dawn on the 6th, they imagined that the surviving Germans had made a final retirement. This proved not to be the case; some 50 or 60 of them had flung themselves flat down in the shell-holes in front of Craters 6 and 7 and the trenches on our left, and had remained crouching there all day. As evening fell, they leapt up suddenly and charged the 31st. A withering rifle fire swept the enemy's groups, which faded out of existence. Some fell and some fled, but a few dropped back again into their shell-holes, and remained there during the night. The strain appears to have been too much for the nerves of the survivors. Driven mad by their position and the fire of our artillery, they leapt up again at dawn on the 7th, and with their rifles slung danced "like Red Indians," as an eye-witness observed, in front of the Canadian lines.

On the evening of the 6th, the 28th were coming up in successive parties to the support of the right of that hard-tried Battalion, and had effected a junction with Major Daly (31st) behind our own craters. Their instructions were to pick up bombers of the 31st and to assault and capture Craters 2 and 3. They actually advanced against Craters 4 and 5. The bombing attack was led by Lieut. V. P. Murphy (25th), who succeeded in establishing himself nearer the hostile craters than any previous advance had done. He was supported by Capt Styles (28th), who exposed himself with the greatest gallantry in the continuous attempt to keep touch with the various scattered units of the 28th and the 31st. But the mud was almost impassable, the darkness intense, the position of the enemy uncertain, and the ground a mere mass of holes.

Dawn, April 7th, 1916.

Dawn found the Canadian infantry still entrenched in Craters 6 and 7, but with no visible progress towards the enemy positions. The attacking parties had lost their way or been overwhelmed by sheer exhaustion. This is the more remarkable, because it is clear that the Germans were throughout the night in position in Craters 4 and 5.

Night, April 6th-7th, 1916.

It thus appears that throughout the night of April 6th-7th, the enemies can only have been separated by the distance of less than forty yards, between Craters 6 and 5. In fact, a few German patrols, as much confused as their opponents, walked straight into the Canadian craters in the dark and were taken prisoners! And yet neither side succeeded in coming to grips with the other. It was as though an impenetrable curtain had fallen between the contending parties of infantry. The mud, the darkness, and the shells made every movement a failure. That such a state of affairs could be possible can only be understood by the insight of imagination or by an actual experience of the ground and the conditions. But a study of the photographs taken by aeroplanes makes it at least intelligible. Among the infinite traceries of lines, trenches new and old, which wrinkle the surface of the chart, the rims of the four great centre craters stand out ominous and distinct. We actually see down into the hollows held by the lurking Germans as one gazes through the sunlit depths of a rock-bound pool to where the tiny monsters of the deep dart in and out of their caves and recesses upon the clear floor of the sea. Away to the right lies Crater 1, a perfect circle of light and shade with its foliated edges like the milling on the rim of a coin. Across a flattish, almost unmarked surface, the Canadian and the British communication trenches drive north and south of it from the strong serrated line of our own trenches, until they strike the intricate tangle of the old German front line. But turn your eyes to the centre and to the ground which lies directly between St. Eloi and the craters. The old outstanding British position on the right crumbles away into a vague tangle of flattened outlines. Behind it the whole surface of the ground is pockmarked with the white dots which indicate shell-holes, and in front of it there is no solid earth at all, but a bewildering labyrinth of minor craters spreading out till they touch the four huge eruptions.

On the left the space is a trifle more open. Craters 6 and 7 held by us can be distinguished as mere holes separated by some forty or fifty yards from the giant rim of Crater 5. From high up it looks so clear, but to the men struggling in the dark over that quagmire, sweating to dig themselves in by daylight under the pitiless hail of death, it appeared confusion worse confounded. Looking down from a great altitude on the passionless picture in high relief it is hard to imagine that here men battled in the mud till they could do so no more, and tasted the bitterness of failure as they fought and died for their country. The photographic record seems cold compared with the ideals and efforts the result of which it enshrines. One turns from it as one might turn from the privacy of the human soul outraged by Omniscience. All this chaos was to the advantage of the Germans once they had seized the dominant position.

Night, April 6th-7th, 1916.

From the rear came continued orders to take the enemy's entrenchments at any cost, and a constant trickle of reinforcements was sent struggling up the communication trenches or dashing across the open in groups the moment the barrage lifted. But in the conditions existing at the front, all these groups seemed to melt away. Units went up and were heard of no more at Headquarters. The bare official reports are tragic. One can select any one at random; for instance, this from Lieut.-Col. Embury, of the 28th:—"I told Capt. A. G. Styles (28th) he was to come around north of the craters. He started off at 11.30 and left part of his men with Major Daly. It was dark and raining hard and we had never seen the ground before. The craters looked just like the ordinary ground. Styles went up and found Lieut. V. P. Murphy (25th) at 4 o'clock a.m., but had no time to fix up for the attack. The men were all in; they had only had three hours' sleep in forty-eight." But it is impossible for the contemporary writer in the space at his disposal to give a clear and detailed picture of the movements of all these units or of the valour displayed by individuals. The fog of war lies heavy on the scene of confusion and heroic effort, and if (which is very unlikely) it is to be lifted at all, it must be by the hand of the future historian. The troops did their best, but the odds both of man and Nature were against them. The 28th Battalion throughout the fighting set a notable example of gallantry and endurance.

That night of April 6th-7th the Germans effected their relief.

They had, by all accounts of prisoners, suffered very severely from the fire of our artillery—but they had held on, retiring by a perverse stroke of irony to our own second line trench dug south of the crater when the bombardment became intolerable. It cannot be questioned that if we had been fully aware of the relative positions of the two forces the British artillery could have blown their opponents bodily out of the craters.

That night, too, the 4th Brigade began to come up to the relief. The 6th Brigade had done its best; it had been fighting continuously for three days and nights; its supply of rations had been intermittent; many of its officers and men had had no sleep for days, and the exhaustion bred of shell-fire and mud was upon it. Its casualties were in all 617 officers and men. The 27th had borne the brunt of the first German onrush and suffered proportionately. Eight of its officers and 209 of its rank and file had been killed or wounded. The 31st, which held its line for the longest period in the Brigade, came next with a roll of 180 casualties. The 29th lost 117, and the 28th, 101. The Brigade had failed, but it had failed gloriously!

April 7th-8th, 1916.

The relief could only be accomplished by degrees. To move large bodies of men up simultaneously was impracticable, and the fighting was therefore continued by mixed battalions of the two brigades. The 4th Brigade, under General Rennie, consisted of the 18th (Western Ontario), commanded by Lieut.-Col. Wigle; 19th (Ontario), under Lieut.-Col. J. T. Maclaren; 20th (Northern and Central Ontario), under Lieut.-Col. C. H. Rogers, and the 21st (Eastern Ontario), under Lieut.-Col. Hughes. In effect, the relief, which lasted over four nights, put the 21st instead of the 27th on the right in the trenches, the 18th replacing the 28th in the centre support position; while the 19th took the place of the 31st on our left and in the Canadian craters. But the Higher Command of the 2nd Division, which exhibited throughout great determination, was not content to await the full relief before it launched a new attack on the enemy.

Night, April 8th-9th, 1916.

On the night of the 8th-9th fresh assault was launched against Craters 2 and 3.

3.30 A.M., April 9th, 1916.

The object of this attack was to effect a lodgment on the north-west side of Crater 2 and on the north side of Crater 3—that is to say, to secure a position where the St. Eloi-Wytschaete road passes through the craters and bends to the right. The assault on the right was led by Capt. Miller, of the 21st, who was wounded during the engagement. He and a small bombing party succeeded in getting to the edge of Crater 2 under a heavy fire, and in the blackness of the night crept up unobserved. Here Pte. Comego had his right arm shattered. In spite of his excruciating agony he managed to control himself when a single sound would have given away the presence of the whole party. They had expected to find only about twenty of the enemy, but, discovering a far stronger force, beat a retreat to secure reinforcements. Fifty more men of the 21st went up with Lieut. Brownlee, who distinguished himself by conspicuous gallantry, to make a renewed attempt. By this time, however, the alarm had been given, and such a tornado of fire was turned on "No Man's Land" that the attack stuck fast. At 3.30 in the morning the exhausted survivors succeeded in struggling back to the trench. In the course of the advance and of vigorous exchange of bombs with the Germans, they had lost three-fourths of their number.

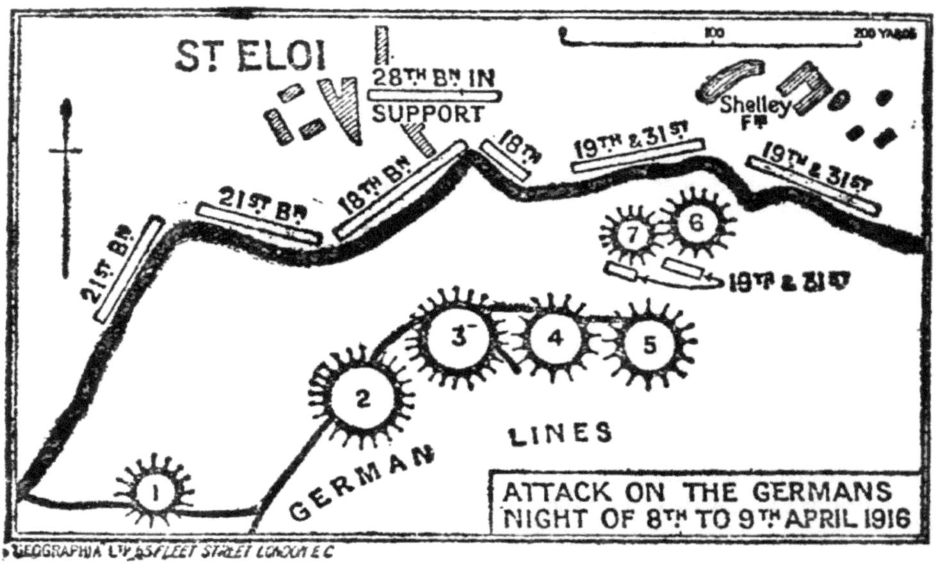

Attack on the Germans Night of 8th to 9th April 1916

Great bravery was displayed by many men of the 21st. Sniper Zacharias used his rifle in the assault until it was blown out of his hands; he then became a grenadier and hurled bombs at the Germans until his party retired. Two lance-corporals, Currie and Henderson, made heroic efforts to drag the wounded back into the trench under heavy and continuous fire. As a result practically all the wounded of the 21st were evacuated by the stretcher-bearers.

The attack on Crater 3 by the 18th met with no better success. Lieut. Kerr, who had reconnoitred the ground on the previous evening, led the party on, but the heavy barrage of the enemy checked the progress, and finally they had to content themselves with re-occupying the old British line and putting an outpost position in advance of it, fifty yards in front of the German crater.

The 18th (Western Ontario) fought throughout with great courage. Lieut. Kerr was wounded, and Lieut. Baxter had been untiring in the most dangerous form of reconnaissance, working on unknown ground; Lieut. Elliott, the signal officer, went out over and over again into the open to establish and keep connection between the front position and battle headquarters, and was well backed by his men. But, as in the case of the 21st, in this attack the great difficulty was to bring in the wounded. Capt. McKeough, Company Sergt.-Major Richardson, Sergt. Cunningham, Sergt. Bowie, and Lance-Cpl. Evans dashed out time after time to bring the casualties in. Private Tom Jones, said to have been in turn a deserter from the British Army, the British Navy, and the American Army, though quite a young boy, lost his life at this stage of the action. He had been helping to carry Lieut. Clarke (18th), who was wounded, into safety, and on returning to guide an officer up, was shot clean through the head, to the grief of his regiment. The attack had suffered heavily, losing 100 men in killed and wounded. In the meantime, the 19th Battalion was engaged in relieving the 31st in the Canadian craters on the night of the 8th and 9th. Lieut. Hooper (19th Batt.), the grenade officer of the battalion, had undertaken the risky work of reconnoitring the position in advance, and Majors Moors and Morrison (19th Batt.) held this very awkward bit of the line in succession. The 19th, in fact, like the 31st, could give very little active assistance to the assaults, for their position in Craters 6 and 7 was dominated by the German Crater 5, and was exposed to heavy shelling. The main object was to hold their own, and this, it may be said, they succeeded in doing. Orders, however, to retake the German positions were peremptory, and, as each wave of assault recoiled under the fire of the enemy, and because of the impossible state of the ground underfoot, a new one was promptly organised for the succeeding night.

Night, April 9th-10th, 1916.

The attack on the night of the 9th was of a extensive character, and achieved at least some measure of success. The 20th were brought up from brigade reserve and thrown into a line between the right of the 18th and the left of the 21st, and pushed into action. The main idea of the Higher Command was a very sound one, if due allowance be made for the extent of their knowledge. The German craters, then supposed to consist only of Craters 2 and 3, were to be attacked simultaneously on three sides.

The 21st were to attack Crater 2 from their own front and through Crater 1, taking their left in reverse, and reoccupy the positions at Sackville Centre and Fredericton Fort which had been held by Capts. Gwynn and Meredith during the morning of April 6th. The 20th, to their left, were to attack Crater 2 from the north-west. The 18th, further to the left of the line, were to attack Craters 2 and 3 from the north. The 19th, continuing the line again to the left, were to close in and assault the Germans on their right flank, and so practically enclose them. The first plan shows the position as it actually was; the second as it was according to the information of the Higher Command.

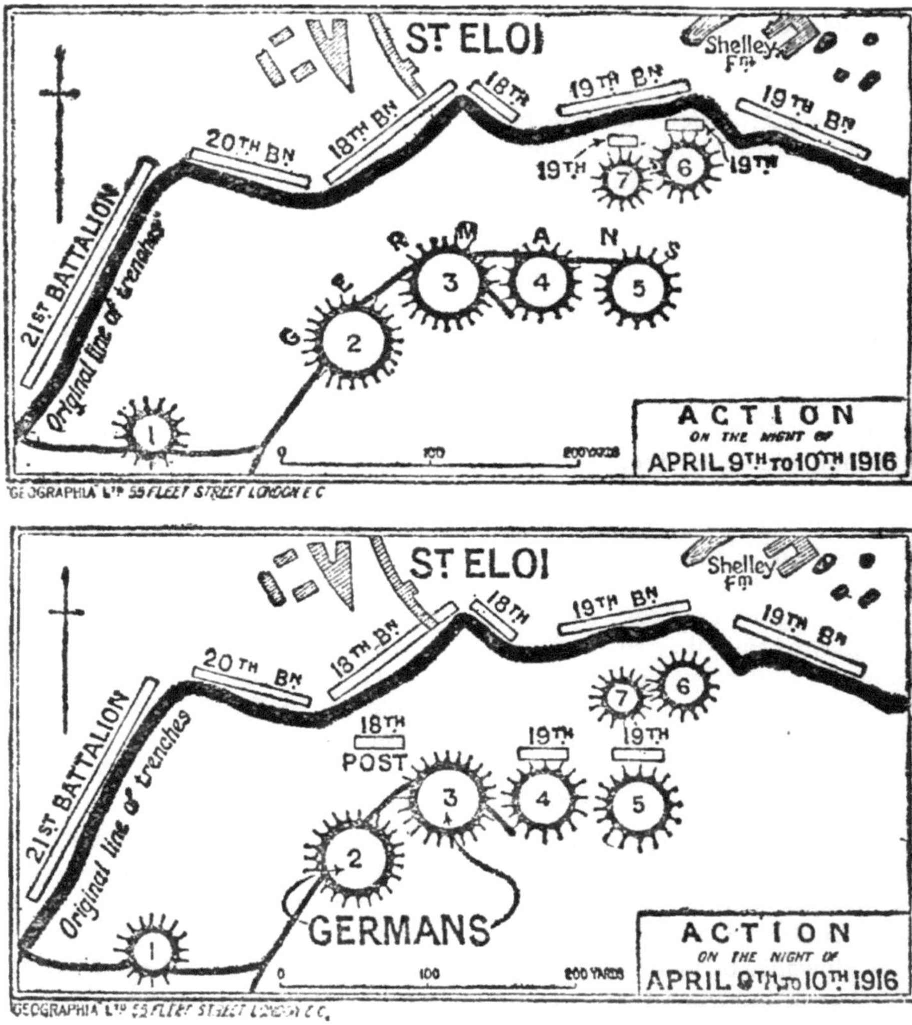

Maps—Action on the Night of April 9th to 10th 1916.

But here again all assaults from the north broke down utterly. The men simply could not get on, and came staggering back into the line at dawn with heavy casualties and in a state bordering on collapse. On the right, however, a glint of success visited our standards. It had been discovered on the previous night that Crater 1 was not in the hands of the enemy. Lieut. Davidson (21st)—taking the place of Capt. Miller who had been wounded in the assault of the 8th—and Lieut. Brownlee once more led a strong party of bombers from our trenches up into Crater 1. Seizing this, they charged into the old German line about Fredericton Fort, where it had been held during the German main attack by Capt. Meredith and Capt Gwynn. They took back this lost ground and advanced north along the trench to capture Crater 2 from behind. This they failed to do, but they established themselves close to its south-west rim. The ground won was retained and consolidated, and the 2nd Division once more held much the same position as it did on the morning of April 6th.

Col. Wigle, of the 18th Battalion, had been in charge of both these successive night attacks, and his account of the failure of his own Battalion and of the 20th to get on in this last attempt throws up in high relief the difficulties confronting the commanders in all these operations. "They had no proper information as to the ground in front of them. They could not find a guide to locate Crater 3 at night—a heavy bombardment retarded progress, and Lieut. Clarke reported that his party could not get through. The Brigade said the attack must proceed. The result of the operation brought no change from the position of the previous night."

The 19th Battalion continued during this assault to maintain the positions in the Canadian craters it had taken over from the 31st Battalion on April 8th, and continued to do so until its relief on the 12th, Lieuts. Thomson and Macdonald commanding the garrison of Crater 7, and Lieuts. Pepler and Cassells of Crater 6. An advanced machine-gun emplacement in a very exposed position was held by Privates D. C. Ballantine, A. W. Sharpe, and W. Hull, for 70 hours without repose or relief. There were many other notable examples of gallantry in the regiment. Cpl. A. F. Lynch went out and dragged in a machine-gun, the entire crew of which had been killed. Private Hagan carried Private Hoffman, who had been wounded in both legs, to a place of safety 500 yards away through a heavy artillery barrage. Lance-Cpl. Bishop and Private Schwann, D.C.M., carried food and water out from the front trench to the garrisons of the craters, who had been cut off from all supplies for 48 hours. This act was done in broad daylight, when to move was almost certain death. The 19th did well.

Nor were the 20th, though less continuously engaged, far behind them in their record of individual heroism. Lieut. C. A. Thomson helped to dress the wounded men of his own and other companies under heavy fire during the night attack of April 9th-10th, though he himself was hit through the leg by a rifle bullet. He remained with his men till dawn and then dragged himself back for first aid—a journey which took four hours. Private Cooke, too, a stretcher-bearer, went on binding up the wounded long after he was hit, and Private B. Asquith carried a comrade to safety single-handed under a heavy fire.

The Lewis gun team of the 20th, under Sergt. Simpson, also exhibited marked courage and endurance. They were under fire continuously from April 5th to 12th, held Crater 6 against an encircling attack of German bombers, repulsed the attack, and took three prisoners.

Wave upon wave of men had been thrust forward in succession to retake the lost positions, yet as each party came up it seemed to melt away in the noise, squalor, and confusion of the front line. The telephones from behind were perpetually jangling with the urgent messages from the Brigade, "You must get on at any cost," and when the wires were cut in spite of the heroic efforts of the regimental signallers to make them good, runner after runner risked his life in a dash across the shell-swept area with the same pressing orders. Urged on by their commanders and their own indomitable spirit, the regiments renewed the attack again and again. But they could not get on. In the daylight the air was full of flying steel, and the bright light showed the assailants to their enemies so plainly that the lines of the attackers withered away under that devastating hail. By night the impenetrable darkness and the chaos of earth and water enveloped each succeeding party before they could get to grips with the enemy, in the dark hours small parties were wandering round trying to find their location in vain. The survivors returned almost fainting with exhaustion to the nearest detachment they could find. Some were left behind as day broke, in the precarious shelter of small holes. Private Warn, of the 29th Battalion, lived for nine days in such a position subsisting on the rations and water-bottles taken from the bodies of men of the 3rd British Division killed in the fighting of the last days of March. Marvellous to relate, he rejoined his unit in safety after his long sojourn with the dead.

The company officers had throughout behaved with unflinching gallantry and vigour, nor had their men failed in any way to second their continued efforts. Man had done his best, but he had been defeated by Nature.

With this assault, then, ended the second phase of the Battle of St. Eloi. The first period had witnessed the success of the German raid on the craters, the second the repeated failure of the counter-attacks; we now enter on the third phase, the consolidation of the line which remained in our hands.

Night, April 11th-12th, 1916.

On the night of the 11th began the relief of the 4th Brigade by the 5th; their casualties had been 14 officers and 389 men.[17]

The whole action must be regarded as a counter-battle fought under the worst possible circumstances. The original advance of the 3rd British Division over the shattered mine craters had met with strong resistance and an unexpected concentration of artillery fire, parallel to that of Verdun. It is probable that the enemy were already planning an attack of their own. They were, however, taken by surprise and lost the first trick in the game. Their reply was instant and effective. Smashing down the ruined trenches in front of them before they could be made good by the defenders under a deluge of high explosive they found a hole in the line and seized the dominant position. After this coup, the weather and the guns combined to make movement on either side almost impossible in a front battered out of all recognition. Had the Germans known it, there were no front-line trenches worthy of the name opposed to them at St. Eloi itself for days, and even the second-line positions had been battered to bits. But, in fact, they could no more advance than we could. The barrage of our artillery prevented, for them too, any heavy concentration behind the craters, and they hung on desperately, as we did, to the ground in their possession. From the beginning General Turner had formed a clear view of the situation on which he based his operations. From the infantry

[17] The 4th Brigade was commanded by Brig.-General Rennie, who displayed marked capacity and ability in handling his command. We may expect for this officer a distinguished future in the Canadian Corps.

point of view the weakness of the position was the extreme narrowness of the front, which enabled the enemy's guns to concentrate on a line the length of which was only from 600 to 1,000 yards. This made successful movement impossible under fire, for there was no cover for the massing of men preparatory to the assault, and the small parties available were cut down in a narrow area by the full weight of the massed guns. On the other hand, the weakness from the point of view of the British and Canadian gunners was the nearness of our lines to those of the enemy and the uncertainty of all precise locations. This latter factor was terribly aggravated by the mistake about Craters 4 and 5. Two alternatives then offered themselves. The first was to make a renewed assault on a far wider front from Ruined Farm or beyond, on the left, to Piccadilly Farm on the right, and so scatter the enemy's shell fire. The second was to get well back from the craters and destroy their garrison by a concentrated hail fire from the heavy guns. It was not practicable to adopt either of these courses, and it was decided to reconstruct the old British line and to hold fast to the two craters in our possession.

Night, April 14th-15th, 1916.

The work of reconstruction fell to the lot of the 5th Brigade under General Watson. As has been stated, on the night of April 11th the moves for the relief of the 4th Brigade began and General Watson took over the line in the early morning. The front was for the moment comparatively quiet. The 26th (New Brunswick) relieved the 19th on the left, the 22nd (French Canadians) took over from the 21st on the right, the 24th (Victoria Rifles) relieved the 18th in the Centre Support position, while the 25th (Nova Scotia) remained for the moment in Brigade Reserve. By April 13th the relief was accomplished. The position taken over by General Watson consisted of the tenable trenches and posts in the old British line, the Craters 6 and 7 and the advanced trenches in Crater 1, and Sackville Centre and outposts to the north. The task of consolidating this last position fell to the 24th (Victoria Rifles). Two very daring reconnaissances were made on the night of the 14th-15th by Lieuts. Robertson and Duclos, and by Lieut. Greenshields and Major Ross, who was in charge of this particular part of the line. As a result, the position of the posts in the old German trench leading into Crater 2 were considerably strengthened and the approaches to Crater 1 were heavily wired. From this time on it may be said that the ground recaptured on the night of the 9th-10th by the 21st passed finally and firmly into our hands. Lieut. Vernon, of the Corps Intelligence Staff, came down during the relief from the Corps Commander to clear up the actual state of affairs. His report was of immense value, though it failed to note the crucial error about the craters, and confirmed the Higher Command in the view that the first necessity was to remake a sound front line. Nowhere, as Brig.-General Watson discovered, were we anywhere as near the German positions as previous reports had led us to imagine. So deep was the mud and slush that no patrols could move, and the greatest difficulty was experienced in carrying up materials for the repair of the line. From the trenches on the right to the trenches near Shelley Farm, in the rear of our own craters was a gaping void held precariously by a few isolated posts. The Brigade, however, set to work tenaciously to make defences out of slush. Basing itself on the line held in the extreme left, it succeeded in re-establishing a considerable part of the line in the direction of the trenches on the right. All this was done under heavy fire, and the repairing of smashed-in parapets occupied as much time as the preparation of the renewed line.

Some author will yet arise to sing the epic of digging. It is of all work the most tedious and dangerous; there is no glory in it; and an infinite amount of labour and risk. Yet the whole safety of the line depends on the exertions of the digging parties. A well-kept line spells comfort and security; a badly-kept one is a purgatory to its occupants. Every battalion and brigade looks askance at the efforts of its predecessors, but none the less rough justice is done in the common opinion of the Army. The 6th Brigade, at any rate, strove valiantly; sandbags were placed in position, and the front was at last protected by coils of barbed wire. In the meantime the position of our troops in the advance craters had for some time been the cause of serious anxiety. Held in succession by garrisons of the 31st, the 19th, and the 25th, throughout the battle they had, except at rare intervals, been cut off from communication with the main body. Reliefs were accomplished by the dashes of the parties in the dark; food and water got up by the same method; and an occasional daring runner got through by daylight, and carrier pigeons were for the first time in the war employed as messengers. The orders were to hold on, but the value of the position was most uncertain. The two small craters lay in advance of our trench well under the dominance of German ground and of the rim of Crater 5. They were joined by a shallow communication trench, along which it was only possible to crawl by daylight, and the right-hand crater was in any case absolutely untenable under artillery fire. Forty yards away lay the Germans, ready to pounce down on the garrison at any moment of the day or night. The defences were negligible, and all attempts to improve them permanently a failure. No man stood upright without the risk of a bullet through his brain.

Night, April 14th, 1916.

The Germans, on the other hand, had, beside the crater, a well-built trench made out of one of our own support trenches dug on April 4th. From this they launched on the night of the 14th four successive bombing attacks against the garrison. All were repulsed by bombers under the command of Lieut. Parish, grenade officer of the 25th. From this point onward the action gradually merged into the ordinary forms of trench warfare except for the peculiar violence of the artillery.

April 16th, 1916.

On the 16th, however, an event of great importance occurred. The gale died out, and the aeroplanes were able to soar aloft once more. The veil which had shrouded our operations was at last lifted, and it was clear that Craters 4 and 5 were in the hands of the Germans and Craters 6 and 7 in those of the Canadians. One final effort was made by the enemy to capture the Canadian craters, but the story of this will be told in the following chapter.

It remains to sum up the action of St. Eloi as a whole.

The 2nd Division was fighting upon historic ground. A few miles to the north lay the battlefield of Ypres, which the 1st Division had made famous in the eyes of the world; near by was Hill 60, from which the 13th British Infantry Brigade had come to the support of the Canadians during the crucial days of April, 1915. At St. Eloi itself, the Princess Patricia's had, a year before, fought a long but unsuccessful action. It is therefore impossible to avoid comparisons between the first and second great actions of the Dominion Army. To do so is to refuse to accept the obvious. The 1st Division lost ground indeed under the gas attack and the steady movement forward of massed Prussian Army Corps. They retreated, but under circumstances which left them with a great and justified reputation. To the 2nd Division was left the more bitter task of fighting for a month under leaden skies above and crumbling mud below, and yet failing to retain their original positions. But they deserved none the less well of Canada. What mortal man could do, they did. The Divisional Command was wise; the Brigadiers thrust their commands forward with unflinching resolution; the Battalion and Company Commanders were both daring, resolute, and prudent; the rank and file shouldered their tasks of exhaustion and danger in a manner well worthy of the best infantry in Europe. It was not given to the 2nd Division to take a part in one of those glittering charges which figure so largely in Press reports and so rarely in actions in the field. Here were no bayonets flashing in the sun, no shouts of a triumphant infantry, but a long struggle against dirt and darkness, the terror of the high explosive, and the sharp spitting of the machine-guns. It is easy to think of war as one triumph reaching to another, and the historians gloss over easily the failure of their national arms. This lesson is, perhaps, not inapposite for a nation already proud in arms but new in history. Wherever in the long confines of the Dominion there comes in the cool of the evening the sense of irreparable loss for a treasured life, let it be remembered that the men who died at St. Eloi died no less nobly than the men who fell at Ypres. The lesson of failure is as much a part of the education of a nation as that of success.

CHAPTER VII

ST. ELOI (CONCLUSION)

The enemy's final effort to capture Canadian trenches—The Higher Command decides to hold on—The precise position of affairs—The 5th Brigade in inferno—Loneliness of the watchers—Carrier pigeons killed by shell-shock—Crater No. 6 abandoned—The enemy's lack of imagination—The power of the British Army "to come again"—Troops of the Allies able to act without support—General Watson on the state of the craters—The report of Lieut. Vernon—Linking up the craters with the old British line—Advantageous position of the Huns—Four attempts to take Canadian craters—The Huns driven back—The assault on Craters 6 and 7—Isolated position of the Canadians—Aeroplanes reveal the true position—Army Commanders blameless—The importance of dominant ground—Difficulties of the Higher Command—The enemy begins an intense bombardment—Many casualties—Permission to surrender—Lieutenant Myers fires his last round—Five survivors—Sergeant Hostel's narrative—The failures at St. Eloi—The garrison of the Canadian craters swept out of existence.

In the meantime the position in the craters became increasingly difficult as the days went on. So grave indeed was the situation that the Higher Command was at one time seriously considering the plan of abandoning them completely so as to give the gunners freer play with the German positions and attempt to blow them bodily out. This solution of the problem was ultimately rejected, and the orders were to hold on at any cost. As brigade relieved brigade this was done in succession by the 31st, the 19th, 24th, 25th, and 26th—the last-named regiment being still in Crater 6 on the morning of April 18th.

Before proceeding, however, to the story of the craters it may be as well to remind the reader, even if a few facts must be repeated, of the precise position of affairs.

Night, April 11th-12th, 1916.

On the night of April 11th-12th, the 5th Brigade carried out its relief of the 4th. On the morning of the 13th the position of the various regiments was as follows:—The 22nd held our trenches on the right, the 25th were in the centre, and the 26th on the left and in the craters. The 24th were in reserve. Compared with the storm of battle which had been raging, the times were comparatively quiet, except for the occupants of the advanced post.

April 15th, 1916.

The rise to the knoll of St. Eloi is a gradual one, but the slope of the ground now gave the Germans the dominating position, and the very force of the explosion of the mines had confirmed their advantage. Looking out from Craters 6 and 7 at night the dimly-seen outlines of Craters 4 and 5 loomed out on the sky-line overshadowing the minor emplacements, which were in the hands of the Canadians. By day, from a distance of about 25 yards, it was possible for the enemy to see right down into the cups of Craters 6 and 7 over the flattened and crumbling edges, and no man moved there save at the peril of his life. The daylight bombardments were fierce and intensive, for the Germans had the range to a nicety with their trench mortars. The evenings were enlivened by periodical bombing assaults from the higher ground. Under these conditions the digging of a proper defensive position could not be carried out, and in this inferno the successive parties of the 5th Brigade continued for five days. One must picture the garrison looking out in the darkness on a serrated ridge illumined moment to moment by the light of star-shells and wondering at what instant the hostile rush would come. Loneliness is a great feature in war; and loneliness here was carried to its extreme. The communication with the shattered defences of the old front-line trenches in the rear was even by night fitful and uncertain. By day all touch over the intervening ground of 40 yards was hopeless, except now and again for a daring runner who took his life in his hand's and usually lost it. The carrier pigeons were killed by shell-shock;[18] the supply of food, water and ammunition was precarious. Many units of the garrison went without any sleep, except the doze of sheer exhaustion, for three or four nights on end—for to sleep soundly might mean to wake to instant death. The ground underfoot was a morass and the sky above charged with falling shell. So terrific was the bombardment that on one occasion Crater 6 had to be abandoned chiefly owing to the annihilation of its defenders.

Under these adverse circumstances the successive regiments of the 5th Brigade held their ground with the customary tenacity of Canadian infantry. The Germans with all their military virtues suffer from one defect of imagination. They can never believe that small bodies of men, unsupported and beyond the control of the Higher Command, will hold on to untenable positions, or will remain fighting units long after they have been beaten by all the rules of war. This error accounts for the failure to pursue after the battle of Le Cateau, and the disregard of the power of the British Army to "come again," which led to the fatal wheel of von Kluck; it also accounts for the German neglect to push their undoubted advantage at various stages of the first and second battles of Ypres. They could not believe that men would resist so boldly who had nothing in reserve.

On a lesser scale the position in the craters and behind them was the same as in these historic combats. The reconstruction of the front or old British line by the 5th Brigade was only beginning; the second line was not in a satisfactory state; the

[18] The last message dating the 15th.

difficulty of bringing up more troops into the advance positions was almost insuperable. The Germans had a chance, had they known it, of pushing through, but the 5th Brigade held the fort until the opportunity had long passed away.

The great concentration of reserves, the massed attack delivered shoulder to shoulder with unflinching courage in the face of a devastating fire, is familiar to the Teutonic mind, which yet seems unable to realise that the democracy of Great Britain, France and Canada can produce men who can do their military duty without the support of carefully-arranged reserves.

As to the state of the craters and the line it may be better to call independent witnesses.

April 12th, 1916.

General Watson had made a tour of the whole position on the morning of the 12th and reported that the 21st Battalion were quite wrong in thinking that in the attack of the 9th-10th they had got anywhere near Crater 2. They were, in fact, never nearer than 70 yards to it. This statement is confirmed by all the evidence, though no doubt the attackers were, in the dark and confusion, unable to ascertain where they were. The General also reported that the first line, that is, the old British line of trenches, was in a very battered state for defence. He regarded the construction work on Crater 1, described in the last chapter, as excellent, and this must go to the credit of the 4th Brigade and the 21st and 24th Battalions.

April 12th, 1916.

On April 12th Lieut. Vernon, of the Intelligence Department, was sent down by the Corps Commander to investigate the situation. He failed to penetrate the error between Craters 4 and 5 and 6 and 7, like everyone else, but his account of the craters is of great interest in view of what followed.

"CRATER No. 7.—This is in our hands, and is a shallow crater about forty yards across; the rims are flat and not high and do not dominate the enemy's new line as to elevation. This crater has no protection from enemy's fire except on the front side (inside), no trenches or parados exist on the rear (north) side, and this side is not occupied by our troops, as it is constantly exposed to rifle and machine-gun fire.

"The communication trench leading to this crater from the north-east is now being improved (fifty men, engineers, working during night), but as yet affords only limited protection; its route includes old mine craters and shell-holes.

"CRATER No. 6.—This is in our hands, and is approached through Crater No. 7 by a ruined shell-wrecked trench along which one has to crawl on hands and knees, and it is constantly sniped at and constantly under observation by enemy flares.

"The crater itself is deep, about forty yards across, and affords much better protection than No. 7. Its rims are higher, but the Germans so dominate it from their trench in front that our garrison has to keep their heads down; the rims are constantly swept by rifle and machine-gun fire. It is built up with some works on the inside facing the enemy, and garrisoned by an officer, men, and machine-gun."

In the light of these facts it was decided to make various arrangements for the improvement of the defence—particularly for the linking-up of the craters with the old British line by a communication trench. It proved impracticable, however, to carry out the whole of the scheme, though 3,000 men were turned on to the various works.

The Germans were in a comparatively enviable position. The lie of the ground was with them and the protection afforded by their own craters adequate. Their knowledge of the precise state of affairs was also more accurate, and in consequence they were better served by their gunners. They possessed in addition the support trenches dug by the 2nd Division on the nights of April 3rd/4th and 5th/6th. They could use the trenches north of the craters as the basis of their own new front line, and the ones south as retiring points whenever our artillery fire became unbearable. None the less, according to the accounts of prisoners, they suffered severely, and the artillery barrage made it impossible for them to bring up strong supports. This did not prevent them taking the offensive as soon as our own counter-attacks had ceased.

Morning, April 14th, 1916.

On the morning of the 14th, as has been related, they four times attempted to take the Canadian Craters 6 and 7 by bombing assaults, but the 25th Battalion repulsed them every time. Simultaneously an attempt was made to oust the garrison of Crater 1. The enemy to the number of 25 charged boldly across the open in broad daylight. This position had, however, as related in the previous chapter, been considerably strengthened, and Lieut. Parish, the grenade officer of the 25th Battalion, who took over the command on April 13th, had extended the outpost line towards Crater 2, and drove back the assailants without much difficulty, but with considerable loss to them. In fact, our position in Crater 1 can never be said to have been seriously threatened, for the ground gave the Germans no special advantage.

10.45, Night, April 15th, 1916.

At dawn on the 15th, the bombing assault on the Craters 6 and 7 began again, this time preluded by a hellish bombardment of trench mortars and heavy guns. Communication with the main position was absolutely broken, and runner after runner failed to get through. Man after man was killed, wounded, or driven back in the attempt. The 25th, however, maintained their position until they were relieved by parties of the 24th on the following day, when Lieut. Lamb took over Crater 7 and Capt. Sutherland Crater 6. At 10.45 p.m. the newcomers had to repulse a strong bombing attack by the enemy. Like others of the very gallant men who held the advance posts, they seem to have been of opinion that their retention served no useful purpose and was in fact impracticable, except at the cost of a continuous drain of human life. They speak of the isolation of the position, of the dominating outlook of the enemy, and of watching that enemy improving his defences without any interference from our guns while they themselves were subjected to an almost continuous fire.

April 16th, 1916.

All this is no doubt true—but it must be remembered that on this day (the 16th) the aeroplanes for the first time were able to soar into the heavens, and look down on the real position of the earth. Up to this date, then, the Higher Command were informed that we were holding essential positions right in the heart of the enemy's line, and that every shell fired by our guns would be a positive danger to the Canadian garrison. It was only as the weather grew calm that the true facts of the case emerged. In any case, the Higher Command of the 2nd Division had no cause to blame itself. General Turner's information from below had been incorrect; in spite of this lack of knowledge his instinct for a practical situation, innate in all real soldiers, had shown itself on every occasion. But the further we get from the front the more difficult it is to arrive at truth, and the Corps and Army Commanders are hardly to be blamed if they were wrongly informed as to facts when Company and Battalion Commanders in the firing line were, with the utmost sincerity, reporting that they occupied points which, as a matter of fact, were never in their possession. The slope of the ground, as at Hooge and Zillebeke, dominated the position; as soon as the Germans held the mound and rise of St. Eloi their advantage of sight was such that the free movements of troops was impossible. Intelligence could not be obtained, and the co-ordination of the various units became a matter of practical impossibility. On the other side of the ridge the Germans, screened from any accurate artillery observation on their immediate front, were able to move with comparative impunity. The only answer was a counter-attack on a far more extended area.

It is one of the fallacies of people who talk about modern warfare to say that ground is nothing. A good trench, forty or fifty yards' fire zone, and sound wire in front will no doubt protect resolute infantry against a frontal attack. But the whole movement and massing of troops for such an attack, the supply of provisions, ammunition and reliefs, the ordinary workaday business which makes the existence of an army possible, can hardly be carried out in the face of an enemy who can watch every move on the board, while the Higher Command can see practically nothing of what is happening on the other side of the hill. It may be possible for troops to carry on under these conditions, but it is neither usual nor expedient.

Noon, April 17th, 1916.

At noon on April 17th, the 24th Battalion was relieved by the 26th; they had been twenty-four hours in the advance post, the ordinary time for anyone occupying a position of great stress and danger. The frequency of the relief speaks more eloquently than words of the strain to which the various garrisons had been subjected.

Night, April 17th, 1916.

The 26th were in their turn relieved by the 29th Battalion of the 6th Brigade on the night of April 18th/19th. These latter troops had suffered severely during the original fighting at St. Eloi; but as the other brigades had done their turn in the trenches it was imperative that the 6th Brigade should relieve them.

April 19th, 1916.

The next day the end came suddenly and the defence collapsed. Lieut. Myers, of the 29th Battalion, with forty men was in occupation of the left-hand Crater 6, and Lieut. Biggs, of the same regiment, held Crater 7 on the right. During the morning all was quiet, but shortly after two o'clock the enemy started an intense bombardment, which made the craters practically untenable. Very few men remained alive or unwounded after three hours. The shelling on the right-hand crater was particularly severe, and some of the survivors got along the shallow communication trench into Crater 6. They discovered, however, that their comrades were in no better case than themselves. The men were buried over and over again, and the rifles, in spite of their breech covers, finally refused to work. When all resistance had been annihilated some forty or fifty Germans started to come across. As far as can be ascertained, Lieut. Biggs appears to have given permission to his few remaining and weaponless men to surrender. Lieut. Myers, who exhibited a most indomitable spirit, resisted to the last, firing one round from a discarded rifle and blazing off his own revolver at the advancing enemy. These were the only shots left in the hands of the defence. Finally, although already wounded, he suggested to the remains of his command that they should endeavour to retire across the fire-swept open country rather than fall into German hands. Five men, two of them wounded, made this desperate attempt, "and as the remainder," says Lieut. Myers, "seemed disinclined to take the risk, I gave them my sanction to surrender, as the Germans were then almost across to the crater." Of the five men and the officer, three were wounded before they started, and only one came in untouched; none the less, they succeeded in making good their escape. Of these, one was Private Harding, who had come in from Crater 7, after having his own brother and three other men killed by his side. They were the only survivors of the garrison—the remainder being all killed or taken prisoners. It is, as a matter of fact, very difficult to conceive and quite impossible to describe exactly what the defenders of the craters had been through, and it is wonderful that the men who escaped retained their sanity. Sergt. H. Bostel, of the 29th, has, however, left such a clear and convincing record of his experience that I prefer to use his own words rather than to give it at second-hand.

3:30 P.M., April 19th, 1916.

"I was one of a party of 40 men under Lieut. Myers, 29th Battalion, and went forward to occupy Crater 6 left at about 12 midnight April 18th. We posted our sentries as soon as we got in and relieved a party of the 29th Battalion under Lieut. Ross. During the morning everything was quiet until about 2 p.m. when the enemy light artillery—whizzbangs, and possibly minenwerfers were firing on Crater 6 left, the one which we were in. This continued for about three-quarters of an hour, during which time we had no casualties whatever, There was no shelling for about one-quarter of an hour, and then they opened up with heavy shells, which fell just on the right front of the crater, and afterwards got direct hits on the centre of the crater, and in my section I had two killed and four wounded. This was about 3.30 p.m. The heavy shelling continued for about half an hour, but there were no casualties, as my section took what cover there was. During the bombardment, Mr. Myers was badly wounded. He, however, gave orders that immediately the bombardment ceased all men were to 'man' the parapet. The bombardment ceased about 4.30 p.m. We then finished dressing the wounded. Sergt. Slaughter went around detailing men to posts and duties. I remained with my section of nine men.

5:15 P.M., April 19th, 1916.

It must have been about 5.15 p.m. when they opened up again, as I remember Sergt. Slaughter inquiring for me about 4.55 p.m. 'what time it was, and if the rifles Were clean and ready?' I might have mentioned that during the bombardment, Mr. Myers tried to get a message through by pigeon, but they were killed by this bombardment. The artillery then opened an intense bombardment which was terrific. Our wounded were killed in this bombardment, being blown to pieces, and many men were buried in their dug-outs. It was impossible for the remainder to render assistance, although several attempts were made. It was raining, and water was flowing from the right crater to the left, and it was practically impossible to move, as the ground within the crater was like porridge except in a few places. During this bombardment we had many casualties. I saw personally eight men knocked out by one large shell. We half expected that an attack would follow after this, and got as many rifles posted as possible. It was noticed shortly after this that the Germans opened up rifle fire from the trenches along the crater. At the same time the bombardment was continued. The fire of the German heavies now seemed to be concentrated on our next crater. Some men came across from the right crater into the left crater. Sergt. Platt told me that the order had been passed along saying that we were to close into the left crater, as there appeared to be less shelling in it. The German rifle fire continued, and we expected that at every moment they would come across. I discussed the question with Sergt. Slaughter of sending back a message, to warn our rear lines, but he said it was hopeless for any man to try to get through that fire in time to be of any assistance, and it was thought that it would be impossible to bring reinforcements up to us in any case. Mr. Myers came out of his dug-out with his wounds bandaged up and shouted out 'Come on, boys; we will make a fight for it.' We all came out of our shelters. I had been buried no less than four times and the shells were splashing mud all over the place. We covered our rifles with sandbags, but it was impossible to keep them in working order, owing to the terrible state of the ground. Sergt. Slaughter left me and went to his own platoon. I calculate that we had fifteen to twenty men left. By this time there were fifty or sixty Germans coming across. I should say there were three rifles actually capable of firing, and these opened up. Mr. Myers used his revolver and then seized a rifle, but was only able to fire one round out of it. I then said to Mr. Myers: 'Are we going to make a fight for it?' and he said 'Yes, boys.' It appeared to us that in the other crater the Germans had got up to the remaining garrison and had overpowered them, as I distinctly saw one or two men put up their hands. They were standing thigh deep in mud, and it seemed absolutely hopeless for them to do anything else but surrender. I saw Mr. Biggs and three or four of his men on the enemy's side of the crater. All this time I might mention that the enemy had a machine-gun playing right across the craters and his artillery fire was extremely accurate on our side of the craters where Mr. Myers and our party were. Shortly after this we decided to retire, as we had no means of putting up any resistance, and rather than be taken prisoners decided to get back and give information and ask for a counter-attack. We then started out with a party of three. Mr. Myers was wounded and had to be assisted, also Private McDonald, who was wounded in the back and neck, and a machine-gun man, I think named Whelan, who was wounded in the face, joined us shortly after we left, and later on one of the pigeon men overtook us. I do not know where he came from. The remainder of our small party in the craters must have been killed or taken prisoners. It was about 11 p.m. when we got back to Voormezeele, where we left the wounded."

April 20th, 1916.

The craters were thus lost. The view that they were untenable was obviously shared by the Germans, who made no attempt to occupy them except by way of roving patrols. On the morning of the 20th Major Tait, of the 29th, and a small party made a bold and complete reconnaissance of Crater 6, which he found quite deserted. "The crater lips have been so knocked about that there is no sign of any edge, and the whole is a mass of slimy mud full of dead bodies." On the same evening Lieut. Jackson, of the 29th, took a patrol over the abandoned ground and found it clear except for a party of five Germans who made off as soon as they were seen. The opinion of the regimental officers on the spot was, however, conclusive against re-entering a position from which they had literally been blown out, and their view was accepted by the Higher Command, whose aeroplane information enabled them to tell that the main crater line had been lost on April 6th, and that the retention of the small craters was merely an embarrassment to our own gunners. The position in Crater 1, maintained throughout the fighting of the 19th, remained definitely in our hands.

The story of the craters is like that of most of the battle of St. Eloi, one of misfortune for the 2nd Division; but it is not one of blame. The successive regiments who held the outposts were from the very outset at a great disadvantage compared with their enemies. They were not, and could not be, properly supported by their own gunners while the enemy's artillery was pounding them to pieces.

They endured the horrors of this experience with fortitude, and repelled the earlier assaults with success. But their defences were like a child's castle on the sand, as wave after wave creeps up the shore on an incoming tide. The outlines became blurred and faded under the remorseless gunfire, until the final wave quietly and calmly swept the 29th out of existence. Of a garrison of eighty men one returned unwounded.

CHAPTER VIII

THE BATTLE OF SANCTUARY WOOD

Moving northwards—The immortal field of Ypres—The greatest of all Canadian battlefields—Description of the ground—Who holds the rim holds the saucer—Advantageous position of the enemy—Sanctuary Wood—Observatory Ridge—The unpleasantness of life and the prevalence of death—Situation of the Canadians—Fortified posts—The German attack begins—The artillery preparation—Jack Johnsons—Whole areas destroyed—A tornado of iron and steel—Canadian trenches swept out of existence—The thunder of high explosives—German guns on the second line—The capture of General Williams—Tragic death of General Mercer—The 4th Canadian Mounted Rifles swallowed up—Heavy casualties—A gallant advance—Machine-guns on Hill 60—Lieuts. Key and Evans make a brave stand—The Princess Pats in the firing line—The exploits of Captain Niven—The gallant-hearted gentleman—A mix-up—Between two fires—Game until the last—Major Critchley—Rescue of men buried alive—Lieut. Glascoe—Canadian guns spotted by the enemy—Attacks repulsed by the Royal Canadians—Plucky deed of Corporal Hood—Loss of sacrifice guns—Lieut. Cotton killed—Faithful unto death—A critical position—The colours of Princess Pats returned to Headquarters—Second Canadian Mounted Rifles move under heavy fire—The enemy loses an opportunity—Energetic action of General Macdonell—The Seventh Brigade in peril—Timely support of the Royal Canadian Regiment—General Butler sends relief—The Fifth Canadian Mounted Rifles hard pressed—Daring reconnaissance of Sergeant Jones—Fifth Canadian Mounted Rifles save the Salient—Heavy losses of the Eighth Brigade—Help at hand.

The fighting since March had, like the Canadians, been moving steadily northward, from the trench raiding opposite Messines and Wytschaete, through the battle of St. Eloi in April, to the successive actions at Sanctuary Wood and Hooge which I am about to record. These actions, which were in scale if not in intensity the greatest of all the Canadian battles, took place but a few miles away from that field of Ypres which the First Division had rendered immortal. The dead who lie in their graves round Langemark and St. Julien might well have stirred in their sleep at the thunder of the Canadian guns. Many men now quick and vigorous were to join them in their last rest, falling in the same spot for the same cause.

In fact, the first action was fought north-east of Ypres, while the present struggle took place south-east and much nearer to it. Anyone who had stood before the war on some high tower within the circle of the vast mediæval ramparts of earth, which have defied even modern artillery, and of the ancient grey walls which still look out across the calm waters of the broad moat and through the poplars which fringe it, would have obtained an excellent view of all save the outer edges of the field of battle. The Menin Road drives out over the flats for a mile, and then for another mile up the gentle slope to the ridge crowned by the ruins of Hooge. This road marks the left and northern boundary of the fighting with the exception of the bombing posts running down to Bellewaarde Beek. This ridge, with one main gap and many irregularities, curves round south-west and runs continuously to Mount Sorrel, where the fighting stops on the south. It represents, as it were, the rim of a saucer of which Ypres is in the central depression: and in war who holds the rim holds the saucer.

Standing on such a position and casting his eye along the ridge from Hooge, the observer sees across a mile or so of green water-meadows striped with the dark lines of high, luxuriant hedges, the northern part covered only by a few isolated and shattered trees, until he comes to Zouave Wood, which runs up into the first and greatest of the gaps. This gap isolates Hooge from the system, and through it the Germans can see right down on to the British trenches in the plain. Farther south the nearer slopes are covered with the great expanse of Sanctuary Wood, once so thick as to be almost impenetrable to the Guards in October, 1914, but now sadly thinned by gun-fire, and crowned by the slight eminences known as Hills 62 and 61.[19] Beyond these comes Mount Sorrel, and the sector of the action is complete; for here the British line breaks suddenly back to the west and to the railway. But between Sanctuary Wood and Mount Sorrel there is a curious feature—Observatory Ridge—a long tongue of higher ground, bare and barren, runs right back due west into the British positions towards Zillebeke village and lake.

June 1st, 1916.

Such was the position occupied by the Third Canadian Division on June 1st, 1916, as seen from the rear—a pleasant prospect if it were not for the signs of devastation, the white-scarred, headless trees, the upcast earth and the growl of the guns which in the salient seem to come from every point on the horizon. Viewed by the Germans from the east, it did not look quite so strong, for they too held high ground dominating slightly in many places the line held by the Canadians.

None the less it is a strong defensive position, and Lord Ernest Hamilton in "The First Seven Divisions" maintains with great show of reason that it was always the natural place from which to protect the town.

High ground may not possess to-day all the importance it had in the warfare of past ages, but the men on the hill still have one great advantage over the

[19] These two hills are called by the Germans Doppelhohe, or "double heights."

men in the hollow: they can see and their enemy is blind. Every trench and every movement of troops can be seen, and artillery fire can be directed and observed with complete accuracy without relying on aeroplanes and balloons, which are imperfect substitutes for direct observation and which bad weather may put out of commission. Furthermore, the life of the infantry in the plain becomes intolerable when every head is liable to show and become the target for immediate fire. Life is too unpleasant and death too prevalent. The Canadian Corps, then, had to hold the plateau at all costs.

This description of the ground may make it easier to understand the positions occupied by the 3rd Division and the 1st Division on its right—for the 2nd Division was still far away on its old ground at St. Eloi, farther to the south, and was not called up to help till a later stage of the action.

The left of the line was held by the 7th Brigade under Brigadier-General A. C. Macdonell, and the right by the 8th Brigade under Brigadier-General Victor Williams. Two companies of the Royal Canadian Regiment, commanded by Lieut.-Colonel C. H. Hill, were firmly astride the Menin Road towards the farther side of the ruins of Hooge village. Their left sloped down through a series of bombing posts to Bellewaarde Beek, where they linked with the 60th British Brigade. Their right extended to the gap, where they were in touch with the Princess Patricia's Canadian Light Infantry. The trenches here had been partially demolished, and an attempt was being made to repair them at the time of the attack. Next to the right came the Princess Patricia's Canadian Light Infantry, under Lieut.-Colonel Buller. They had two companies in the front line, the left-hand one on the slight rise on the northern boundary of Sanctuary Wood, the right-hand one in another gap or dip, so that the regiment had a depression on either side of its position. In the southern section of Sanctuary Wood they met the line of the 1st Canadian Mounted Rifles of the 8th Brigade under Lieut.-Colonel Shaw.[20]

This last battalion held Hills 62 and 61 with three companies in the firing line and one just behind, but its junction with the Princess Patricia's was slightly broken at the dip. Next on the right came the 4th Canadian Mounted Rifles Battalion under Colonel Ussher, with three companies in the firing line holding Mount Sorrel. Two platoons were just in rear in the support trenches and in the communication trench leading to Headquarters. Here the 8th Brigade ended and the 2nd Brigade of the 1st Division took on the line.

Behind this front line there was a support line on the left of the position. From the Menin Road the strong and excellent support line trenches drive south-east. This line was held by the support company of the Royal Canadian Regiment and the support company of the Princess Patricia's Canadian Light Infantry, each backing their respective regiments in the front trenches. At a point north-east of Maple Copse and in the middle of Sanctuary Wood this well-marked support line ceased and broke into two separate systems of trenches. In the first place a series of communication trenches broke back sharply to Maple Copse and the south-west, making an acute angle, or Apex, facing the Germans. From this Apex the support line continued, though not at all points in a fully completed condition,

[20] One company of the Princess Patricia's was in support.

close behind our front-line trenches on Hill 62 and Mount Sorrel.[21] Behind these again was a series of Fortified Posts covering, in a somewhat irregular pattern, the ground between Zouave Wood and the southern slopes of Observatory Ridge. This in effect completed the system of front line and support defence. Further back, a second line nearer Ypres, known, as the G.H.Q. trenches, represented the last barrier. It will be observed that there was no trench between Maple Copse and Square Wood.

The Fortified Posts on the north were held by the support battalion, the 5th Canadian Mounted Rifles, under Lieut.-Colonel Baker, and on the south were in possession of the spare platoons of the 4th Canadian Mounted Rifles and were in rear of their lines. One fort, however, was in the hands of the Princess Patricia's Canadian Light Infantry. Maple Copse was occupied by a company and a half of the 5th Canadian Mounted Rifles, and the remainder of the latter were back in reserve. With them were the 42nd Battalion (Royal Highlanders of Canada) under Lieut.-Colonel Cantlie in support of the 7th Brigade, and also the remaining company of the Royal Canadian Regiment. A glance at the map will make the positions of the various units and the general scheme of defence clear, and tiring as such a recapitulation of companies and regiments may be, it is necessary if the story is to be in the least intelligible. The 49th (Edmonton Regiment), under Lieut.-Colonel Griesbach, was the reserve battalion of the 7th Brigade, and the 2nd Canadian Mounted Rifles of the 8th. The 9th Brigade was in Divisional Reserve.

June 2nd, early morning.

Such were the dispositions of the corps, now under Gen. Sir Julian Byng, who had on May 28th succeeded Gen. Alderson, when the storm finally broke.[22] There had been warnings already. The enemy had been driving "T" saps[23] out in front of their lines and linking them up so as to form a new trench in advance of the old one. Lieut.-Colonel Odlum, of the 7th (British Columbia) Battalion, launched a daring plan of counter construction at one place against the works and definitely checked their progress. The shelling of the last few days before the attack had been peculiarly heavy, and it is probable that the Higher Command had other information of impending mischief. It was undoubtedly this fact which induced Major-General Mercer and Brigadier-General Williams to make their tour of the trenches on that fateful early morning of June. They left at six in the morning and

[21] In consequence of this forking of the trenches in Sanctuary Wood, there are just behind the Hill 62 position two support positions, one behind the other—the first close to the front trenches and the second formed by the westward bend of the Apex. I use the term "support trenches" as meaning the first of these two lines, and in addition, of course, the trench running from the Menin Road to the point of the Apex.

[22] Lieutenant-General the Hon. Sir Julian Byng, K.C.B., M.V.O., was born in 1862, and joined the 10th Royal Hussars in his 21st year. In 1901 he commanded that regiment, having done distinguished service in the Sudan, 1884, and in the South African War. He commanded the 3rd Cavalry Division with great brilliancy during the opening stages of the campaign in France.

[23] A "T" sap is one of a series constructed in the form of a letter "T," so that the top of the "T" may be driven out left and right, and, linking up with the others, form a new trench in advance.

reached the Battalion Headquarters of the 4th Canadian Mounted Rifles before eight o'clock. General Mercer was accompanied by his A.D.C., Lieut. Gooderham, and General Williams by Capt. Fraser, the Brigade Orderly Officer. Colonel Ussher conducted them up the communication trench at about a quarter past eight, and the party had either reached the front trench or was about to enter it when with a sudden crash the enemy's guns opened.

The 3rd Division was now to experience in its full fury the artillery preparation of the summer of 1916. All that had gone before was as nothing to this. The bombardment of 1915 had been feeble in comparison, and those of 1914 a mere sun-shower as compared to tropical rain. The soldiers of the 1st Division when they landed in France had, with their native humour, come to laugh at the Jack Johnsons from the 11-inch howitzers, though these were formidable to an army which then had no guns of an equal range. But a preparation in the modern style leaves very few remaining to laugh. The 2nd Division had a taste of the new shelling at St. Eloi and its dangers had been intensified by a bad position and wretched trenches. But even so, all agreed that there was no comparison between the gunfire of April and of June, which was the heaviest endured by British troops up to that time. The Germans were directing their efforts against a strong position and sound trenches, yet they swept both out of existence as the autumn wheat is mowed down by the reaper. It was not merely a line they destroyed, but a whole area.

June 2nd, 8.30 A.M.-1.15 P.M.

Indeed, the storm which burst on the 3rd Division at 8.30 that June morning was like a tropical tornado which presses men flat to the ground and suffocates them with the mere force of the wind, which uproots forests and hurls them headlong, obliterates all ancient landmarks and the houses and shelters of men and beasts, and leaves behind nothing but a tangled desolation from which a few survivors creep out scarcely sane enough to realise the catastrophe or to attempt to repair the damage. But here the blinding crashes overhead were not those of thunder and lightning, but of high explosive. The fragments which drove through the air were not bits of wood or masses of vegetation. They were steel and iron fragments which pierced the flesh, as the shock of the explosion stopped the heart and threw cascades of earth over bodies in which life still beat feebly or in which it was already extinct. The solid trenches melted away, and mounds and craters appeared where none existed before. A litter of broken wood, burst sandbags, and human remains cumbered the earth where it was not merciful enough to bury them. And this tornado of man was let loose on a few acres which contained, perhaps, two or three thousand troops, and continued for the space of about four hours.

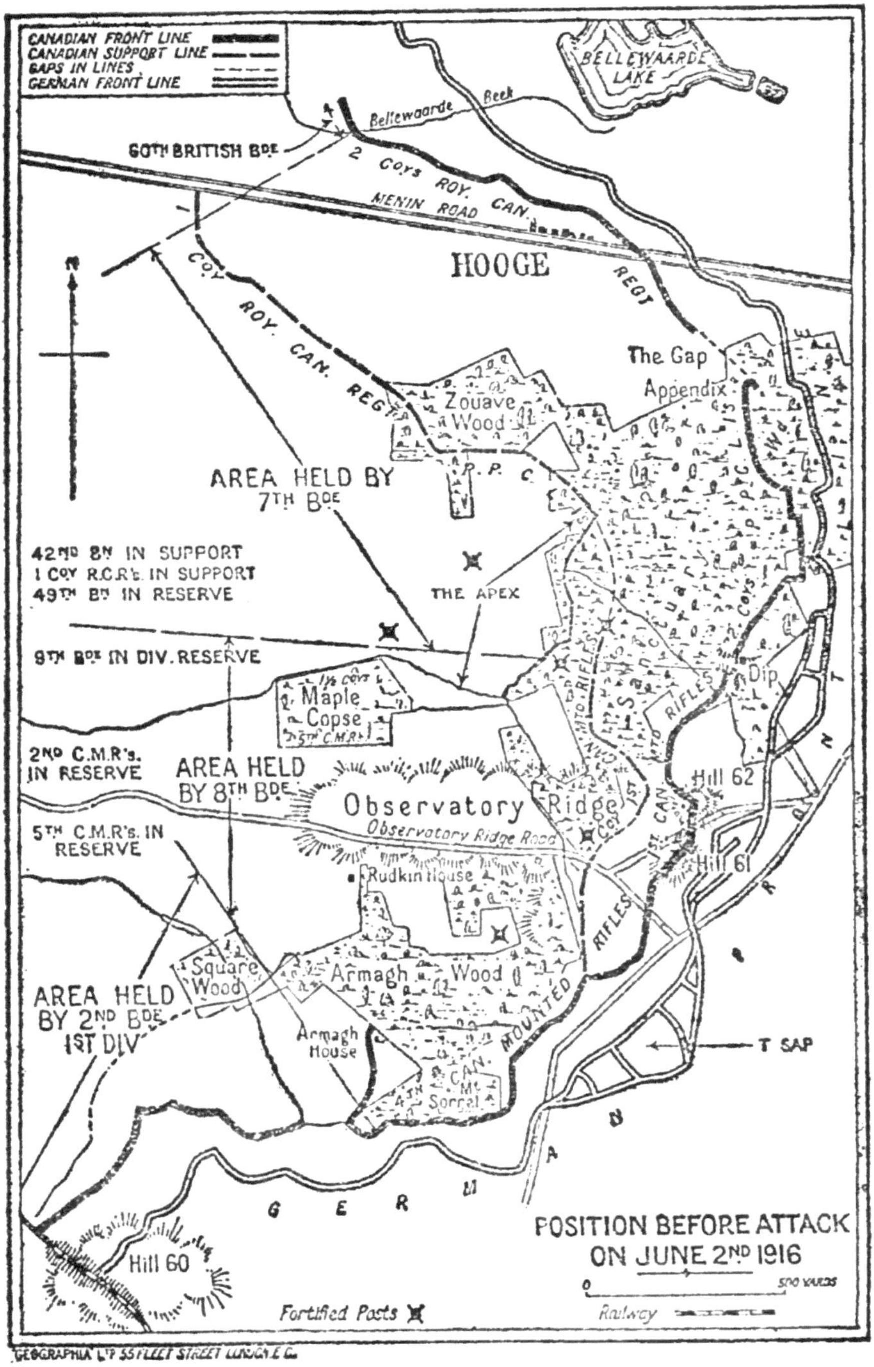

Map—Sanctuary Wood area.—Position before Attack on June 2nd 1916

At the end, although the awful noise goes on, the shower of steel ceases. The guns have lifted to the second line. Here and there groups of survivors creep out, wild-eyed or stupefied, like men just risen from the tomb, to see the solid lines of the enemy advancing at a walk or a jog-trot. Every man acts according to his instinct. A few lie where they are and chance being taken prisoners. Some make a rush and crawl for the ruined communication trenches and face the barrage once more in the hope of rejoining their comrades. Another group resists desperately, grasping what rude and broken weapons remain to it, and dies in a hopeless struggle. Such in effect is the story of the front and support line companies of the 1st and 4th Canadian Mounted Rifles and the right-hand company of the Princess Patricia's between 8.30 and 1.15 of June 2nd, as their casualties will prove. That story must, however, be told in greater detail; but isolated facts cannot be understood without their environment.

The Generals and their Staffs were caught by the outbreak of this Inferno. It is idle to go into the question as to exactly how, when, and where the Divisional General died. There are many ways into such a controversy and no way out. All that is certain is that one of the first shells burst close to the Staff, wounding Brigadier-General Williams[24] and stunning Major-General Mercer. None the less, shortly afterwards General Mercer sent back a message, the last to come through from Mount Sorrel, asking for the howitzers to be turned on. After that he tried to get back to his post behind the lines and failed. Some say he remained with the 4th Canadian Mounted Rifles Battalion for a time and was seen moving up and down. Soon, at any rate, he was seen no more by living men. He must have made another attempt to get back to his post and been killed on the way. His body was found with three wounds on it in Armagh Wood. He was buried at Poperinghe. There lie the mortal remains of Lieut.-Colonel Hart-McHarg and Lieut.-Colonel Birchall, who served under him in the 4th Battalion of the 1st Brigade of the 1st Division. It is tragic to think that such a brilliant soldier, who had risen to the command of a division by sheer force of ability, should have died just as his new command was going into its first big action and needed his services so greatly.

The trenches of the 4th Canadian Mounted Rifles and their garrisons thus vanished, and nothing more was heard of them save for the stories of small isolated parties which escaped. The last trench on the right and round the western bend of the salient escaped a little more lightly. The garrison held on till night fell, and then the survivors, finding the Germans coming up behind them in Armagh Wood, made good their escape to the lines of the 2nd Brigade on their right. Colonel Ussher collected some of the support company in a roofed-in trench, hoping to keep them under cover there until the German attack. Almost immediately heavy shells blocked both ends of the tunnel and many were stifled before the party could break out of this living grave. This was the last attempt at any organised resistance. Major Dennison fought a rearguard action at point-blank range with the advancing Germans, and eventually got back into the second line with five men. Meanwhile, the shelling on the support line had been almost equally intense.

[24] Brigadier-General Williams was taken prisoner. The Canadian Corps was unfortunate in thus losing the services of a soldier of such wide experience and proved skill so soon after he had taken over a brigade.

The Fortified Posts held by the 4th Canadian Mounted Rifles were blown to pieces and the platoons in them. One garrison perished and of the second garrison three men got away. In all some thirty or forty men of the 4th Canadian Mounted Rifles got away and were rallied behind the support line. Their casualties were 637; the regiment had simply ceased to exist.[25]

On their left the 1st Canadian Mounted Rifles Battalion had fared little better. All through the morning, their advance and support trenches being flattened out section by section, the survivors rallied in isolated groups wherever cover was left. In face of the attack these retired, some on the trenches in the Apex, and some on the Battalion Headquarters, where Colonel Shaw and the support company were preparing to put up a vigorous resistance. The casualties of the front companies speak for themselves. Of one company fifteen came out alive, of the second company fifteen, of the third twenty-three.

June 2nd, 1.15 P.M.

The German assault was delivered just after one o'clock, when their guns lifted from the front trenches and was preluded by the blowing up of mines, which were, however, outside our trenches and had no effect on the ultimate issue. The attack was launched from the south-west, for it was plainly visible to our men in the trenches by Hill 60. The watchers saw in the clear air four successive lines of grey-clad figures carrying packs and greatcoats advancing in the distance with the assurance of those who neither dread nor expect resistance; behind came the engineers with the material to make good the position. An indignant rapping from the machine-guns on Hill 60 greeted them; but the tide flowed on, unheeding. The lines reached Mount Sorrel and disappeared. The enemy, by attacking the corner of the line, advanced in effect "en échelon"—that is to say, their left flank reached Mount Sorrel and cleared it somewhat before their centre attacked the 1st Canadian Mounted Rifles. The result was that Colonel Shaw in his redoubt found his right flank exposed and was the object of a concentric attack. None the less, the garrison put up a heroic fight against machine-guns, rifle-fire, and grenades. Colonel Shaw fell, and with him Major Palmer and his Adjutant, Lieutenant Rowles. Finally, when all the officers but two and most of the N.C.O.'s were killed or wounded, and the position was in danger of being surrounded, Lieuts. Key and Evans led the fifteen survivors back into a Fortified Post just in front of the Apex, where they collected some stragglers from other units and held on until relieved the following day. This dogged defence was of the utmost value, for the second line at this point was desperately weak and quite unable to resist a resolute assault.[26] Of the

---

[25] The chaplain of the regiment, Capt. A. G. Wilken, was in the trenches at the time of the attack. He acted as guide to a party of volunteer stretcher-bearers, who brought out the wounded and returned carrying up ammunition to the front line. He was killed during the final assault.

[26] Lieut. Evans was greatly assisted in his defence by Private Murphy, of the Machine Gun Company of the 8th Brigade, who beat off every German attack, although his gun was twice buried by shell-fire. Lieut. Beatty of the same Company also showed conspicuous gallantry and ability in organising the machine-gun defence of the second line. Finally he was shot through the leg, but continued at his duty until he fainted from loss of blood.

support company and Battalion Headquarters about seventy-one men survived. The total casualties of the regiment were 367. It was now the turn of the Princess Patricia's to withstand the assault, which came upon them at about 1.30 p.m.

June 2nd, 1.30 P.M.

Regiments which possess some special name as opposed to ordinary battalions, which are designated by numbers, and which are therefore picked out by over-zealous correspondents for particular praise for their share of work which all have done equally, are not always popular. This is certainly the case in the Imperial service; and yet no Line regiment would grudge the Guards their reputation, for what they have won in praise they have earned, and they have worn their laurels with a studious modesty.

The Princess Patricia's had two companies in the firing line, one in the communication trench leading up to it past Battalion Headquarters with a tail in the support line, and a fourth entirely in the support line trenches. The right-hand company in the firing line was, like the Canadian Mounted Rifle Regiments, blown out of its trenches, and the survivors took ground in communication trenches held by the support company. At 1.30 p.m. the German wave lapped round the left of all except the front-line company commanded by Captain Niven, which turned about and volleyed into the Germans' right rear.

This company kept its position in the front line and maintained it for eighteen hours after the bombardment began, although the enemy attempted to penetrate the gap on the left and had seized the dip to the right of the trenches on the rise which they held. Capt. Niven had with one hand to fend off attempts to bomb his men at right and left down the trench, and with the other to turn and enfilade with excellent result the Germans who were pressing in on either flank. Yet he, who was in command, is chiefly anxious to explain in his report that this was the result of a pure accident, as the enemy had over-ranged his trench and the heavies and trench mortars were bursting twenty yards behind, save for the right platoon, which mustered only three survivors. The enemy then attacked the Princess Patricia's Canadian Light Infantry companies in the communication trenches and began to bomb his way to the support line and the Apex line, which possessed at that time scarcely any defenders. Colonel Buller rallied the support platoons in the communication trench and pushed them up to a counter-attack to save the support line. Not satisfied with the rate of their progress through the shattered trench, he climbed outside to urge them on, and was killed instantly.[27] He possessed one of those fearless and impetuous natures which made him the fitting commander of a famous regiment and brought him the soldier's death he would have desired.

June 2nd, 2 P.M.

There followed a dark and bloody *mêlée* between the Germans and the Ca-

[27] General Macdonell says of Colonel Buller: "He fell as the splendid soldier and gallant-hearted gentleman would have wished, in the forefront of the battle at the head of his regiment, all ranks of which, it is not too much to say, idolised him. The Empire can ill afford to lose such a man, a 'Chevalier sans peur et sans reproche.'"

nadians in the communication trenches, the former trying to press on and rush the support line and the latter trying to build blocks down the communication trenches to stave them off until that line could be fully manned. At one time the Princess Patricia's in the communication trench, though attacked across the open simultaneously on both sides, resisted the enemy, thus emulating the traditions of the famous British regiment which, when attacked from behind, simply turned its rear rank about and fired in both directions.[28]

Major Critchley, Staff Captain of the 7th Infantry Brigade, going up after we had retaken the communication trenches, said that he found the bodies of the Princess Patricia's Canadian Light Infantry lying in succession behind six blocks in the trench, showing that in their retirement they had held each block until a new one was built. In effect, the garrison of each block had perished while the new one behind was being built. The losses were, of course, very severe, but in the meantime the reserve company of the regiment had come up into the support line behind, and the vital position was saved; for if the support line had gone, the whole of the Ypres salient would at that hour in the day have gone with it, as the subsequent argument will show. Colonel Buller and his men held the fort at the critical hour, and gave Brigadier-General Macdonell time to bring up his reserves.[29]

June 2nd, 9 P.M.

In the meantime, Captain Niven, some hundred yards to the north-west, was still clinging to the knoll of trenches in the front line amid an encircling tide of Germans. As has been already stated, his right-hand platoon had been destroyed by the bombardment and Lieut. Hagerty, its commander, killed. Lieut. Molson then took charge, and with great gallantry dug out some of the men buried alive, although the trench was ranged to a nicety. He was shot through the jaw, and the section was abandoned in the end. Lieut. Triggs, in the nearest sector, was severely wounded soon afterwards, and Lieut. Irwin, the only remaining subaltern, was hit later on in the day. Captain Niven, though hit himself, continued to command and move about, as he was by this time the only remaining officer of his company. The telephone dug-out was smashed in and all communication with the battalion lost. None the less, two heroic runners managed to get through and to report that the company were still holding out. Some of the worst cases of wounded were even carried back by the stretcher-bearers under an appalling fire to the support line. At dusk Lieut. Glascoe was sent up from Battalion Headquarters, and Captain Niven handed over his command and attempted to go back and report to Battalion Headquarters. In the course of his wanderings he came to a dressing station, and, after his wound had been dressed, started once more for his isolated company, which after eighteen hours was still left among the encircling Germans as lonely as the

[28] The Gloucester Regiment (28th Line) at Abercrombie's landing in Egypt in 1801. The regiment was accorded the right of wearing its badges both in front and back of its headgear.

[29] During this fierce engagement Capt. J. D. Macgregor, the doctor of the P.P.C.L.I., displayed the greatest devotion, remaining three days at his post in the firing line without rest dressing the injuries of the wounded, often in places where there was no cover from fire.

survivors of the Flood on Mount Ararat. He was promptly hit again in the breast.

At 2.30 a.m. of the 3rd Lieut. Glascoe, seeing that the whole surviving party would shortly be completely surrounded, exercised a wise discretion and got his remnant safely back to the support line. "During the bombardment," says Captain Niven, who certainly has a right to be heard, "this company behaved splendidly, every man holding his own and inflicting heavy losses on the enemy wherever the opportunity occurred."[30]

It was during the general retirement from the east of Sanctuary Wood that two of our guns were lost. Those guns were 18-pounders, and had been brought up to within 400 yards of the front line and established in gun-pits. They were to be used only in case of emergency, as their fire would be sure to disclose their position to the enemy. Owing to their position and purpose they were known as "sacrifice guns." Lieut. C. P. Cotton, of the 1st Divisional Artillery, was in command of them.

A German aeroplane found these guns on Friday morning (June 2nd), and particular attention was immediately paid to them in the midst of the general bombardment of our trenches and positions. Lieut. Cotton's gun-crews suffered, and he reinforced them with Sappers James E. Hood and Chambers, who were in charge of an emergency wireless station situated within a few yards of the gun-pits.

Cotton opened fire at 1.45 in the afternoon, and, assisted by his three surviving gunners and the two sappers, continued to fire until the enemy came over Observatory Ridge to within a few yards of the gun-pits. He then ordered a retirement. Sapper Hood rushed into his wireless dug-out, destroyed his instrument, and then escaped with a bullet through the bone of his arm. Lieut. Cotton and the others of the gun-crews were not so fortunate. They died near the gun-pits—they and their guns having served their desperate purpose to the end—and so they too made the great sacrifice.

The attack still continued to spread up to our left. Between two and three o'clock in the afternoon the extreme German right had come up to assault our extreme left at Hooge. Two attacks were however, repulsed with great loss to the enemy by the Royal Canadian Regiment.

June 2nd, 2 P.M.-3 P.M.

None the less, the position at three o'clock was one of the very gravest danger. On a frontage of three battalions the Germans had overwhelmed our front and right support lines on the crest of the ridge and annihilated or decimated the defending regiments. From Maple Copse they could be seen advancing in strong force on the high ground of Observatory Ridge into the very heart of our position, and they were also attacking farther north down the various communication

---

[30] Casualties: Officers, the Princess Patricia's:—*Killed*: Colonel Buller, Major Jones, Captain Cornish, Lieuts. MacDonnell, Wanklin, Hagerty, De Bay, Fyfe. *Wounded*: Major Gault, Captain and Adjutant Martin, Captain Niven, Lieuts. Scott, McDougall, Currie, Irwin, Triggs, Glascoe. 8 killed, 9 wounded—17 out of 22 present at action.

trenches which led to the support line.[31] Our left at Hooge had held firm, but it was now utterly in the air, save for Captain Niven and his men, and the triumphant enemy were rapidly sweeping behind that line of defence. The support trenches having been taken on Hill 62 and Mount Sorrel, there was nothing in front of the German left and centre except the Apex line to Maple Copse. It was, therefore, a matter of life and death to hold on to these left-hand support trenches to the Apex and to Maple Copse. But the line was very weakly held for the task of resisting 2,000 Germans attacking from higher ground and flushed with victory. There were, in fact, about three companies of the 5th Canadian Mounted Rifles, the remains of the 1st and 4th Canadian Mounted Rifles, perhaps a hundred all told, and what was left of three companies of the Princess Patricia's Canadian Light Infantry. The situation looked so dangerous that the famous colours of the Princess Patricia's were entrusted to Lieut. Scott, who took them back to Brigade Headquarters to avoid any possibility of their capture. To the left, from Zouave Wood to Menin Road, was one company of the Royal Canadian Regiment in support of their companies in the front line trenches, who could not abandon their ground. In addition, the Staffs of the 3rd Division and the 8th Brigade, who were primarily concerned, had lost their commanding officers. From Mount Sorrel and the 4th Canadian Mounted Rifles they had had no news since 9.15 a.m., and did not know whether General Mercer and General Williams were alive or dead, or whether the trenches there still held. On the other hand, the 1st Canadian Mounted Rifles had continued to report till just before the German attack at 1.15 p.m. that they were holding their ground and were in no need of reinforcements. None the less, at noon the 2nd Canadian Mounted Rifles were moved up from Brigade Reserve to Zillebeke under heavy barrage fire.

The three factors which prevented a serious disaster were undoubtedly the hesitation of the enemy to pursue an advantage, the strenuous resistance of the 5th Canadian Mounted Rifles under Colonel Baker, and the energetic action of General Macdonell of the 7th Brigade in taking advantage of the precious moments of delay and pushing every man he could command, beg or borrow into the threatened section.[32]

The Germans at Le Cateau, and at the first and second battles of Ypres, had always stopped just when victory seemed within their grasp. Nor on this occasion were they wanting to themselves. There are, however, no doubt explanations. One was in a document found on the body of a German officer which laid down precisely the position they were to occupy and entrench, and this they had attained

[31] These bodies were unquestionably strong German patrols. They developed in this action a course of procedure now generally adopted, but then new. The assaulting column sends out in advance large parties, whose duties are not merely reconnaissance, but the occupation of advance positions in front of the captured line, which are to be taken by fighting if necessary and used to repel counter-attacks.

[32] Valuable reconnoitring work was done in this connection by Lieut. E. Basset, of the 21st Battalion, who was attached to Gen. Macdonell's staff for instruction. It is a curious fact that nearly all the officers from the home regiments out for this purpose were wounded in the fighting of June.

except in the neighbourhood of Rudkin House.[33] Our barrage was heavy behind them, and it was not until 9 p.m. that they were reinforced by an additional two thousand men in spite of our heavy artillery.

June 2nd, afternoon and evening.

By two o'clock the right of the 7th Brigade was in grave peril. The Brigadier at once ordered up the reserve company of the Royal Canadian Regiment to help. Already ten minutes before he had sent up two companies of his support battalion, the 42nd, to assist the hard-pressed 5th Canadian Mounted Rifles in Maple Copse and beyond. These two companies undoubtedly just saved the situation, and a delay of an hour or so in dispatching them might have proved fatal. The remaining two companies of the 42nd, which were back in Ypres and beyond, were ordered to come up to the support line trenches. The 49th (Edmonton) Battalion (Col. Griesbach), which was right back in Brigade Reserve, was ordered up to the Ypres ramparts, and reached there about 8.30 p.m. Not content with this, at 3 p.m. the Brigadier asked General Butler, of the 60th British Brigade, on his left, to lend him a couple of companies to help hold the support line. The request was granted, and two companies of the King's Royal Rifles took up the left-hand section, south of the Menin Road, thus enabling the Royal Canadian Regiment Companies to shift farther to their right and strengthen the critical point of resistance at the Apex.

June 2nd, 5 P.M.-6 P.M.

By 5 or 6 p.m. General Macdonell had got into the support line and Apex line five entirely fresh companies—a welcome relief to the nerve-worn and shattered units which, under the most tremendous shell-fire, had been struggling there from eight in the morning against heavy odds. He had also the 49th well up in reserve, while the 8th Brigade had three companies of the 2nd Canadian Mounted Rifles up on the right of the 5th Canadian Mounted Rifles in Maple Copse in the communication trench running back in the direction of Zillebeke. The reinforcements thus amounted to eight fresh companies or two battalions. It is impossible to speak too highly of the resource, vigour, and moral courage of the General, who took the situation in charge on his own initiative, or of the dash of the men who came up through the barrage over flat ground, every yard of which could be seen by the enemy.

For the Brigade and Divisional Staffs the period was one of doubt and anxiety. Information was hard to get from the front, and what news came in was generally bad. Between five and six in the evening General Hoare Nairne, C.R.A.[34] took command of the 3rd Division, and Lieut.-Colonel Bott, 2nd Canadian Mounted Rifles, of the 8th Brigade.[35] But to the units hastily gathered under Lieut. Evans in

[33] The Germans had laid down two alternative lines to take and entrench. One, "the gold line," in case of complete success, another, "the iron line," farther back, in case of a partial success. In effect, they reached the gold line.

[34] Commander of the Artillery of the 3rd Division. This was the Lahore division lent to the Canadian Corps, since the 3rd Divisional Artillery had not yet left England.

[35] Maj. G. A. Stevens (Royal Fusiliers), Brigade-Major of the 8th Brigade, took command in place of Brigadier-General Williams, and commanded it with marked ability from

the Fortified Post, to the Princess Patricia's Canadian Light Infantry, and the 5th Canadian Mounted Rifles, the strain was well-nigh intolerable, for the shelling on the support line had been almost as intense as that on the first line. The 5th Canadian Mounted Rifles were nearly blown out of Maple Copse, and had to shift from trench to trench more than once as the Germans got the range, but they held on. On the left the enemy had in no way abandoned his intention of getting into our support line, and about 2.30 p.m. some forty succeeded in rushing it.[36] There was a sharp, short hand-to-hand struggle, in which the Princess Patricia's bayoneted the lot. The occupants of the Fortified Post at Maple Copse were annihilated by shell-fire, and Maple Copse, held by the 5th Canadian Mounted Rifles, was so heavily shelled that the whole wood was smashed flat. They had to make new trenches, as the old ones became untenable. This was done under the eyes and fire of the enemy, who loomed over them on Observatory Ridge in unknown numbers and from invisible positions.

Major Hugh Walkem arrived with the first relief—a company of the 42nd—about 2 p.m., and finally got into position in the Apex between the Canadian Mounted Rifles and the Princess Patricia's. The other company of the 42nd took up a place in the support trenches.[37]

Through all this period there were constant rumours, fortunately untrue, that the Germans had penetrated the line at one point or another. It was here that Sergeant Jones, 42nd (Royal Highlanders of Canada), made a peculiarly daring reconnaissance, lying out all night within thirty yards of the enemy and observing the line of their digging and the direction of their fire.

In the meanwhile, the 2nd Canadian Infantry Brigade on the right was also in a position of grave peril, for the enemy in Armagh Wood were practically behind its left rear. At 2 p.m. they were already in Armagh House, but were chased out by a patrol of the 5th Battalion under Captain Collum. The only course left open to the 5th Battalion (Western Cavalry), which held the line here, was to throw its left out at right angles to its main line of trenches along a communication, and not a firing, trench in the direction of Square Wood, and to establish themselves firmly in the wood itself. This they did, and remained till evening watching the movements of the enemy, who were entrenching themselves firmly on the ridge just behind Rudkin House. To the north the Canadian Mounted Rifles were in Maple Copse 600 yards away, but the ground between was fire-swept and trenchless. In the meantime, the 7th Battalion (British Columbia) was brought up to support the 5th Battalion (Western Cavalry). The 2nd Brigade offered to make a counter-attack in the course of the afternoon with the ten platoons available in this line, but the offer was rejected by the 1st Division, which considered, rightly enough, that the force was insufficient for so long a frontage. The Germans, therefore, remained

6.30 a.m., June 2nd, until relieved by Lieut.-Col. Bott.

[36] These were strong combative patrols sent out according to the new plan mentioned above.

[37] Capt. Molson and Lieut. Ewing, of the 42nd Battalion, both showed great resolution in holding out with their men at the Apex during the critical hours of the German attack. Capt. Molson was wounded at the Ypres ramparts on the way up; Lieut. Ewing was also wounded later, but both went on throughout the engagement.

undisturbed. None the less, the Brigade was warned that a counter-attack would almost certainly be made as soon as sufficient reserves came up.

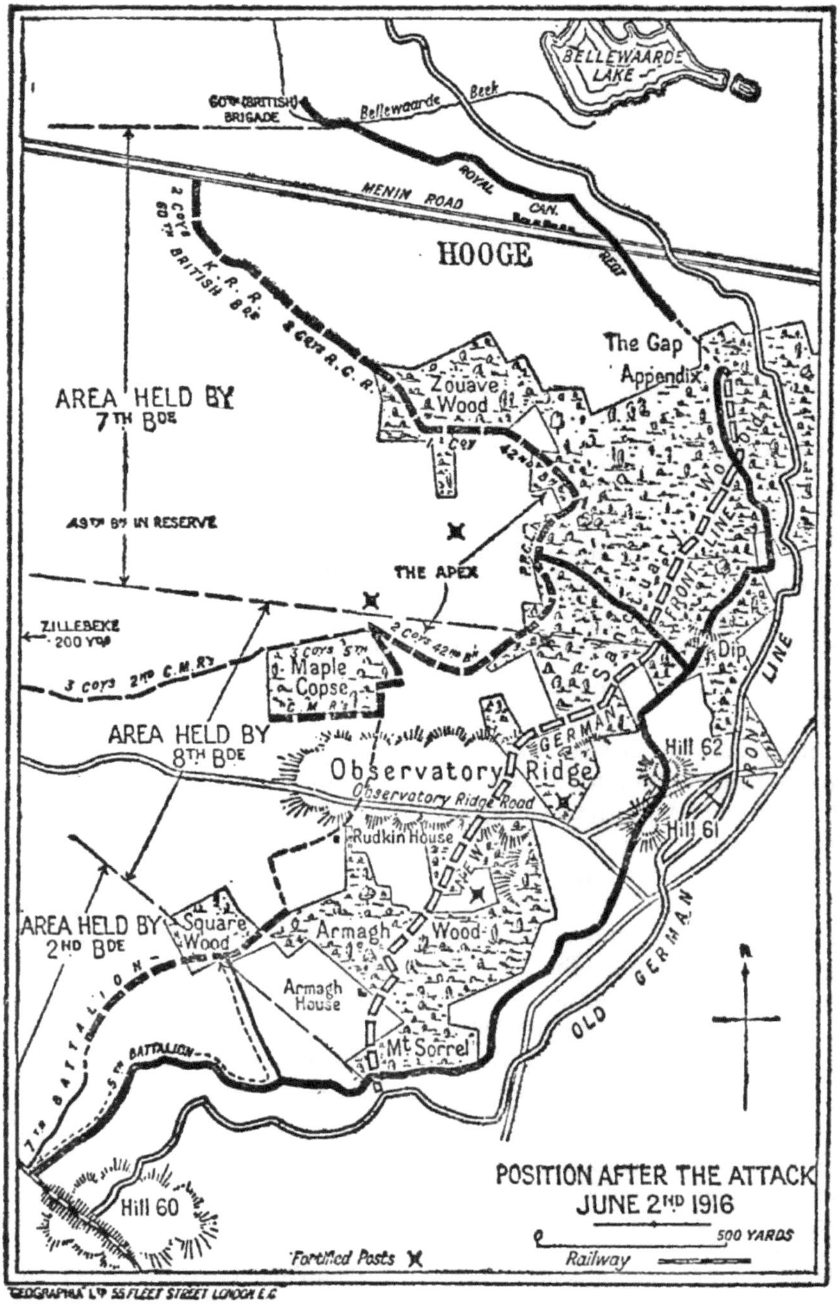

Map—Sanctuary Wood—Position after the Attack June 2nd 1916

June 2nd, 6 P.M.

One counter-attack of a minor character was attempted from the Maple Copse side of the trenchless area by the 3rd Division. The 2nd Canadian Mounted Rifles, three companies strong, had arrived in the trenches in front of Zillebeke at 6 p.m. They linked up with the 7th Battalion of the 2nd Brigade on the right, who had come up to support the 5th Battalion of their Brigade, and attempted to create out of the old trenches there a third line in case the enemy should break through.

June 2nd, 9 P.M.

Finally, as dusk drew on, two companies of the 2nd Canadian Mounted Rifles were ordered forward to Maple Copse to attempt a counter-attack on the enemy at Rudkin House. It was eleven o'clock when they reached the Copse and met Major Allen, of the 2nd C.M.R.'s. Colonel Baker had just fallen mortally wounded while walking up and down behind a new trench his men were digging under heavy fire and encouraging them by his coolness and example.[38]

The 5th Canadian Mounted Rifles succeeded in maintaining their position in Maple Copse. Shelled to pieces for hour after hour, and hunted from cover to cover, they yet held on, and this fact was in no small measure due to the great firmness and heroic disregard of death exhibited by Colonel Baker. He inspired his men by sheer personal magnetism and by the example of a splendid devotion to duty. Other men did their share in saving the line; still, but for him it might not have been saved at all, and in that case June the 2nd would have been associated with a great disaster to our arms.

June 2nd, 11 P.M.

The attack of two companies of the 2nd C.M.R.'s in the dark against an unknown German position held by troops whose numbers it was impossible to estimate was not a very promising venture, and it was not pressed home, the attackers being set to the more feasible task of trying to dig a trench linking up Square Wood and Maple Copse. The Battalion sustained very heavy losses. This attempt likewise failed, the shell-fire in the open proving too heavy; but Captain Leduc, of the 2nd Canadian Mounted Rifles, advanced with great daring as far as Rudkin House and satisfied himself—as proved to be the case—that the enemy's new line was being built well behind it.

June 2nd, midnight.

The 8th Brigade had by now suffered between 1,800 and 1,900 casualties out of their total strength, and it was time for some fresh troops to take a hand in the game.[39]

---

[38] Major Draper took over the command of the 5th C.M.R.'s when Col. Baker fell. Although hit himself, he carried his Colonel, mortally wounded, out of action, and then returned to conduct the defence.

[39] Colonel Hill's defence of Hooge from June 2nd to 5th will always be remembered as a fine military feat. There was nothing to prevent the Germans, after they had broken through the main line, rolling up his right flank and rear except the coolness and courage of

The losses, indeed, in both the 7th and 8th Brigades had been heavy, but the support line, in spite of its extraordinary zigzag conformation and the wide gaps which intersected it, remained firm. On the left the Royal Canadian Regiment still held its original position with a resolute calm, though its right was only supported by Capt. Niven's company, and they retired at dawn on June 3rd. Behind it and in the centre the support line trenches were intact, and the Princess Patricia's Canadian Light Infantry and the 42nd still clung to their positions; just in front of them Lieut. Evans was still holding the Fortified Post, and no shelling could shift the Canadian Mounted Rifles from Maple Copse, and beyond that to the south the 5th Battalion of the 1st Division were in Square Wood and the front line leading to Hill 60. General Macdonell was up and down his front encouraging his men by his very presence—and, indeed, there was much need of encouragement. The movements of the Germans on the overlooking heights were shrouded in darkness and uncertainty. They had been heavily reinforced.[40] There was no remission of the shell-fire, which alone gave flashes of light in the darkness except for the white flares which occasionally illumined the ridges in front, and might portend the sudden assault of an overwhelming enemy.

Help, however, was at hand. By the early afternoon of the 2nd the Higher Command had been alive to the danger of the attack, and were informed as to the true position. The determination to retake the lost trenches was arrived at, and as darkness fell the corps began to move in the direction of the enemy. Everywhere in the night was heard the tramp of marching men, and the dim outlines of endless columns flowing steadily towards the east were visible on every road.

---

his regiment and the skill of his own dispositions.

[40] Our outposts by Hill 60 reported strong masses of Germans moving up at 9 p.m., June 2nd, towards Mount Sorrel.

CHAPTER IX

THE COUNTER-ATTACK

Method of counter-attack—Successful efforts of the French—The question of time—Attacks which failed—Precipitancy of main counter-attack—Enemy reinforced—The assaulting forces—Inadequate system of railways—Failure of well-laid plans—Value of armoured cables—A stroke of misfortune—Uncertainty as to the enemy's positions—A test of endurance—Defective communications—Artillery unable to support infantry—An American officer gives a lead—The death of Major Stuart—Observatory Ridge—Enemy well supplied with machine-guns—The fatal trench—Heavy casualties—Gallant attempt of the 15th Battalion—The 14th Battalion digs itself in under heavy fire—The fateful gap bridged—Lieut. Beaton and Sergt. Topham—The Higher Command misinformed—Misfortunes of the 52nd and 60th Battalions—The Princess Pats cheer their comrades—Gallant officers of the 49th—Main object of the counter-attack fails—The road to Ypres blocked to the enemy—The 3rd Division wins its spurs—A prospect of defeat turned into an achievement of victory.

The doctrine of the counter-attack is one of the most simple in theory, and yet it appears to be one of the most difficult to apply effectively in practice. The idea is to take advantage of that confusion which must always beset an enemy in a victorious advance, and to strike him violently with the impact of new and well-organised troops from the second or support line of the defenders. The French have reduced this method to a fine art by punishing the Germans severely in their advance on a lightly held trench, allowing them to occupy it, and then turning them out at the point of the bayonet by a strong counter-attack from troops ready in the support line trenches just behind. It may also be used in the last resort to rally broken troops returning on their own line and threatening confusion to all concerned, or to repel an enemy adverse to bayonet fighting, rather than allow him to get into one's own trench.

All these methods of counter-attacking are largely questions of timing, like the blow delivered by a skilled boxer. You cannot hit too soon, but if you hit too late you fail. The time limit for the launching of this assault in the later stages of modern warfare is practically decided by the interval which it takes an enemy to get into some kind of cover and bring up his machine-guns. After that the confusion in the ranks of the opponents has vanished, the machine-guns are waiting, and artillery preparation is ineffective, as the gunners have not yet had time to locate and register the enemy positions with sufficient accuracy to make sure of putting those machine-guns out of action.

This chapter is the record of a counter-attack which failed, but it is only fair to the brigades which undertook the assault to point out that it took place eighteen hours after the Germans had made their first rush and many hours after they had fortified their new positions. During these eighteen hours it had been impossible to locate with any exactitude the new lines taken up by the Germans, so that while our artillery peppered the whole ridge very effectively, they could not concentrate on and wipe out trenches of the existence and position of which they were unaware.

It has been pointed out in the last chapter that the real counter-attack of the afternoon, or evening, of June 2nd could not be delivered because there were not at hand troops in sufficient force to attempt the task. Gunnery had gone too fast in its development for infantry tactics. The rim of the saucer, which could have been held against all odds eighteen months before, had been carried by the new artillery, and yet it was in effect the last and only defence of the Ypres salient. It is not possible to-day to defend on a single line of defence, and yet the Canadian Corps had been compelled by the logic of events and the policy of its predecessors to do so. Indeed, since Lord Ernest Hamilton wrote of the Mount Sorrel position as "the natural line," the whole science of defence had undergone a drastic change owing to the increased sweeping power of heavy artillery. A position must have "lungs," as Verdun proved—first lines which can be lost without overwhelming consequences. In the northern section of the Ypres salient there were at least three defensible sets of trenches with good sweeping ranges of fire, one behind the other, but here in the south-east the configuration of the ground did not permit of a dual or triple system. Lose one position of defence and you lose all. This fact no doubt accounts for the anxiety of the Corps and for the haste with which the main counter-attack was launched.

The original decision to attack was taken before 4 p.m. on June 2nd, and the Divisional Commanders of the 1st and 3rd Divisions were aware of it shortly afterwards, although the actual operation orders were not issued until 9.45 p.m. that day.

June 2nd, 9.45 P.M.

The real difficulty was to get the troops up in time for an attack at dawn. In the ordinary course of events the natural troops to undertake such a task are the support and reserve battalions of the brigades which have lost the position, if a prompt decision is to be reached before the enemy can build himself in. But so serious had been the fighting of the morning that of these the 49th Battalion (Edmonton Regiment), Colonel Griesbach, alone had not yet been drawn into the fighting in the front line. The 5th Canadian Mounted Rifles, the 2nd Canadian Mounted Rifles, and the 42nd Battalion (Royal Highlanders), under Lieut.-Col. Cantlie, were already used up. Furthermore, it was known that at 9 o'clock on the night of the 2nd the Germans had been heavily reinforced, and a rough guess might have put their numbers at anything between four and five thousand. A strong assailing force was therefore necessary. The 3rd Brigade of the 1st Division, which was in corps reserve, and two battalions of the 9th Brigade of the 3rd Division, 52nd Battalion, New Ontario Regiment, under Lieut.-Colonel Hay, and the 60th Battalion (Victoria Rifles), under Lieut.-Colonel Gascoigne, were therefore sent up. Two battalions of the 2nd Brigade of the 1st Division, 5th Battalion (Western Cavalry), under Lieut.-Colonel Dyer, and the 8th Battalion (Winnipeg Rifles), under Major Humble, were already in the trenches on the right of the line, and had, with the exception of the 5th Battalion, been only slightly engaged. The 7th (British Columbia) Battalion, under Lieut.-Colonel Odlum, and the 10th (Western Canada) Battalion, under Lieut.-Colonel Rattray, were in support and reserve.

June 3rd, 2 A.M.

The new troops then at the disposal of the General Officer Commanding in charge of the attack were the 7th and 10th Battalions (2nd Brigade), General Lipsett, the 13th, 14th, 15th and 16th Battalions (3rd Brigade), General Tuxford, the 49th of the 7th Brigade, and the 52nd and 60th of the 9th Brigade, making a total of nine battalions. The 58th and 43rd Battalions of the 9th Brigade were not made use of in the fighting at the time. All these were placed under the command of General Hoare-Nairne, of the 3rd Division. That officer, in the conference which preceded the formation of the plan, had put forward the view that, rather than make a frontal assault across the open, it would be better to start from what I have called the Apex of the defence (the projecting angle between Zouave Wood and Maple Copse) and bomb a way up the various communication trenches towards Hill 62 into the heart of the enemy's country and then spread right and left along our own original line. It was agreed, however, that such an advance through an intricate tangle of trenches involved first-hand knowledge of the ground on the part of the troops engaged; otherwise the result would be confusion worse confounded. None of the fresh troops available had this knowledge, and it was therefore decided somewhat reluctantly to risk the frontal assault. The attack was originally to be at dawn and to be delivered on a wide frontage—both precautions to obviate the deadly effect of the machine-guns. On the right, Colonel Rattray, with the 7th in advance and the 10th close in support, was to carry the south aspect of Observatory Ridge, and finally Mount Sorrel. Brigadier-General Lipsett, the Commander of the 2nd Brigade, was to see that this attack conformed with the movements of the centre battalions under General Tuxford of the 3rd Brigade. These two were old comrades, and well accustomed to work together; they decided to set up common Brigade Headquarters. The centre was the 3rd Brigade—the 15th Battalion (48th Highlanders) under Lieut.-Colonel Bent advancing on the left of the 7th, with the 16th Battalion (Canadian Scottish) under Lieut.-Colonel Leckie in support and the 14th Battalion (Royal Montreal Regiment), under Major McCombe to the left again, with the 13th Battalion (Royal Highlanders) under Lieut.-Colonel Buchanan close behind it. The right of the 3rd Brigade was Square Wood and the left Maple Copse, with Observatory Ridge Road as the point of junction between its two battalions. The objective of the 3rd Brigade was Hill 62. Farther north still, and not in immediate contact, the 49th Battalion of the 7th Brigade was to attack through the southern section of Sanctuary Wood and the 52nd Battalion of the 9th Brigade to the north again, while the 60th Battalion acted as support. Their aim was the position between Hill 62 and the Royal Canadian Regiment, still in place at Hooge. Such in brief was the plan. It was to prove, unfortunately, as fallible in execution as sweeping measures hurriedly conceived under the stress of war are apt to be.

June 3rd, 4.15 A.M.

There were two main difficulties: to get the troops up in time and to co-ordinate the artillery and the infantry so as to get the preparation and the assault to move as if by clockwork. But time was the great enemy. The original attack, as has been stated, was timed for 2 a.m. on June 3rd. The 3rd Brigade was back in Corps Reserve, and found the roads blocked with ambulances, transport, and ammunition.[41] It struggled vigorously, but could not get into position until 4.15 a.m. on June 3rd, and the 2nd Brigade, which was already on the spot, could not attack without it. This upset the whole of the arrangements with the artillery, and these had to be rectified under conditions which were far from satisfactory for accurate Staff work. The telephone lines were constantly broken, and the heroic runners were frequently killed.[42] The armoured cables[43] were the main stand-by. On the left the 49th were ready at 2.10 a.m., but without their left-hand battalion (the 52nd) or their support (the 60th). As a result of these delays, the attack was delivered in broad daylight, in a succession of waves, against hidden machine-guns, so that the enemy's fire was concentrated on each section in turn. The signal was

[41] It is impossible to pass over the check thus experienced by the 3rd Brigade without commenting on the reason for much misfortune to the British Armies during the two years of war on the Western front—the inadequate system of light railways. I have witnessed on many occasions blocks on the roads in Flanders caused by ambulance and transport wagons going down and infantry and ammunition wagons coming up, whereby hours were lost, very often at critical moments. Many of these checks might have been avoided altogether if a system of light railways had been constructed behind the trenches as soon as it became apparent that trench warfare had rendered the contending armies immobile for a long period of time. Since Sir Douglas Haig took command there has been a great improvement in this direction, but it is difficult to make up for lost time. I could not help thinking of the contrast between this delay and the rapidity and skill with which Sir William Mackenzie drove his railway across the Canadian prairies, not unlike the plains and plateaus of Flanders. The military leaders, indeed, with their technical staff training, lagged far behind in a task which would have been accomplished rapidly by experts like Sir Herbert Holt. Possibly, however, they had not the requisite authority from the Government to employ civilians in engineering tasks and in transportation problems. It must be added, however, that there were two principal difficulties which it took time to overcome: the shortage of shipping to carry over the material, and the dual, and sometimes triple, control of the railways by the British, French, and Belgian authorities.

[42] Among them Private H. Johnston, of the 2nd Battalion, is entitled to special mention for his absolute indifference to danger when carrying important despatches.

[43] The armoured cable is an underground telephone system, protected by armour from damage and destruction by shell fire. It is recorded in the diaries of the Canadian Divisions that the system of steel cables on this front was hit by shells fifty-seven times during the fighting in June without communication being broken.

to have been six green rockets fired by the 3rd Division Staff as soon as all the troops were ready. But this was, of course, a night and not a day warning, and by a crowning stroke of misfortune many of the rockets fired in daylight were faulty, and fourteen had to be discharged before the requisite number was reached.

June 3rd, dawn.

The day dawned dull and stormy, with dashes of driving rain which drenched the troops, many of whom had been marching all night. And though the day broke, the signal to attack still tarried hour after hour. The 7th and 10th Battalions on the right had been in position since before 2 a.m., and in waiting on the others had lost the precious hours of darkness. The same fate had befallen the 49th on the left, which waited interminably for the battalions of the 9th Brigade which never came. The 49th Battalion was given permission to charge at 2 a.m., but their Commander preferred to wait for the 52nd and 60th rather than risk ruining the whole affair by an isolated effort. The 14th and 15th were ready by 4.15 a.m. As the chilled soldiers of the 7th, 14th, and 15th peered out in the dull grey light they saw in front of them some hundred yards of open ground, and behind a tangled, irregular piece of woodland, sloping up to a low crest. Somewhere in this thicket lay the enemy's trenches, but the precise spot was largely a matter of guesswork, not of certainty.

The time of waiting for the charge is one of tense anxiety. As the company commanders consult their watches and note the passage of the minutes, the men string themselves up for a final effort. The next few seconds will carry them over the parapet through the shell fire and machine-gun fire into the enemy trenches if they are fortunate, but in any case to a fate which no man can predict. Here the moments of nervous strain were prolonged hour after hour until endurance must have become an agony. But the spirit of the counter-attacking battalions on the right never faltered, and when the time came at last they advanced to the assault in the face of a devastating fire with their customary resolution and gallantry.

June 3rd, 7.00 A.M.

The artillery preparation was from the first, in the opinion of competent witnesses, not adequate for the task of clearing the way for the infantry. The assault, as we know, had been ordered for 2 a.m. on June 3rd. The time had to be altered owing to the delay in the arrival of the infantry in some parts of the field. The new assault was timed for 7 a.m., June 3rd, but in one case it was postponed for another hour owing to the constant breakdown of all telephone communication between the Higher Command, the Battalion Commander and the gunners. These last had indeed a hard task in any event. The trenches in front of them had been dug by the Germans since the assault, and were neither ranged by observers nor photographed by our aircraft. The heavy rain and brooding mists had robbed the guns of the vision which is essential to accuracy. They fired blindly into the positions which the enemy might be supposed to occupy, and could not give the infantry the unfailing support which it expects and almost invariably receives.

At last it came! The green rockets were fired at 7.10 a.m. of June 3rd, and those battalions which were ready went over the parapet. Major Stewart, an officer of the Canadian Forces, formerly in the regular U.S.A. Army, was wounded in giving the 7th a lead over the parapet at 7.37 a.m., as they were clearly puzzled as to whether the signal had been given or not. His orderly stopped behind to bandage his wound, and both were killed in an instant by a shell. The 7th Battalion, closely supported by the 10th, attacked on the extreme right of the position with the view of clearing the south edge of Observatory Ridge, and so getting through to Mount Sorrel. It was impossible to go straight for the objective while the Ridge remained in German hands. The task was a very difficult one, and it is not surprising that they failed. They were exposed to an enfilade fire from the position on Hill 60 held by the enemy,[44] who as the 7th Battalion dashed out from the trench, could see our troops with perfect distinctness. The enemy were plentifully supplied with machine-guns, and had even wired their front in the eighteen hours in which they had enjoyed undisturbed possession. They had a particularly new strong trench just behind Armagh Wood, which held up the whole centre of the assault, for it had been in no way impaired by the artillery preparation. Lieut. Elliott and Lieut. Carstairs, each with a company of the 7th, attacked on the right, and Captain Holmes with two companies of the same Battalion and one of the 10th under Captain Fisher on the left. Captain Holmes found it impossible to get on, and finally dug himself in about forty yards in front of the enemy; Captain Fisher, pressing up to his assistance, was shot through the head and killed. Meanwhile a party on the extreme left found a hole in the enemy's line, and, turning the fatal trench, broke right through. But the Germans had reconstructed the battered Fortified Post, once held by the C.M.R.'s at this place, and manned it with machine-guns, which simply swept the bold adventurers out of existence. Few returned. On the right, Lieut. Elliott fought his way forward and turned the south end of the German position, reaching the original trench line just south of Mount Sorrel. Here, however, he was caught in the right rear by the German machine-guns on Hill 60. His party suffered heavy casualties and he was wounded. They were not able to hold their ground. Lieut. Carstairs' company fared no better. The attack on the right had broken down, and to press it was mere suicide on a large scale. There was no alternative but for the 2nd Brigade to get back and turn on the guns.

June 3rd, 8.35 A.M.

Next, to the north, came the 15th Battalion, who attacked at 8.35 a.m. They were already astride the end of the Ridge, but the ground in front of them had absolutely no cover, and after pushing to just beyond Rudkin House they were compelled to stop and dig themselves in under a withering fire.

June 3rd, 8.17 A.M.

The 14th Battalion (Royal Montreal Regiment) was to continue the attack on the north, its right connecting with the 15th Battalion on Observatory Ridge. The connection was duly made earlier in the night, and the Battalion was in position to attack at 4.15 a.m. in the morning of June 3rd. It is of the essence of an attack made on a broad frontage that it prevents the concentration of enemy fire at any one point in the line, and it is therefore essential that the various assaults should

[44] Positions on Hill 60 were held by the enemy and ourselves.

be simultaneous. This, unfortunately, was not the case with the 14th Battalion. Although the regiment had been ready for some hours and had been notified that the artillery preparation would begin at 6.15 a.m. and last till about 7 o'clock, a subsequent message was received to the effect that the bombardment would not begin until 7.45 a.m., and therefore terminate at 8.15. The battalion in consequence advanced to the attack at 8.17 in broad daylight against machine-guns, an hour after the first assault had taken place. In spite of these adverse circumstances, the 14th Battalion went forward without flinching and ultimately linked itself up with the 15th at Rudkin House on the right and with Maple Copse on its left. Here the regiment dug itself in under the fire of the enemy, and so with the 15th bridged the fatal gap between Square Wood and Maple Copse. The casualties in the 14th were 387.[45] Two notable feats of arms were performed on both flanks of the 14th Battalion. Lieut. Beaton and his platoon pushed right up to the German lines on the right of the regiment and maintained himself there until midnight of the 3rd-4th. On the left Sergeant Topham and fourteen men broke clean through the enemy and reached a point not far from our own original front line. They were, of course, completely unsupported, and soon found themselves practically surrounded by the enemy. Of Sergeant Topham's party of fifteen, two succeeded in making a safe return.

These stories, however, of isolated bodies getting through the first German line and penetrating to our trenches reached the Higher Command and conveyed to them a totally erroneous view of the actual situation. In consequence, although the right and centre attack had stuck fast after an advance of 200 or 300 yards, the left was urged forward later in the day under the impression that the whole enemy position was being carried.[46]

June 3rd, 7.00 A.M.

The position on the extreme left, where the 49th and 60th[47] were to attack through Sanctuary Wood, was a peculiar one. The 49th Battalion was in position by 2.10 a.m., the regiment having moved steadily to its objective under heavy fire, merely panting for the fray. It had not yet been engaged in any great general action, and was anxious to give its proofs—which, indeed, it did most nobly. Unfortunately, the 52nd and 60th Battalions failed to arrive in time for the assault, which took place at 7 a.m. on June 3rd. They were caught in heavy barrages in the only communication trench which led them to their points of assembly, and all the senior officers who understood the plan were either killed or wounded. The two regiments became mixed up in the mile-long trench. The 60th, however, eventually reached the position originally allotted to them as supporting battalion in the

[45] The 14th was commanded by Major McCombe (formerly Captain in the 3rd Victoria Rifles, Montreal) during the temporary absence of Lieut.-Colonel Clarke. Major McCombe, who had already been once wounded in action, showed great gallantry and ability in the attack.

[46] During the fighting of this and the following night Sergeant Brayton, of the 14th, exhibited conspicuous courage in the work of carrying the wounded lying in the open.

[47] The 52nd Battalion had been detailed for attack with the 49th Battalion, but in the night march was overtaken by the 60th. In consequence, their *rôles* were reversed.

support trenches, and these lines they maintained all day of the 3rd under heavy fire, relieving the P.P.C.L.I. that night. Colonel Griesbach, who was in charge of the whole assault, and had therefore handed over the command of his regiment to Major Weaver (Major Weaver was hit in the barrage and handed over his command to Major Hobbins), twice walked back across the open through a sleet of steel to consult by telephone with his Brigadier and to try to find someone in command of the 52nd or 60th. In the latter effort he failed, and these regiments took no part in the assault. Colonel Griesbach succeeded, however, in getting on the telephone with General Macdonell, to whom he explained the situation. The General speaks very highly of the clear grasp of affairs which Colonel Griesbach displayed.

June 3rd, 7 A.M.

By now, however, the morning had come, and there were no assembly trenches to shelter large bodies of men for the assault through Sanctuary Wood. The 49th were sheltering in what cover they could find in the Apex, and the support line in Sanctuary Wood. The 52nd and 60th were far behind, and it became a question whether to assault with the 49th alone or to abandon the attack altogether. Colonel Griesbach decided that it would be dangerous to let down the battalions on his right, even though the main plan on the left had gone awry, and at 7 o'clock the 49th climbed the parapet and attacked across the open. As they passed through and to the right of the Princess Patricia's attenuated companies, these stood up and cheered a new battalion going out to win its battle honours. The Princess Patricia's Canadian Light Infantry, in fact, seem to have contemplated the action which ensued over ground on which they had just fought in the spirit of an elder brother watching a younger one snowing his mettle.

The attack of the 49th was well planned and carried out in a very gallant manner, the officers leading their men, revolver in hand, to within point-blank range of the enemy. In this manner Captain McNaughton and Lieut. F. W. Scott fell at the high tide of the assault. Five officers were killed and eight wounded. But the effort was an isolated one, and was persisted in far too long under the erroneous impression that the 2nd and 3rd Brigades had recaptured the old front line and were urgently in need of support on their left to make the whole position good.

June 3rd, afternoon

The 49th, at any rate, succeeded in making a very considerable advance and in establishing blocks in Sanctuary Wood and in rendering the apex of the new front line comparatively safe from assault. Finally, on advice from the officers of the Princess Patricia's they desisted from any further attempt to advance to the old front line, and rested content with the security of the new line which their own gallantry and persistence had achieved.

June 3rd, 6 P.M.

By 6 p.m. of the evening of June 3rd it was known that the counter-attack had failed in its main object. The strange stories about capturing the original trenches had withered away, by their lack of proof and by their intrinsic absurdity. The enemy neither fainted nor failed, but remained roughly where he stood at the beginning of the day, though he had been thrust back here and there. None the less, the failure had achieved certain important objects. It had made good the line which now ran continuously from the Menin Road to Hill 60 in a shape which, though irregular, was firm. The deadly danger of the afternoon of June 2nd no longer existed. The fatal gap had been closed. The spirit of the Canadians had risen in the face of adversity and proved to the Württembergers that as long as the Corps stood in the entrance there was no easy road to what remained of the famous city of Ypres. The 1st Division had saved the town from entrance by the north a year before; the Corps had protected it from the tramp of German infantry advancing from the south. That heap of stone and rubble, with its one projecting pinnacle, still remained inviolate and inviolable. The line was not a good one, but it was a line still.

Finally, the regiments of the 3rd Division had proved themselves in action on the big scale, and so had entered into the fellowship of arms of the Canadian Corps. It has not been necessary to dwell at any length on the 1st Division, which, from brigadiers down to privates, behaved with the skill and courage of experienced veterans.

But if this chapter is one of failure it is not devoid of consolation. The 3rd Division in its first great fight had won its battle honours. Deprived at the very outset of the encounter of the services of its General and one of his brigadiers, assailed by the fiercest bombardment British troops had yet encountered, with a first line swept out of existence and a second line full of rending gaps, it yet held on and changed the fortunes of the third battle of Ypres until the prospect of an overwhelming defeat was turned into the achievement of a final victory.

CHAPTER X

A LULL IN THE STORM. THE FIGHT FOR HOOGE

Relief of the front-line Battalions—Heavy losses of the Seventh Brigade—Good work of the Third Pioneer Battalion—Sudden advance of the enemy—The Knoll of Hooge—The Menin Road—Description of the scene—The 28th relieves the Royal Canadians—Heavy bombardment by the enemy—The importance of the Knoll of Hooge—The enemy springs four mines under the first-line trenches—A company of the 28th perishes—A terrific explosion—Fierce fighting of the 6th June—Effective work of Captain Styles—The enemy in dangerous proximity to our support line—Former tragedies in Zouave Wood—Serious casualties of the 6th Brigade—The effective loss of the village of Hooge—Preparations for retaliation.

After the storm which had blown for thirty hours since the morning of June 2nd, a kind of lull settled down on the field. The artillery bombardments on both sides showed that the fighting was by no means finished, but the infantry remained on the ground where the assault of June 3rd had left them. It was now necessary to relieve the decimated front-line battalions.

June 4th, 8.30 A.M.

The 6th Brigade was in reserve of the 2nd Division, and it was decided to bring it up to the Hooge section on the left, but this move was not finally completed until the night of the 5th-6th, when the Royal Canadian Regiment was relieved by the 28th (North-West) Battalion. At 8.30 a.m. on the 4th the battalions of the 2nd and 3rd Brigades in the firing line were relieved by the 1st Brigade; the 1st Battalion (Ontario Regiment) under Lieut.-Colonel Hodson took the place of the 7th and 10th from the old line to Square Wood; and the 2nd Battalion (Eastern Ontario) was substituted for the 15th and 14th in the new trench from Square Wood to Maple Copse. On the following day the 43rd, 52nd, 58th, and 60th Battalions, 9th Brigade, relieved the Princess Patricia's Canadian Light Infantry and the 49th Battalion in the centre of the position at 12.45 p.m., and these regiments were able to go back for a well-deserved rest.

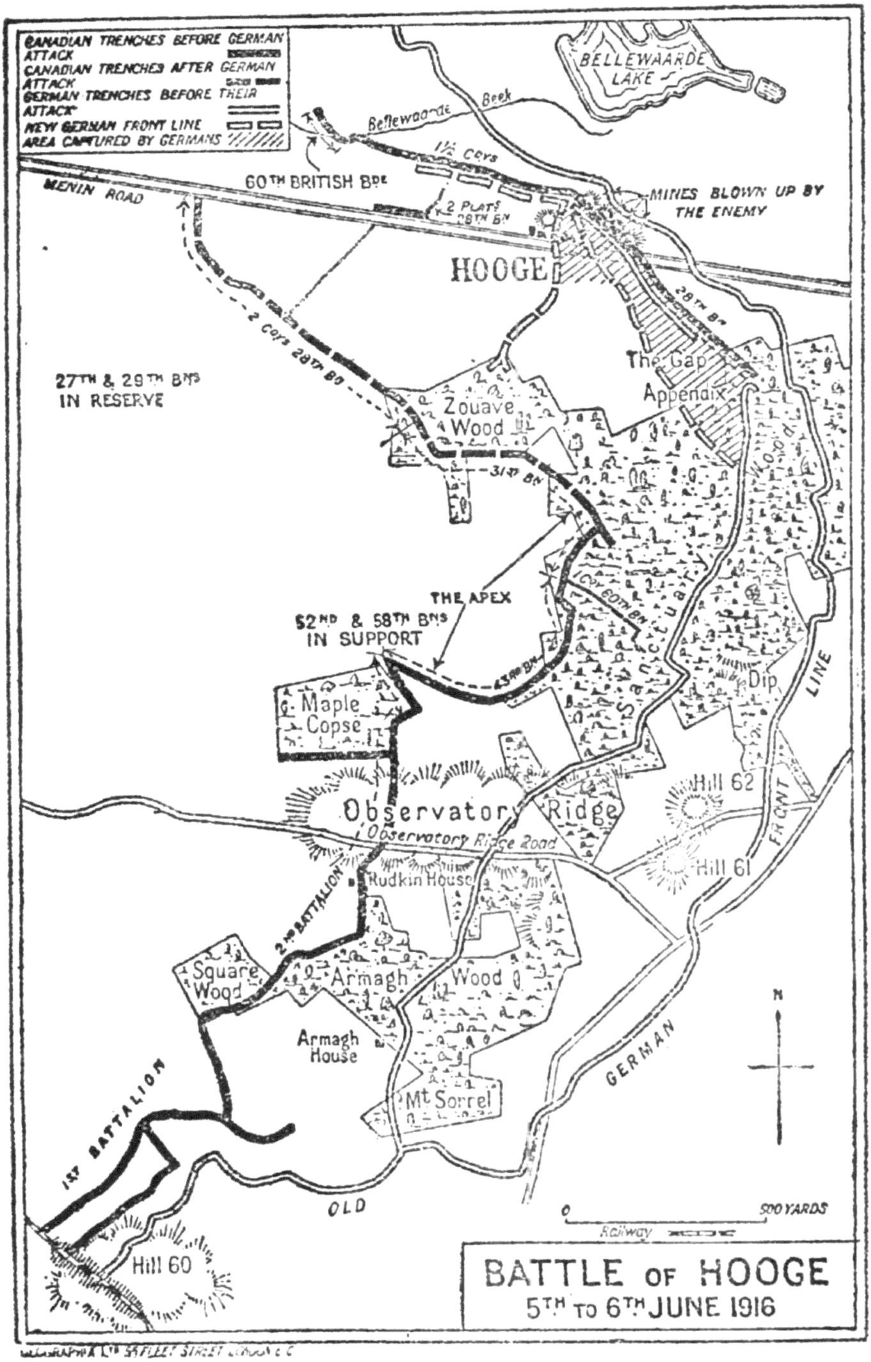

Map—Battle of Hooge 5th to 6th June 1916

June 5th

The casualties of the 7th Brigade had indeed been severe, totalling in all 45 officers and 1,051 men, and making up with those sustained by the 8th Brigade considerably more than 3,000, apart from the losses incurred by the 60th and 52nd Battalions of the 9th Brigade. The effect of the action can be seen by giving the rifle strength of the Brigade as it came out of the fighting. This was as follows:—Royal Canadian Regiment, 500; the Princess Patricia's Canadian Light Infantry, 210; 42nd Battalion, 460; 49th Battalion, 450; or 1,620 to a Brigade, which, if it had been at the full strength of 900 rifles to a battalion, would have numbered 3,600, or nearly three to one of the actual survivors. They had left their trenches, however, sensibly improved, chiefly owing to the efforts of the 3rd Pioneer Battalion, commanded by Lieut.-Colonel Holmes, which all through the action continued to make good the new front line and to dig trenches in support of it. This work was indeed essential, as it must be remembered that the larger part of the new position had never been intended for defence at all.

Night, 4th-5th.

In the meantime, it became clear that the situation could not be left as it was. Officers' patrols had been out on the night of the 4th-5th and had located the enemy's position fairly accurately. But while the Higher Command was planning the counterstroke, the enemy moved suddenly against the only part of the front line which remained in our possession.

The knoll of Hooge, if it hardly formed part of Mount Sorrel Ridge system, was yet an eminence of great importance, for from it one could look straight down to the walls of Ypres. It had in consequence changed hands over and over again, until the chateau, stables, and tiny village were nothing but a rubble heap of bricks stained with the best blood of Great Britain and Canada. Its last adventure had been in the summer of 1915, when it was lost on July 31st and retaken by the 6th Division on August 8th. Since then, however, the advance trenches had been pushed forward until they were right at the east end of the village and looked down on Lake Bellewaarde. On the left the ground falls swiftly, too, to Bellewaarde Beek, on the other side of which was the 60th British Brigade. The line here was exposed and open to the Germans on the higher ground, and was only held by a series of bombing posts.

On the night of the 5th-6th the 28th Battalion came up to relieve the Royal Canadian Regiment. The direct way up to Hooge is the Menin Road, straight from the historic gate. But you will not take that way unless you are anxious for death, for it is ranged to the last millimetre. The battalion will turn outside the gate, which has seen so many armies and generations pass, and skirt the edge of the calm and stagnant moat. Then it will turn through the long grass and water meadows such as fringe the Thames, and finally into the communication trenches. After this descent it is a question of a long struggle up the communication trenches, of clawing one's way through abandoned telephone wires which conspire in the effort to strangle, and of climbing and leaping shell-holes where the German guns have struck the trench with accuracy. Finally comes the Menin Road again. The great causeway runs straight with the rectitude of a Roman road. But there is added to it modern engineering, which has raised it twenty feet above the ground on each side. The road is lined with poplars, now mostly decapitated and scarred. Now and again, as the relieving battalion advances, a high, shrill noise will be heard overhead, followed by the flash and detonation of shells among the shattered trees. The 28th Battalion, used to these manifestations, plodded steadily up to the relief of the Royal Canadian Regiment on the night of June 5th.

Night of June 5th.

There are three lines of trenches of great importance in the Hooge position. The front-line trenches are now pushed forward to the extreme limit of the village beyond the crater the British blew up in August, 1915—for these look down into the valley of the Germans, though they are, in their turn, somewhat commanded by the enemy's heights at Bellewaarde Farm. These trenches connect with the British on the left of this rise beyond Bellewaarde Beek, and on the right stretch as far as the gap which leads down to Zouave Wood.

Some two hundred yards behind lies a support line, a good trench leading down to the Beek. Its field of fire is limited by the slope of the ground upwards towards the front-line trenches. North-east it commands a good field of fire, and proved, in consequence, useful to the 28th Battalion when the front line had been abandoned. Behind the support line the machine-guns were concentrated for the defence, and behind that again was another set of trenches.

The disposition of the 6th Brigade was as follows:—One and a half companies of the 28th in the front line and in bombing posts. The remaining two platoons and the machine-gun sections were in the support line. The machine-gun sections consisted of three Colt guns left by the 7th Brigade,[48] two Lewis guns of the Royal Canadian Regiment, one Colt gun of the 6th Brigade Machine-Gun Company, and in addition a Stokes gun. The other two companies of the 28th were in support trenches by the Menin Road. The 31st Battalion was in reserve along with a company of the 60th Battalion of the 9th Brigade, which it was found impossible to relieve at the last moment on the night of the 5th-6th. The 29th and 27th were in Brigade reserve. Shortly after midnight the 6th Brigade was in position. The shelling during the night was very heavy, and the relief was, in consequence, accomplished under some difficulties, but as these bursts of fury died away time after time there was no particular reason to suspect an attack of the German infantry. At 7 a.m. on the 6th an unprecedented bombardment began once more, and lasted until the very moment of the assault at Hooge seven hours later.

June 6th, 7 A.M.

One vital fact was entirely unknown to the Royal Canadian Regiment and the 7th Brigade. The Germans in planning their attack on Mount Sorrel and Hill 62 had not in the least forgotten the importance of the knoll at Hooge. It was nec-

[48] Under Lieut. Ziegler. When Lieut. Ziegler was wounded Lance-Corporal James took over the command. The assistance of these guns was invaluable in repelling the attacks.

essary to capture it if the new line was to be made complete and the Ypres salient finally broken. Their right wing had, as has been recorded, lapped round in the direction of the village and had been driven back by the sturdy fire of its defenders. But long before this they had made their plans and had driven four mines right under the front-line trenches. When the hour of attack at 2 p.m. came the mines were sprung simultaneously.

June 6th, 2 P.M.

The aeroplane photographs after the event show them actually overlapping in the craters they threw up. The explosion was horrible, and one entire company of the 28th perished in it almost to the last man. Many of the remaining company of the 28th were involved in the catastrophe; the bombing posts were abandoned and the survivors concentrated in the support trenches. Yet so tremendous was the noise of the artillery preparation that the garrisons in the Fortified Posts behind were quite unaware that any mines had been exploded until the survivors began to arrive, although they were but a little distance from the scene of this tremendous detonation.

June 6th, afternoon.

After this the day of the 6th witnessed some very fierce fighting. The Germans had already taken the whole Canadian front line from the gap to Mount Sorrel on the morning of June 2nd, and were determined to carry the remainder at Hooge on the 6th. Soon after the mines had exploded they came forward in the usual formation with packs on their shoulders like men expecting no resistance. So far as the front line was concerned they were right; otherwise they made an error. They occupied the remains of the trenches in Hooge and assaulted the 60th British Brigade opposite Bellewaarde Farm, but were repulsed with considerable loss by the resolute infantry of the British Brigade which had neither been mined at all nor bombarded to any considerable extent. The enemy then came straight down the line of the Menin Road both on the right- and the left-hand sides. By this time, however, the resistance, in spite of the continuous bombardment. had been organised by Captain Styles, of the 28th, who was fortunate in having at his disposal in the support line such an exceptionally strong force of machine-guns.

The battle was back on the old line always occupied when Hooge is lost, and was defended with the greatest obstinacy by the Canadian infantry and gunners. On the left-hand side of the causeway the enemy got as far down the hill as Bellewaarde Beek, but any further advance was swept out of existence by the machine-guns in the support line. On our right side of the Menin Road the attack appeared more dangerous. The enemy succeeded in jumping from shell hole to shell hole, and attained dangerous proximity to our support line. But here again the 28th drove them back by rifle and machine-gun fire.[49]

[49] The advance of the enemy down the communication trench north of the Menin Road was checked by Lieut. Gilmour, of the 28th, who put up a block just beyond the support trench nearest to the front and drove them back with bombs.

June 6th, 3.30 P.M.

By 3.30 p.m. on June 6th the attack on the support line had been repulsed for the moment by Captain Styles and the machine-guns, but it persisted on the right-hand side of the road all the afternoon. At about 4 o'clock the enemy determined to attack the support trenches now held by the 31st. Their avenue of approach was obvious. It was through the gap and down by the Zouave Wood. This is an old field of battle, fought over until every yard of earth is covered with the relics of the slain. Here in October of 1914 seven hundred of the Prussian Guard broke clean through the British front line, and paused as though bewildered when they found they had attained their object. They were immediately caught in reverse by the fire of the 7th Division, still holding the slope of the ridge to the right and left, and charged from the support trenches by the 52nd (Oxfordshire Light Infantry), who killed them to a man. For many months afterwards their piled bodies still cumbered the ground. The Germans, undismayed by this precedent, attacked down Zouave Wood at 4 o'clock and renewed their attempts during the course of the evening. The support trenches are good ones, the field of fire excellent, the wood itself devoid of all substantial cover, and the enemy gained nothing by the attempt except a heavy list of casualties. Hooge had gone, but the support line still remained.[50] The main attacks were delivered in two waves at five yards' interval and fifty yards' distance. But although all the main attacks were repelled, the Germans succeeded in establishing small posts down our old communication trenches in the Zouave Wood area.

Early on the night of the 6th-7th the bombardment, which had been applied to the whole area for nearly seventeen hours, died away. None the less, the casualties of the 6th Brigade were serious—20 officers and 580 men.

June 6-7th, night.

The whole line, then, had gone, and Ypres remained open to its assailants. This is the first reflection on the loss of the village of Hooge. But all the time that attack was going on, and some time before it, the powers that be had been brooding darkly over methods of retaliation and reconquest. It was time to teach the enemy that two could play at the game of the new artillery preparation, and ground lost by that method could as speedily be regained. In the next chapter we shall see how these plans evolved themselves and what the result of the trial was. As it is, on the night of the 6th, the Germans were sitting on the rim of the saucer imagining that in the third battle of Ypres they had at last conquered the salient.

---

[50] Capt. W. E. Manhard, of the 8th Field Company R.E., showed great gallantry and devotion to duty in making the new front line secure. His splendid example was an inspiration to all ranks working under him.

CHAPTER XI

THE FINAL VICTORY

Canadians take the initiative—The Anglo-French offensive—Good fellowship between the Imperial and Canadian Army—British Brigade supports the Canadians—The Württembergers and the Canadians—General Burstall commands formidable assembly of heavy guns—Aeroplane photographs—Battalions massed in strength—Divisional Commanders—Artillery pounds the German position—The enemy demoralised—The advance to the assault—Intense artillery preparation—A struggle between weapons of attack and methods of defence—Unforeseen developments of trench warfare—The significance of the Battle of the Marne—The use of gas a failure—Terrific force of great guns—Mr. Lloyd George and the industrial development of England—The 3rd Toronto Battalion advances—The centre attack—A daring scheme to baffle the enemy—The front line moves forward unnoticed—German listening post captured—The forward rush—The bayonets clear the trenches—Captain Bell-Irving's daring exploit—The 16th and the 3rd Battalions recapture the heights—The 13th Battalion to the charge—Machine-gun fight and bombing encounters—Hill 62 in Canadian hands—Real gain of the day—Counter-attacks dispersed—The enemy dazed by the suddenness and the success of the onset—Splendid arrangement and precision of the attack in face of difficulties—Ypres salient reconquered with bayonet in semi-darkness—A devastated territory—The natural green blotted out—Earth churned up into masses of mud—The sight after the battle—Where captains and soldiers lie—Those we shall remember—Defeat turned into victory.

It is difficult to penetrate the mind of the German Headquarters Staff. The enemy had, by a profuse expenditure of ammunition and a great concentration of heavy guns, conquered the last defensive position which guarded Ypres on the south-east. The Canadians lay below them in hastily constructed trenches on the flat, where every move was visible to the keen observers on the heights above. One would imagine that the next step would be to turn the guns on again to destroy far weaker positions, to break the salient finally, and to compel the retirement of two army corps to posts far back in the rear. Yet after June 6th the Germans made no move and allowed the initiative to pass into Canadian hands. The best explanation of this singular line of conduct has been suggested by the Army Commander, who held that the sole object of the attack was to compel the British to move troops from other parts of the line.

The idea of the Anglo-French offensive in the summer of 1916 had long been a nightmare to the great Headquarters Staff. They dreamt of the continual piling up of men and munitions from beyond the narrow seas at some pre-arranged point; they believed that a vigorous offensive at one or two places would disturb their opponents and confuse the threatened move. According to this theory, Verdun and the third battle of Ypres were defensive-offensive operations. Neither action prevented the offensive at the Somme. However that may be, the Germans remained impassive after their first two strokes, while the Canadian Corps devoted itself in quietness and confidence to the preparation of the real attack. They borrowed liberally both in men and guns from the army corps on their right and left, but no general reserve of the British Army was shifted to imperil the great offensive on the Somme. There has been nothing pleasanter in the course of the campaign than the feeling of good comradeship, common among soldiers, which subsisted between the Imperial Service and the Canadian Corps. The Canadian Corps had borne the brunt of the fighting on the Ypres salient, and, as far as they were concerned, to ask was to have. A British brigade was moved into the St. Eloi district, so as to set the 2nd Division free for retaliation. A reserve cavalry division of the British Army was moved up at once to occupy the third line in order that the Canadian generals might have no doubt as to their freedom of action in moving to the final assault against the captured positions. The Higher Command now had the reserves necessary to make them secure in an advance, and they certainly needed such security. In the fighting which ensued between June 2nd and 14th every Brigade of the Canadian Corps was fully engaged, and many of them suffered severe casualties. None the less, they endured until the end and the Canadians regained the lost ground. Their attitude is best summed up by the remark of a senior Staff Officer, who, basing prejudice on military knowledge, declared "that this was a personal matter between the Württembergers and the Canadians and that the Canadians were going to win." Troops animated by this spirit are not likely to fail.

But the work of the real counter-attack had to be done behind the lines. The failure of the first effort had been due to lack of artillery preparation on unknown trenches. None the less, the heavy guns were on the march. Some were asked for from neighbouring Army Corps, others were freely offered as a voluntary contribution to the gallantry of the Canadian infantry. The new reinforcements were stupendous.

General Burstall, of the Canadian Corps, thus commanded one of the greatest assemblages of guns ever concentrated on the British front. I have described already the effect of the enemy's bombardment on the Canadian front. The Germans were now about to get a little of their own medicine back. The guns were divided into groups, the trenches accurately ranged, and each battery was given its definite and proper objective.

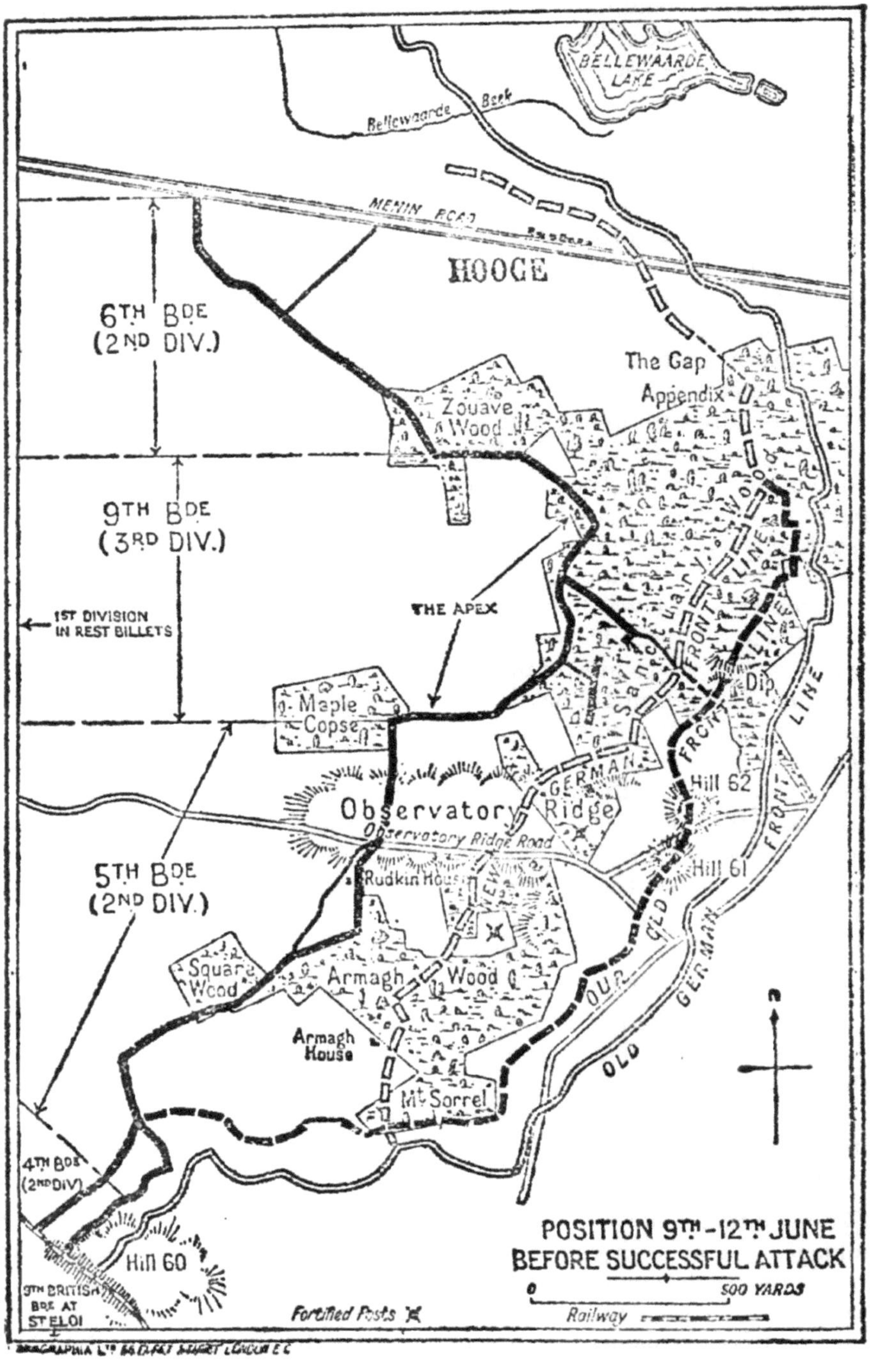

Map—Position 9th-12th June before Successful Attack

On the other side of the line, one must conceive the Germans toiling mightily, with the assiduity of coral insects, to make good what they seem to have imagined was to be their permanent home. Their industry was certainly marvellous. When the weather grew clear again and the aeroplane photographs could be taken, they showed no fewer than eight communication trenches driven up from the old German line to the new one, and an entire and excellent support line, dug just west of our own original front trench, now battered almost out of recognition, while the assault revealed deep dug-outs innumerable. So, from June 4th to June 12th the powers of offence and defence got ready, one for the other.

June 4th-12th.

But while the heavy guns were being brought into position, it was necessary to reorganise the infantry and to mass the Corps for a strong and concerted attack. An immediate assault had been put out of the question by the failure of June 3rd. The enemy's trenches had to be located accurately before the fire of the guns could be directed upon them. For some days after the 3rd the weather remained unfavourable, and in the heavy rains and mists it was impossible for our aircraft to obtain good photographs, or for the ranging shots of our guns to be observed adequately. This delay gave us an opportunity for the reorganisation of the infantry, preparatory to a general assault, and it is, after all, by the infantry that the final issue will be decided. The Canadian battalions were therefore massed in great strength for the night of the 12th-13th.

June 8-9th.

The 9th British Brigade took over the St. Eloi sector, and thus released the 2nd Division, which was enabled to take over the ground on the northern sector, while the 1st Division prepared for the attack, and recuperated its forces in rest billets. When the reliefs had been accomplished the position on June 8th was as follows: 6th Brigade of the 2nd Division at Hooge, and 9th Brigade of the 3rd Division from Zouave Wood to Maple Copse; 5th Brigade of the 2nd Division in line of Maple Copse to Hill 60; 4th Brigade of 2nd Division from Hill 60 to Ypres-Commes Canal; 9th British Brigade in the St. Eloi sector.

The accompanying sketch will make the position of June 9th quite clear. The 2nd Division were to hold the line while the attacking brigades were reorganised. The 1st Division was given the post of honour; but its formation was entirely altered for the purpose of the battle. It was necessary to secure two elements: knowledge of the ground and a sufficient number of battalions which had not been too severely punished in the action of June 3rd. Further, it was essential to secure the conjoint services of the two Brigadiers, General Tuxford and General Lipsett, who were familiar with the locality and accustomed to work together. With these objects in view the 1st Division was redistributed in the following manner:—

June 12th.

General Lipsett took command of the 1st, 3rd, 7th and 8th Battalions for the right attack. General Tuxford took command of the 2nd, 4th, 13th and 16th Battalions for the left attack, while General Hughes remained as Divisional Reserve with the 5th, 10th, 14th and 15th Battalions to push the matter through should any disaster overtake the leading regiments. The map will show the disposition of our forces and the great mass of infantry assembled for the purpose of retaking the lost position.

June 11-12th, night.

The 2nd Division was relieved by the 1st Division on the night of the 11th-12th preceding the attack at dawn of the 12th-13th. The artillery in the meantime had not been idle. Apart from pounding the German position in a regular and methodical spirit, it had indulged in the last few days in bursts of intensive fire, which seemed to herald an infantry assault which did not take place. By this time the Germans were first of all demoralised by being kept on perpetual tenterhooks, and finally lulled into a false security. So much was this the case that our final attack, though preceded by three-quarters of an hour's intense preparation, caught them in the middle of a relief.[51]

June 12th, 8.30 P.M.

The frontage of the attack was one of three battalions, the 3rd, 16th and 13th, from right to left. Strong reserves were behind, and on both flanks demonstrations would be made, the 7th loosing smoke bombs from Hill 60 and confusing the enemy with a bombing attack, while the 58th made a severe bombing attack up the well-fought-over communication trenches by the Apex on the left of the 1st Division, and were to link up finally with the captured position. In the evening of June 12th, at 8.30, a tremendous bombardment was directed on the German trenches before the last light failed; at 12.45 a.m. of June 13th the tempest of the guns would be let loose once more, and at 1.30 the guns would lift and the battalions advance to the assault in successive lines, each supporting regiment occupying trenches in front of them as soon as they were vacated by their predecessors. The Staff preparations had been complete and were crowned with success. In this, as in previous operations of the 1st Division told in this volume, Major-General Currie exhibited the skill and resolution which he had shown in so marked a degree at the second battle of Ypres. He achieved, however, so great a reputation at that action that it would seem almost superfluous to mention that the conduct of affairs in his hands was efficient and successful. He was greatly assisted in his operations by Lieut.-Colonel Kearsley, the Chief Staff Officer of the Division. Brigadier-General Harington, of the Corps Staff, did much to perfect the plan of operations. He left the Canadians, much to their regret, shortly after the action to take up a superior command. He stayed long enough, however, to see an action which had begun as a reverse turned into a striking triumph. But the main credit must be given to General Byng, who well sustained his previous military reputation in laying down the outline of the plan which brought success, and in supervising its preparation.

[51] The greatest possible assistance to the attack was given by Capt. Godwin and the trench mortar batteries of the 1st Division. These mortars kept up so heavy a fire on Hill 60 that the enfilade fire which had largely stopped the night attack on June 3rd was kept down completely. Capt. Godwin was unfortunately killed.

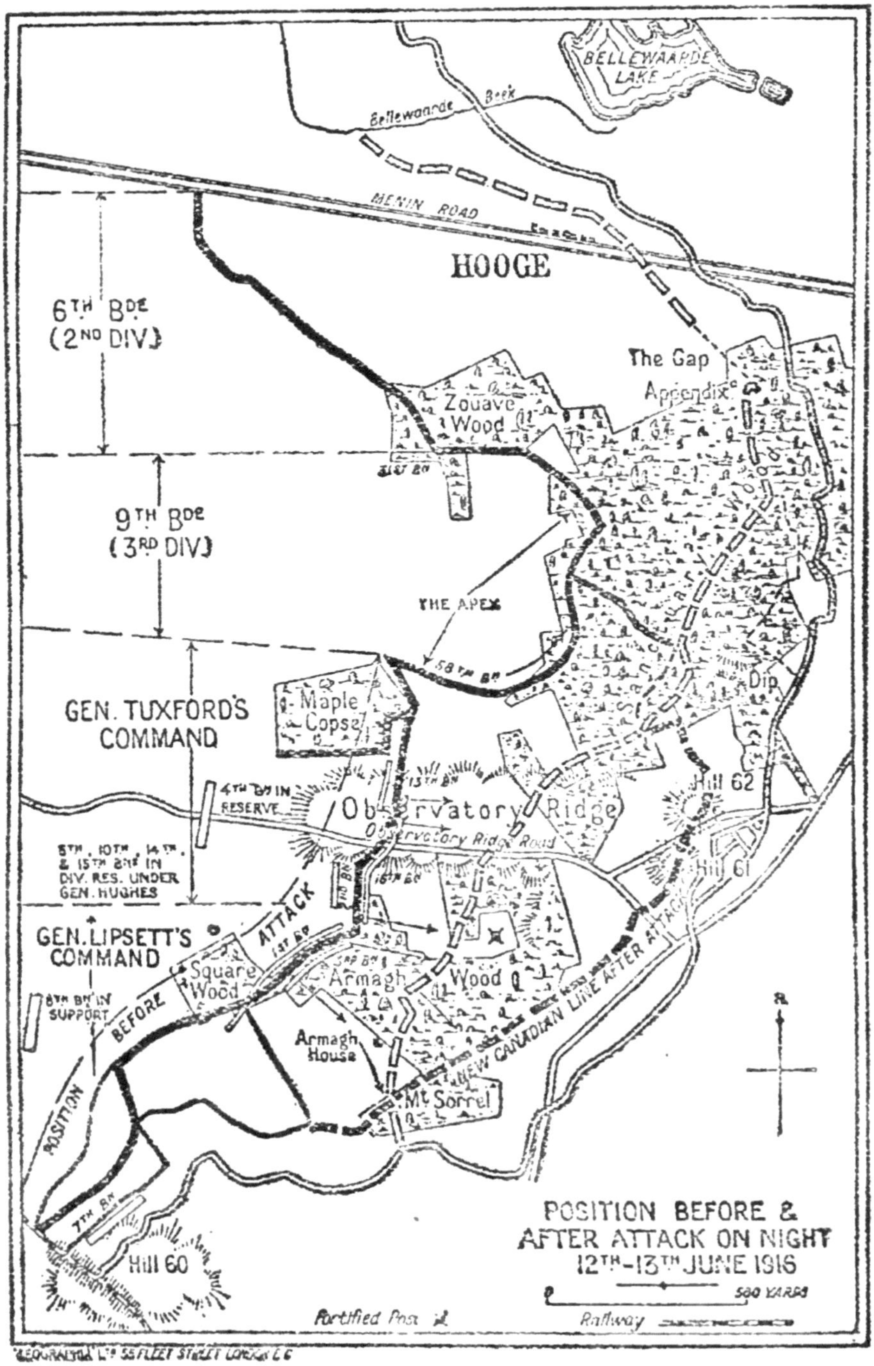

Map—Position before & after Attack on Night 12th-13th June 1916

It had been agreed that, in the event of a check taking place anywhere, flares should be sent up to indicate the position stormed by the assailants, and for this purpose the objectives were divided into four successive lines. It would, perhaps, be unwise to give further details of these arrangements, and one may be content to remark that they worked admirably. Finally, when the 3rd Battalion arrived at Mount Sorrel on the right, the 16th at Hill 62 in the centre, and the 13th to the old lines to the north of this, a red flare from each section would be the signal that the whole position was taken.

June 12-13th, night.

The weather throughout the attack was of the vilest description, the rain coming down in torrents; but it was not, as subsequent events will show, altogether unfavourable to the successful prosecution of the adventure. The new wire which had been placed along the front by the 2nd Division was removed early in the night of the 12th, for to do so before would have been to evoke suspicion; and planks were placed across the trenches to allow the supports to cross them quickly.

June 13th, 12.45 A.M.

Then at 12.45 the guns began. For three-quarters of an hour the air was full of the preparation. An enormous force of heavy artillery had been assembled, against which no ordinary parapet or traverse would stand for an instant. The 18-pounders reached an astonishing total, with several Belgian field guns in addition. It is true that the whole of this artillery would not be turned on the actual field of battle. Some of it was to be employed for purposes subsidiary to the action. None the less, a great battery of guns of all calibres pointed their muzzles towards the Germans on Hill 62 and Mount Sorrel. The enemy's positions on Mount Sorrel and Hill 62 were to be shelled upon a frontage of 1,500 and to a depth of 1,000 yards, while it was the ambition of the artillery to break to pieces, day in and day out, some 10,000 yards of German trenches, so that when the moment for the assault arrived the infantry could go forward, in General Burstall's words, with slung rifles. This ambition they very nearly fulfilled, as the light casualty lists of the 1st Division show. The infantry would be the first to acknowledge the immense debt they owed to the artillery behind them.

War, while it is in one sense a contest between two opponents, is also a struggle between the weapons of offence and the methods of defence. A strange kind of attack suddenly grows formidable, and after winning one or two resounding victories is countered by the cunning brains which organise an appropriate form of resistance. On the other hand, man raises what appears to be an impregnable bar to the forward progress of armies; instantly, far away, perhaps in laboratories beyond the seas, human intelligence is contriving to break the bar and to prove that it is impossible for any one force to say to another, "So far shalt thou go and no farther." In this interplay of forces the functions of the infantry, cavalry and artillery are constantly changing. Now one has, for a short period, a greater superiority and importance, and then the circle swings round and

"The spoke which is to-day on top
To-morrow's on the ground."

In all these calculations, each side is fallible until it has gained by experience.

It is a general and very fallacious view that the Germans foresaw all these developments of war and prepared for them, while the Allies were caught napping. Nothing could be more untrue. The Germans were better prepared for all possible eventualities than anyone else, but no soldier in any army foresaw the actual course which modern warfare would take. As a matter of fact, the development of trench warfare and the reign of the machine-gun was so fatal a blow to German prospects that it is improbable that they would have declared war at all if they had thought it anything more than a bare possibility. To them it was a matter of life and death to keep the armies on the move—life if they could crush the French and British armies in the field and then turn back on Russia; death if they were condemned to a static defence while the invincible resources of the Allies in men and money accumulated slowly on either front. History decided at the Marne in favour of the latter alternative.

From the date of the Aisne the infantry in defence gained a decided superiority over the artillery in attack and kept it for many months after the race to Calais had locked the lines in Western Europe. The enemy possessed indeed a great superiority in heavy guns, but it was not sufficient to blow out of its position a resolute corps or army. The deadlock was complete. The gunners could not destroy the trenches and the machine-gun emplacements sufficiently to allow the infantry to advance, and time was on our side. It was in the attempt to break through this impasse that gas was first used at Ypres; but after that terrible experience the defence produced the gas helmet, and the new weapon broke in the German's hands.

Then began the race between the contending armies to produce guns and shells of such size and in such quantities as would blast a whole area with death, bury the machine-guns and the garrisons, destroy the superiority of the infantry in defence, and give the game once more into the hands of the offensive. In this race we were slow starters. The generals took time to realise the necessities of the new situation, and it was not until the cyclonic energy of Mr. Lloyd George was harnessed to the work of the Munitions Department that the vast industrial resources of Great Britain were really brought into play. It was a work which required not only the energy of genius, but the tact of a consummate man of affairs conversant with all the details of civilian life. But presently the machine began to work and to gather momentum in its course. Every private concern adapted to the task was taken over and pressed into the work. The factories smoked on every hillside and the furnaces flared in every city. The vast metal tubes of the guns took shape, and a tremendous volume of shells began to flow in ever-increasing numbers across the Channel. By the summer the work was well in hand and the guns were ready to overpower the defence of the German defenders and clear the way for the 1st Division. On that June night Mr. Lloyd George was fighting on Canada's side.

June 13th, 1.30 A.M.

Then, as the guns lifted, the infantry charged. On the right Lieut.-Col. Allan led the 3rd Toronto Battalion forward, with the 1st Battalion close in support. So dense was the brushwood in Armagh Wood that in the first stages they went forward in the curious formation of sections in file. Advancing with great dash, they got in advance of the enemy's barrage before the latter could be turned on to our trenches, and took the Germans' front line. One of our Fortified Posts, then in the enemy's hands, turned a machine-gun and rifle fire on them, but the fort was taken by assault and the garrison bayoneted in the fighting. This Fortified Post represented the left of the 3rd Battalion, and thenceforward they met with little opposition here and in the centre, except attacks from isolated bombing posts, and their casualties were almost entirely due to enemy shell fire. They rushed a position somewhere in the region of their old line on Mount Sorrel, as soon as our guns lifted to the old German line, and were the first of the attackers to signal that the final objective had been reached at ten minutes past two in the morning of June 13th, forty minutes from the commencement of the action.

June 13th, 2.10 A.M.

The right-hand company, however, working up the old front line British trenches, was somewhat delayed by an obstinate resistance, but with the assistance of a company of the 1st Battalion it also pushed through.

The night of the attack was, as has been stated, dark and squally. The rain blew in great gusts, drenching the waiting battalions to the skin and filling the assembly trenches knee-deep in water. But these conditions suggested to the mind of Colonel J. E. Leckie, of the 16th Battalion, or centre attack, a particularly daring scheme. Two of his subalterns, Lieuts. Adams[52] and Scroggie, had been for some days reconnoitring and crawling about the ground in front, with the view of guiding the Battalion during the actual assault.[53] In the course of these investigations they had come across an old trench marked on no map and about 100 yards in front of the Canadian first line. Such a trench is a common feature on ground which has been much fought over. It was suggested that if the leading lines of the Battalion crept up during the night to this new position they would be 100 yards nearer their objective and would probably escape the German artillery fire, which would break out on our front line the instant our guns lifted and the attack was seen to be imminent. Such a course had great advantages. On the other hand, Colonel Leckie had to consider the fact that an encounter with a patrol or a listening post of the enemy would give away the secret of an attack the prospect of which had, so far, been sedulously guarded from reaching the ears of the enemy. A premature brush on the part of a company with even a small section of the enemy would have meant flares and infantry firing along the whole line and the plan would have stood disclosed. Colonel Leckie decided to take the risk and the responsibility. His regiment was drawn up for the assault on a frontage of two half-companies in four

[52] Lieut. Adams was killed in the attack.

[53] A reconnaissance was also undertaken on the night of the 12th to try to estimate the accuracy of our shooting in the bombardment beginning at 8.30 p.m.

successive lines. The first two lines were passed successfully up to the unmarked trench without any suspicion of their intention reaching the enemy. The margin between success and failure was, however, narrow to the last inch. The Germans had actually put out a listening post well in front of their line, but the advance guards of the 16th (Canadian Scottish) passed by it in the dark. By the time the Germans discovered the presence of the Canadians they were hemmed in in front and rear, and remained quiescent until dawn led to their discovery and surrender. Of course, they ought to have fired their rifles and given the alarm at any cost to themselves.

But the manoeuvre succeeded, like many risky chances taken in war. The enemy's shells missed the two front lines completely as the 16th Battalion charged straight into the German positions. The two supporting lines, on the other hand, suffered somewhat severely from ranged shell-fire as they climbed the parapet. The first two waves of the assault met, indeed, with little resistance owing to the unexpected rapidity of their advance—a plan since extensively adopted in the fighting on the Somme.

Isolated German parties of bombers or machine-gunners still put up a fleeting resistance. In the face of these assaults the Canadian infantry moved steadily on with the quietude of fate. The second two waves of the 16th, on approaching the German front line, were met in places by machine-gun fire and by a bombing resistance, in which Captain Wood, an American Army officer whose services were very valuable to the Canadians, was killed. The trench was soon taken and the enemy who resisted were bayoneted. The survivors, who were taken prisoners, appeared to be dazed and to possess neither rifles nor equipment. About thirty yards behind this line, however, a machine-gun was still in action and was causing many casualties in our ranks. Captain Bell-Irving dashed out from the line, got behind the gun, shot three of the team with his revolver, and, picking up a rifle, charged in from the rear and killed the remaining gunners with the bayonet. Line after line was carried in this fashion until the 16th were able to put up the red flares, which signalled to the division that they had recaptured the heights and stood once more on their old ground or in its immediate vicinity. Although not so quick to arrive as the 3rd Battalion, they were soon in touch with it, and the new line was linked up.

Meanwhile, on the left the 13th Battalion (Royal Highlanders of Canada), under Lieut.-Colonel Buchanan, had advanced at a given signal. The German artillery had ranged their assembly trenches during our own bombardment and inflicted somewhat severe losses on them before they climbed the parapet at the correct moment. They set out in the usual formation of four waves on a frontage of two half companies, the first two waves under Major Perry and the last two under Major McCuaig, and, advancing across broken ground under heavy shell fire, reached their first objective. Here they were held up for a time by a machine-gun on their left front; a bombing party had to be sent round its rear to destroy it before the regiment could proceed. Finally, after some isolated bombing encounters in the communication trenches, the 13th broke through to the north of Hill 62 and linked up with the 16th on their right.[54] The circle from left to right was now com-

[54] The Staff Direction of General Tuxford's Brigade was admirable throughout, and

plete, for the 58th (Colonel Genet), fighting their way slowly up the communication trenches on the left of the 13th, finally established touch with them. The main action was over shortly after 2.30 on the morning of June 13th.

June 13th, 2.30 A.M.

On the right the 1st Division had not, as they thought, retaken the precise position held by the 3rd Division on June 1st, although in the heat of the assault they were fully convinced that they had done so, and, in fact, succeeded in doing so on the following day. The Germans had built a new support trench somewhat to the west of the original British line, and this was in very good condition. In the meantime, a fortnight of rain and heavy bombardments, both from British and German guns, had practically obliterated the old first line. In the confusion of the final onrush in a half-light the company commanders of the various battalions occupied at once the first sound trench which obviously held a dominating position looking towards the east, and, in doing this, they no doubt stopped on the right 50 yards short of their objective. Such an error must be regarded as trivial by those who understand the conditions of modern warfare; it is a mistake which is bound to be made over and over again, even by the best infantry in the world, and is a far less dangerous offence than the opposing one of overcharging the position. Bombing posts were at once established down the German communication trenches and all measures taken against threatened counter-attacks. Immediately behind the assaulting waves came the Pioneers carrying on them the materials for consolidating and making good the captured trench the very instant it was clear of the enemy. In this work, Major W. B. Lindsay, of the Engineers, especially distinguished himself. The enemy, indeed, threatened a counter-attack, but their concentrations were, however, dispersed by our gun-fire. The enemy, in fact, had been surprised, and appeared to be dazed by the suddenness and the success of the onset, and the various reliefs of the assaulting battalions were carried out successfully, though under heavy shellfire.

It may be pointed out in summarising the action that no military movement can be realised without a consideration of its environment. The advance of the Canadians to the final counter-assault took place in the semi-darkness which precedes the dawn. The wildness of the elements tended to produce confusion if it added security from observation. There was enough light to distinguish the features and uniform of the enemy from our own and to give the officers a general sense of their direction. In the gloomy rainstorm, just before daybreak, the 1st Division advanced in a long succession of four lines, one close behind the other, on the frontage of three companies. Each regiment maintained its correct line of attack on the objective; each leading company was reinforced at the proper moment by the company which was marching steadily behind. The fury of the German shell-fire in no way discomposed the orderly advance of these disciplined battalions. In the shadows of the shattered woods which surrounded them it was easy to be deflected from the true course by the sudden spurt of machine-gun fire from an undestroyed emplacement, or to be checked by bombs thrown by

for this special credit should be given to the work of the Brigade Major—Major Clarke—and to Captains Urquart and Clarke Kennedy.

isolated detachments of Germans. But the regiments moved steadily forward in the darkness, over a ground ravaged both by British and German artillery until no landmarks remained. Here and there patches of barbed wire still stood out to show that a trench had once existed behind it. The orders were to use the bayonet until light came, for fear of firing into the other detachments. Through this chaos of shattered trees and earth the Canadian infantry moved steadily forward, and as the dawn broke once more on a ruined countryside it saw the assailants unshaken in discipline and correct in alignment—masters once more of the heights which defend the salient of Ypres.

Captain Papineau, of the Corps Staff, on June 16th surveyed the field of battle after the Canadian Corps had re-established itself in its old positions. His impressions are well worth recording. Looking north from the works which we still maintain on Hill 60, he was able to survey most of the ground over which the ebb and flow of battle had raged during the preceding fortnight. The first impression was one of blight—as though a devastating plague had suddenly descended upon these woods and fields and hills, had blotted out the natural green of Nature, and churned up the earth into sordid masses of mud. The blaze of sunshine and the blue sky flecked with slow-moving clouds could not wipe out the ugliness of the prospect. Man had defaced Nature until the charm of Nature had vanished.

Gaunt and grey and menacing, the prospect of the low hills swept out from the feet of the observers. Below were the shattered remains of Square Wood and Armagh Wood. Observatory Ridge, lost and recaptured, stood in front, its coppices full of the memories of hidden machine-guns. Behind there peeped out the higher grounds of Hills 61 and 62, to which the remains of Sanctuary Wood still climbed upwards. On the right rose Mount Sorrel, where the grim earth and shattered trunks still met the clear sky. Behind, in contrast, the green fields of high grass stretching towards Ypres ringed this land of death. The uncut crops, grown wild, had attained an unwonted luxuriance. Here and there a bunch of scarlet poppies might have drawn their intense colour from the gallant blood which had soaked the earth beneath. The unkempt hedgerows, no longer tall and neat, ran back to the city behind, and the beheaded and scarred poplars remained as mute witnesses to the strife of man. Yet Nature was attempting to assert herself, and through this summer's growth of verdure to cover the riot of battle.

Scattered beneath this innocent mantle of green are innumerable shell holes, old crumbling trenches full of the memories and odours of death, graves and graveyards marked by the crosses commemorating the long-forgotten captains once well loved by their regiments, and of humble privates perhaps still remembered. The torn and trampled equipment, the empty ammunition boxes, the remains here and there of shattered bodies, which human care and energy had been unable to bury, all await the healing tide of Nature which will cover them in its due time. On the roads behind lie the bodies of dead horses, with the flies thick on their congealed sides, killed in the effort to bring up to the assaulting battalions the necessities of war and livelihood. Yet of these, too, the poet has written that their cups are the calm pools and the winding rivers, and that care never breaks their healthy slumbers. Even over all that quiet countryside has come the continued spray of bursting shells, week after week and month after month, and if you look closely into every field and tree and ruined house, every yard of that wide landscape will show its wounds. We shall remember when the time of reckoning comes.

Even as the observers watched the field of conflict on June 16th, sudden clouds like giant powder-puffs leapt into the sky, and the air carried less swiftly the sound of bursting shrapnel. They looked into Square Wood, which was a wood no longer. In it there was no speck of green—only grey mud, slowly crusting in the sun, and bare, white, lifeless stalks to mark what had once been trees. But against the sky-line the new Canadian trenches ran, marked by the new outlines of red earth, to show that we held once again the lines of Mount Sorrel. The experience had been a hard one; the cost of life severe; the energies of the whole Corps had been required to balance the advantage the Württembergers had gained over us in the early days of June, and no regiment had been exempt from a share in the trial. Yet the task was accomplished, and defeat was turned into victory.

CHAPTER XII

"CANADA IN FLANDERS"

Conclusion—Canada will meet new necessities with fresh exertions—The Military co-operation of all parts of the Empire to lead to closer Political Union—Significance of the title "Canada in Flanders"—French General's views—British Infantry have never had to protect their own soil—Devotion of Australians and Canadians for an ideal—They felt the Empire was in danger—Lack of foresight in England—Prevision of Mr. Hughes, General Botha, and Sir Robert Borden—Recrimination in War-time useless, but the feeling for closer union and more responsibility growing overseas—Difficulty of organising this sentiment in a constitutional form without imperilling the liberty of the Dominions—Perils of refusing to do so—Controversy between Captain Papineau and Mr. Bourassa—Risk of reaction after the War—"Admit us to your Councils"—Reorganisation of Imperial resources the first constructive task for the Statesmen of the Empire.

It is more than a year ago since, in the last chapter of the first volume of "Canada in Flanders," these words were written:—

"After incredible hardships patiently supported, after desperate battles stubbornly contested, the work of the Canadians is still incomplete. But they will complete it, meeting new necessities with fresh exertions, for it is the work of civilisation and of liberty." These words still contain some truth in relation to the conditions of to-day. The work is still incomplete. But in the interval which has passed the dimensions of the task have wholly altered. In this war success depended, as Mr. Churchill once pointed out, not upon episodes, but upon tendencies. And in the last ten months the tendencies have all marched with the terrible inevitableness of a Greek tragedy towards the doom of the Central Powers.

In that development the Canadians have played their part. They will continue to play it, "meeting new necessities with fresh exertions," until the happy day when peace is dictated upon the terms which the Allies require. And then they will return to the farm, the bank, the university, the shop, and the ranch, as the seven thousand returned who fought in our South African quarrel. But is it possible that they should return without having stamped upon the loose constitution of the Empire articles at once more formal and more mutual than those with which until this war we have on the whole been content?

It does not seem possible, and it is certainly not desirable, that this remarkable military co-operation should be so unfruitful in constitutional result. In this final chapter of the second volume—the last volume in which it is likely that the present writer will be able to undertake the responsibility of authorship—he may perhaps be forgiven if he allows himself the intrusion of a more personal note than has been consistent with the scope of that part of the work which has preceded it.

"Canada in Flanders" suggests many reflections to a mind either acquainted with the past or imaginative in relation to the future. It speaks of achievement; and it also speaks of the agony of lingering death; it recalls Ypres, which will perhaps be in the history of Young Canada what Verdun is in the history of Old France; it recalls, too, the truncated bodies of the maimed who have offered the sacrifice of radiant youth and health upon a shrine the reality of which to them may perhaps sometimes have seemed a little remote. "Canada in Flanders," if confined to the military activities of Canadians in that unlovable country, would awake these and many other tragic and glorious memories. The pages which precede these words are a contribution and an effort to do justice to this branch of the subject.

But to the title "Canada in Flanders" must be conceded the relevance of some other observations which as a Canadian I think ought to be made, because it is plain that the Empire is still in an evolutionary stage; because plans and policies involving great changes are being boldly canvassed; because I myself am in favour of great changes; and, finally, because to see the facts as they really are is a condition precedent to fruitful development.

The first step in such a consideration is to examine shortly the nature, the significance, and the inevitable consequences of the Dominion's contribution to the necessities of this gigantic struggle.

The degree of heroism which has been constantly displayed by Canadians of all ranks will be admitted by all who have read these pages. The moral grandeur of their deeds can only receive justice from those who keep in mind considerations which are sometimes overlooked, but which are nevertheless of immense importance.

A very distinguished French General—a General than whom none more distinguished has been discovered by France in this war—and very few by any country in any war—was good enough once to discuss with me the respective qualities of the French and British infantry. Our conversation took place under circumstances which invited and won from him both sympathy and candour. He spoke of the soldiers of France in words so eloquent, so full of personal reminiscence, so charged with emotion, so vibrant with a wholly attractive pride, that for the first time I fully understood how deep and how pure are the wells from which the patriotism of this immortal nation is distilled. Then he began to speak of the British forces. Of these he made this penetrating observation: "To the British of all nations this singular tribute must be paid: that their infantry has never been engaged in any protracted war without a universal admission that it was the equal of any infantry in the world; and yet that it has never been afforded the supreme incentive to soldiers, that of fighting on their own soil, and for their own women and children at the moment and on the scene of their instant peril.

"In Flanders, under Marlborough, in the Peninsula and at Waterloo, under Wellington, your infantry have compelled the admiration of the world. And yet, my friend, they have never responded, as we have, to this appeal:—

"'Soldiers! facing you are the men who still occupy the sacred soil of France: who have ravished your women: and murdered old men, your compatriots. Soldiers, advance to avenge your country and those of your blood and race whom a savage enemy has done to death!'"

Deeply moved by a tribute made with so much feeling, tact, and sympathy, I ventured to ask, "Do not these remarks of yours, General, apply with even more force to the troops of the great self-governing Dominions who from so far have come to sustain with their lives the fortunes of the Allies upon soil so remote?"

His reply stated so clearly and with such insight the view on which I desire to insist that I venture to reproduce it. "Nothing," he said, "in the history of the world has ever been known quite like it. My countrymen are fighting within fifty miles of Paris to push back and chastise the vile and leprous race which has violated the chastity of our beautiful France. But the Australians at the Dardanelles and the Canadians at Ypres fought with supreme and absolute devotion for what to many of them must have seemed simple abstractions, and that nation which will support for an abstraction the horror of this war of all wars, will ever hold the highest place in the records of human valour."

I recall this conversation because it illustrates my point.

In a sense it is true that the majority of Australian and Canadian soldiers understand generally that they are fighting for the existence of the Empire, and in particular for the independence of that part of the Empire to which each respectively belongs; but the conclusion can only be a general one, the outcome rather of intuition than of exact knowledge. Australia is far, far remote from European quarrels. Canada has no neighbour but the United States. The shearer from Australia and the lumberman from Canada have come to help the Empire; but they would, I suspect, rather fight for six months than spend six minutes in attempting a lucid exposition of the motives which proved decisive to each individual volunteer. And, indeed, how could they—simple men far away from the heart of the Empire—be expected to have grasped the nature of the German menace when the whole of a great historic party in England was blind to it six months before the war broke out? Was a bank clerk in Toronto, or a book-keeper in Sydney, or a squatter in Rhodesia, to appreciate the ultimate tendency of German policy when the Chairman of the National Union of Liberal Federations, himself a Privy Councillor, was declaring that as a business man he preferred the sanctions of International Law to the protection of the British Fleet; when members of Parliament were forming each year a powerful committee to fight the Naval Estimates; when official invitations to suspend shipbuilding programmes gave annual indulgence to the Teuton sense of humour; when German editors and professors in yearly deputations exploited the simplicity of their silly hosts; and when, finally, statesmen in high places paid periodic and public tribute to the sincerity and humanity of German *Kultur*?

To ask these questions is to answer them. The majority of those who stood to the Colours did so because they saw that at that moment the Empire was in peril. The circumstance that neither they nor their leaders were responsible for the policy which brought us, wholly unprepared on the military side, to the most gigantic struggle in history, seemed to them no sufficient reason for refusing to fight while the fight lasted. But it may be pointed out that many of their leaders had a very clear vision of the dangers in our path. They saw the European situation from a distance, and perhaps for that reason in truer perspective. Mr. Hughes, the Prime Minister of Australia, who unites with profound knowledge of affairs dauntless courage and the analytical power of a trained mind, has always believed this struggle must come. General Botha—in many ways the most romantic figure in the Empire to-day—adroit politician, skilful general, chivalrous soldier, faithful friend—returned from a visit to the German Army manoeuvres some years ago with the same apprehension branded upon his mind. Sir Robert Borden, only four years ago, in introducing his naval proposals in the Canadian Parliament, used these prophetic words:—

"But to-day while the clouds are heavy, and we hear the booming of the distant thunder, and see the lightning flash above the horizon, we cannot and we will not wait and deliberate until the impending storm has burst upon us in fury and with disaster."

The leaders, then, of political thought in the Dominions had arrived at sound conclusions by observation and inference from known facts. And having formed these conclusions, they decided, when war came, to throw their whole strength into the scale, though they were well aware of the errors of judgment that had paralysed preparation in England. The rank and file volunteered in hundreds of thousands, and then in more hundreds of thousands, because they saw that recrimination as to past responsibility was at that moment futile, and that there and then the Empire was in mortal peril. From thousands of miles the flower of the youth of the Empire have come and trained, and fought and died, or have drifted back broken after the war to the Dominions whence they set out. And the men who have done these things, uncompelled and uncompellable, have accepted our military and diplomatic direction of the war, even when they disagreed with it, without question and without complaint. Nothing nobler has been uttered in the war than the answer, made in the Australian Parliament, by the Prime Minister to a Member who gave expression to the bitter grief with which Australia learned of the definite abandonment of the Dardanelles adventure.

"Not upon us," said he, "have these great burdens and responsibilities been cast. Not by one word or even one doubt will I add to the anxieties of those from whom decisions have been required."

It is a commonplace that no such phenomenon as the great rally of the Dominions has ever been witnessed in history. None of the Great Empires of the world has ever conceded so much freedom to its constituent parts or been rewarded by so much devotion. And it is well known that the whole world—our friends and our enemies alike—have been amazed at the spectacle of Imperial solidarity which the war has exhibited. "For the purposes of a European war," wrote one of Germany's many military philosophers, "the British Colonies, even if they remain faithful, may be ignored." To-day this gallant theorist—the nursling of Treitschke—is, one may presume, somewhat better informed.

It may perhaps be urged that, after all, the very co-operation of which so much has been said has become possible under the undefined, impalpable, and sentimental Union which has hitherto prevailed throughout the Empire; that the task of translating in the twin fields of Defence and Diplomacy informal into formal representations of the Dominions is very hard to reconcile with the complete domestic independence of each unit; and that all our most valuable constitutional doctrines have been the fruit of an evolutionary and not of a conscious or studied process. This is true. But it ignores a real peril to the Empire. In all things physical, mental, and moral, great activities are followed by great reactions. And the violence of the reaction is generally determined by the violence of the activity. The efforts made by all parties in this War have been stupendous. It is certain that these exertions will be followed in every belligerent country by violent reactions. The Dominions will not escape the influence of these currents of opinion. "The captains and the kings depart," but there remain the memory of the dead, the presence everywhere of the maimed, and perhaps to many of the bereaved the anxiety of financial pressure. Canada has been and is overwhelmingly loyal, but none the less a student of Imperial affairs should give attention to the recent correspondence between Mr. Bourassa and Capt. Papineau. Similar problems survive even the immense influence and prestige of General Botha in South Africa. In Australia and New Zealand the loyalty which is endemic in these stubborn and homogeneous peoples is reinforced by obvious local inducements to a centripetal policy. But even here there are forces which at a time of reaction are certain to become both articulate and critical. In measuring the probable extent and seriousness of such a reaction the student of politics will not forget the lessons of the South African War. The glamour of war is dissipated: material gains are forgotten: there survive commercial and industrial dislocations, the stale but strident advertisement of war scandals, and the abiding, grinding pressure of war taxation. The khaki election in England was followed by the *débâcle* of 1906, and by the accession to power of a Parliament which consisted to a greater extent than any House of Commons which had ever existed in England of pacifists, idealists, and demagogues to whom not only the thought of war, but even of preparation for war, was abhorrent.

But the country in which this reaction against the South African War took place was, after all, the country whose Government, elected by themselves, was responsible for the diplomacy which led up to that war and for the conduct of the war when once it was declared. The danger in the case of the self-governing Dominions is that the reaction is certain to be supported by opponents of the War with the argument that those who have made contributions relatively so immense were never consulted as to the policy, and have merely been called in to support the consequences of other men's bungling. It is sufficient to say that such a campaign might become formidable.

There is only one remedy. It is not attempted here to work out the details; and, indeed, their elaboration might most usefully engage the exclusive work of the twelve ablest statesmen in the united Empire. But without making any such attempt, it may be broadly claimed that both in the interests of the Mother Country and of the Dominions, and of that Empire of which they are equally the legatees, the close of the War will mark the moment when the claim of Sir Robert Borden, "Admit us to your councils," will become irresistible. It is important that this claim should be recognised now. With every year that passes it will become more important. The Dominions have played a great part in this War and one which will never be forgotten. But they are still in their infancy. Their adult strength has yet to be tested. There may never be another world struggle. Should such an occasion unhappily arise, it is at least likely to be remote in time. And the more remote it be, the more decisive is the part which our kinsmen in the Outer Empire may hope to play.

Do not, at least, let us fail in the attempt to keep our friends for want of imagination.

Burke, in a splendid and memorable passage, dealing with those Colonies which the folly of our ancestors lost, spoke to a deaf audience of the swift development of our old American Colonies:—

"Whether I put the present numbers too high or too low is a matter of little moment. Such is the strength with which population shoots in that part of the world that, state the numbers as high as we will, whilst the dispute continues, the exaggeration ends. Whilst we are discussing any given magnitude they are grown to it. Whilst we spend our time in deliberating on the mode of governing 2,000,000 we shall find we have millions more to manage. Your children do not grow faster from infancy to manhood than they spread from families to communities, and from villages to nations."

Such will be the growth of these great communities which have given us their lives in this War. Let us welcome, and, if it be possible, let us increase their proven attachment. Nor let us for one moment forget, among the great tasks with which peace will confront us, that the reorganisation of our Imperial resources is the first constructive task which awaits the statesmen of the Empire. If this indeed be realised, the work will not have been done in vain which has been done by "Canada in Flanders."

APPENDIX

Extracts from the third supplement of the *London Gazette* of Friday, May 29th, 1916. In the Despatch from Sir Douglas Haig, G.C.B., Commander-in-Chief British Forces in France, of May 19th, the following references are made to the Canadian troops:—

SECTION 10.

During the period under review the forces under my command have been considerably augmented by the arrival of new formations from home, and the transfer of others released from service in the Near East. This increase has made possible the relief of a French Army, to which I have already referred, at the time of the Battle of Verdun. Among the newly arrived forces is the "Anzac" Corps. With them, the Canadians, and a portion of the South African Overseas Force which has also arrived, the Dominions now furnish a valuable part of the Imperial Forces in France.

SECTION 8.

The following units were specially brought to the notice of the Commander-in-Chief for good work in carrying out or repelling local attacks an raids:

1st Divisional Artillery,
22nd Canadian Howitzer Brigade,
5th Canadian Infantry Battalion,
7th Canadian Infantry Battalion,
29th Canadian Infantry Battalion,
49th Canadian Infantry Battalion.

SECTION 6.

St. Eloi.

6. On March 27th our troops made an attack with the object of straightening out the line at St. Eloi, and cutting away the small German salient which encroached on the semicircle of our line in the Ypres salient to a depth of about 100 yards over a front of some 600 yards. The operation was begun by the firing of six very large mines; the charge was so heavy that the explosion was felt in towns several miles behind the lines, and large numbers of the enemy were killed. Half a minute after the explosion our infantry attack was launched, aiming at the German Second Line. The right attack met with little opposition, and captured its

assigned objective; but the left attack was not so successful, and a gap was left in possession of the Germans, through which they entered one of the craters. The following days were spent by both sides in heavy bombardment and in unsuccessful attacks, intended on our part to capture the remaining trenches, and on the part of the Germans to drive us from the positions we had occupied. In the very early morning of April 3rd we succeeded in recapturing the crater and the trenches still held by the enemy, thereby securing the whole of our original objective. We had, moreover, captured five officers and 195 men in the first attack on March 27th, and five officers and 80 men in the attack on April 3rd. The work of consolidating our new position, however, proved extremely difficult, owing to the wet soil, heavy shelling and mine explosions; though pumps were brought up and efforts at draining were instituted, the result achieved was comparatively small. By dint of much heavy work the Brigade holding these trenches succeeded in reducing the water in the trenches by two feet by the morning of the 5th. This state of affairs could not, even so, be regarded as satisfactory; and during the 5th the enemy's bombardment increased in intensity, and the new trenches practically ceased to exist. On the morning of the 6th the enemy attacked with one battalion supported by another; he penetrated our new line, and gained the two westernmost craters. It is difficult to follow in detail the fighting of the next three weeks, which consisted in repeated attacks by both sides on more or less isolated mine craters, the trench lines having been destroyed by shell fire. Great efforts were made to maintain communication with the garrisons of these advanced posts, and with considerable success. But there were periods of uncertainty, and some misconception as to the state of affairs arose. On the 11th it was reported to me that we had recaptured all that remained of the position won by us on March 27th and April 3rd. This report, probably due to old craters having been mistaken for new ones, was subsequently found to be incorrect. The new craters, being exposed to the enemy's view and to the full weight of his artillery fire, have proved untenable, and at the present time our troops are occupying trenches roughly in the general line which was held by them before the 27th.

In a subsequent despatch, dated December 23rd, 1916, issued in a Supplement to the London Gazette of December 29th, the following references to the activities of Canadian troops during June appears:—

> While my final preparations were in progress the enemy made two unsuccessful attempts to interfere with my arrangements. The first, directed on May 21st against our positions on the Vimy Ridge, south and south-east of Souchez, resulted in a small enemy gain of no strategic or tactical importance; and rather than weaken my offensive by involving additional troops in the task of recovering the lost ground, I decided to consolidate a position in rear of our original line.
>
> The second enemy attack was delivered on June 2nd on a front of over one and a half miles from Mount Sorrel to Hooge, and succeeded in penetrating to a maximum depth of 700 yards. As the southern part of the lost position commanded our trench-

es, I judged it necessary to recover it, and by an attack launched on June 13th, carefully prepared and well executed, this was successfully accomplished by the troops on the spot.

Neither of these enemy attacks succeeded in delaying the preparations for the major operations which I had in view.

END OF VOL. II.

Lector House believes that a society develops through a two-fold approach of continuous learning and adaptation, which is derived from the study of classic literary works spread across the historic timeline of literature records. Therefore, we aim at reviving, repairing and redeveloping all those inaccessible or damaged but historically as well as culturally important literature across subjects so that the future generations may have an opportunity to study and learn from past works to embark upon a journey of creating a better future.

This book is a result of an effort made by Lector House towards making a contribution to the preservation and repair of original ancient works which might hold historical significance to the approach of continuous learning across subjects.

HAPPY READING & LEARNING!

LECTOR HOUSE
LECTOR HOUSE LLP
E-MAIL: info@lectorhouse.com

9 789356 146082

Printed by Libri Plureos GmbH in Hamburg,
Germany

9 789356 146082